STRANGE HISTORIES

STRANGE HISTORIES

The trial of the pig, the walking dead,
and other matters of fact from the
medieval and Renaissance worlds

Darren Oldridge

Routledge
Taylor & Francis Group

LONDON AND NEW YORK

First published 2005
by Routledge
2 Park Square, Milton Park, Abingdon, Oxon OX14 4RN

Simultaneously published in the USA and Canada
by Routledge
270 Madison Avenue, New York, NY 10016

Routledge is an imprint of the Taylor & Francis Group

Typset in Ehrhardt by M Rules
Printed and bound in Great Britain by
MPG Books Ltd, Bodmin

British Library Cataloguing in Publication Data
A catalogue record for this book is available from the British Library

Library of Congress Cataloguing in Publication Data
Strange histories: the trial of the pig, the walking dead,
and other matters of fact from the medieval and
renaissance worlds / Darren Oldridge.
p. cm.
Includes bibliographical references.
1. Belief and doubt – History. 2. Witchcraft – History.
I. Title. BD215.O53 2005
001.9′09–dc22

ISBN 0-415-28860-6

For Emma

CONTENTS

PLATES

PREFACE

This is not a conventional history book. I have not written an account of the social and political developments of the late medieval and Renaissance ages. Rather, I have tried to reconstruct the thinking of men and women who accepted as normal ideas that now seem to be absurd: the existence of witches and roaming cadavers, trial by ordeal, the capital punishment of animals, and much else besides. I have also attempted to revive moral arguments that now appear to be abhorrent: that God sometimes wants people to suffer on earth, and that killing heretics is necessary and just. These ideas are, by their very nature, shocking to modern readers. This is precisely why they are included here. As historians have often noted, our failure to comprehend the beliefs of people in the past is a measure of the distance that separates us from them. It is the very strangeness of these ideas – from a modern perspective – that makes them worth looking at. If we can begin to understand why a French judge warned people about demonically possessed apples in 1602, we might start to unravel the intellectual context in which he lived.

Despite the deliberately bizarre content of the pages that follow, this book is not intended as a freak show of misconceived opinions. A better analogy is an old photograph album in which recognisably normal people appear in strangely outdated clothes. As anyone who has seen themselves in this context will know, one of the first responses is to think, "How could I possibly have thought I looked good in that?" In a similar spirit, this book invites readers to ask how people in the distant past could have believed in things that now seem crazy. Equally, it invites them to see that these people were *not* crazy – any more than the fashion victims in the old pictures. The analogy can be taken a step further. If we can see how our old clothes now look ridiculous, we might reflect on the transient nature of fashion itself. If people once accepted things that now seem strange or cruel, what should we make of our own commonplace assumptions? This book will, I hope, lead readers towards this new perspective.

Specialists in the period may, I hope, find material here to interest them, but this book is written for the general reader. It aims to introduce unfamiliar ideas from the past to a non-specialist audience. For this reason, I have kept academic references and theoretical jargon to a minimum, though I hope that my intellectual debts are acknowledged in the notes at the end of the book.

I would like to thank Vicky Peters, my editor, for her generous support throughout the project. I am also grateful to Meg Barker for persuading me to stick with it in the early stages. My partner Emma Tuckfield has kept me sane through all this strangeness, and has provided constant supplies of encouragement and love. This book is dedicated to her.

I

Introduction

Strange Worlds

A remarkable trial was held in Rothenbach in the Black Forest in 1485. A woman suspected of witchcraft was arraigned before the seignorial court of the Count of Fürstenberg. Instead of relying on human judgment to determine the verdict, the Count decided to place the matter in the hands of God. The suspected witch was subjected to "the trial by red-hot iron". This procedure required the accused person to take an iron from a furnace and carry it for three paces. Their hand would be bound for three days and then the wound would be inspected. They were declared innocent if the wound had healed cleanly, but condemned if it was found to be weeping or discoloured. The accused woman submitted to the ordeal with impressive confidence. According to one account, "she carried the red-hot iron not only for the stipulated three paces but for six, and offered to carry it even farther". She was eventually acquitted and freed. The case later reached the attention of the Dominican friars Heinrich Krämer and Jacob Sprenger, who condemned the verdict in their influential treatise on witchcraft, the *Malleus Maleficarum* (1486). They claimed the decision was unsafe because the ordeal was open to demonic manipulation. The devil, as a master of natural science, may have protected the woman's hand "by invisibly interposing some other substance" between her skin and the iron. This led them to warn judges in future cases to avoid the ordeal.[1]

What should we make of these events? To people living in the modern west, nothing in the episode appears to make sense. The woman was accused of a crime that is now regarded as impossible, and she was set free by a process that seems completely arbitrary. When Krämer and Sprenger condemned the proceedings, they ignored the obvious problems that modern readers would point out: the apparent randomness and unfairness of the ordeal, not to mention its brutality. Instead, they based their objections on the supposed power of the devil, and assumed the unfortunate suspect was guilty as charged. Episodes like this test the ability of modern thinkers to understand the past, and provoke responses that demonstrate the sheer difficulty of this task. People often dismiss such events as "superstitious". It is also frequently assumed that those involved in them were irrational: their behaviour derived from stupidity or some kind of hysteria. More darkly, some people may suspect that such actions were driven by ulterior motives: those responsible were exploiting popular credulity as an excuse for financial gain or sadism. Others might argue that ignorance and poor education were to blame. The people involved simply "didn't know better".

These reactions are understandable, but they bear little relation to the surviving evidence. One of the first things to strike any reader of medieval and Renaissance writings on witchcraft is the painstaking, often tedious scholarship they contain. Whatever else we may think of these texts, they do not appear to have been produced by hysterics. Books like the *Malleus Maleficarum* were based on extensive and highly conventional learning, rooted in the Bible and the philosophy of the Church Fathers. The most serious allegations against witches – that they gathered at night to kill babies and worship the devil – were found mainly in the writings of educated men. While the legal prosecution of witches was exceptional in many respects, there is little in the surviving records to suggest it was normally characterised by malice or a cavalier disregard for justice. Equally, the practice of trial by ordeal took place in a spirit of seriousness and attention to correct procedure that belies the view that it was based on cruelty. In some cases, the suspects themselves asked to undergo the ordeal, confident in the belief that God would judge them truly. As the *Malleus Maleficarum* noted sourly, this was the case with the accused woman at Rothenbach. By the time of this incident, the use of the ordeal was rare, but until its decline in the thirteenth century, its application was supported by some of the most thoughtful and devout Christians in western Europe.

This book will argue that concepts like "superstition" and ignorance do little to help us understand the vanished world of the witch of Rothenbach. On the contrary, they actually prevent us from seeing that world as it probably was: a community of men and women who were no less reasonable and well intentioned than we are. It is not only simplistic to view these people as hysterical: it also denies their humanity. To regard them as irrational is no less insulting – or mistaken – than to view African tribespeople as "savages". The idea that the pre-modern world was befogged with superstition also separates us from the past. The romantic nineteenth-century historian Thomas Carlyle affirmed this point as he contemplated the ruined English abbey of Bury St Edmunds:

> Let us know always that this *was* a world, and not a void infinite of
> grey haze, with phantasms swimming in it. These old St
> Edmundsbury walls, I say, were not peopled with phantasms; but
> with men of flesh and blood, made altogether as we are. Had thou

and I then been, who knows but we ourselves had taken refuge from an evil time, and fled to dwell here?[2]

Carlyle was a conservative Christian who yearned gloomily for an idealised past. But he also challenged the arrogant assumption that the modern age was intellectually superior to its predecessors. He denied that the extinct society of the Suffolk monks was any less reasonable than his own, and implied that the beliefs of its inhabitants – and presumably those of his contemporaries as well – were shaped by the conditions in which they chanced to live. These simple ideas provide the basis for this book. However peculiar they now seem, the beliefs of pre-modern people were normally a rational response to the intellectual and social context in which they were expressed.

This leads to the idea of "strangeness". When something appears to be strange, this often means it is outside our normal experience. It is strange to put a pig on trial, to execute a dead man, or to attempt to conjure a spirit. By the same token, an idea may seem strange if it is unfamiliar. Historians of witchcraft have noted that allegations of the crime were more readily believed when they included well-known motifs: the bad reputation of the supposed witch, their threats to their neighbours, and "unusual" afflictions. The sheer familiarity of these ingredients made accusations more plausible. In an important recent study of the *Malleus Maleficarum*, Hans Peter Broedel has shown how its authors placed the widely held beliefs of late-medieval villagers in a context acceptable to Renaissance intellectuals. Their vision of witchcraft proved more successful than the work of other writers because it "was more closely aligned with the perceived reality of their contemporaries". For much the same reason, the *Malleus Maleficarum* seems utterly incredible today. This observation may seem banal, but it has an important implication. If the feeling of strangeness results from unfamiliarity, then this feeling depends largely on what we are normally used to doing and believing. Saying something is strange is just another way of saying, "This is not what I do", or "This is not what I believe". Its strangeness would vanish if we were transported, as Carlyle imagined, into another world where different assumptions prevailed.[3]

Our own lives are filled with experiences and beliefs that are peculiar to our culture, and would seem bizarre to anyone outside it. We do not need to look far for examples. The ability to read is a good illustration. For the great majority of western people, the habit of literacy makes it impossible to scan the shelves of a newsagent's shop without noticing the titles of magazines. When we walk down the high street, we recognise the words on posters and shop-window displays without even trying to do so. These actions are automatic; they feel as natural as breathing. But reading is an acquired skill that can only be mastered through years of practice. Moreover, mass literacy is a comparatively recent phenomenon: only a fraction of the European population could read in the fifteenth century. More remarkably, it is quite likely that widespread literacy is an exception to the normal pattern of human culture: anthropologists and historians have argued convincingly that reading has emerged in only a minority of human societies. In reading this book, you may well be doing something that runs counter to normal human experience. From the perspective of most people who have ever lived, the activity you are engaged in would appear to be truly strange.[4]

If familiarity is one measure of strangeness, another is "making sense". Many strange beliefs strike us as nonsensical. It is not only unusual to acquit a suspected criminal because she can carry a hot iron for six paces; it also seems absurd. Here it is useful to borrow a concept from anthropology. The American anthropologist Clifford Geertz has argued that people always understand their life experiences in the context of a "system of belief". This is "the framework of beliefs, expressive symbols, and values in terms of which individuals define their world, express their feelings, and make their judgments". Belief systems are not created from scratch. Women and men are born into them, and accept them in much the same way that they accept their physical environment. Geertz notes that systems of belief change over time, so "historically defined standards of judgment" usually determine how people make sense of things. "Common-sense" judgments reflect the prevailing beliefs of particular communities, which often differ from one another. Ideas can be regarded as rational if they are consistent with prevailing knowledge. When we are familiar with the dominant assumptions of a certain culture – such as our own – we tend to regard the behaviour of people who act in conformity with these assumptions as perfectly sensible; when we have little understanding of the beliefs of another society, many of the acts that routinely occur within it may strike us as absurd.[5]

In the period covered by this book – from the late Middle Ages to the beginnings of modern science at the end of the seventeenth century – the prevailing system of belief permitted many ideas that now seem unfamiliar or ridiculous. Can the dead walk? Most people in medieval Europe believed they could, and orthodox Christians assumed this would happen en masse at the time of the Last Judgment. Can witches fly? Even the most trenchant opponents of the persecution of witchcraft in sixteenth-century Europe believed this was possible. Just like us, the people who accepted these things relied on a body of knowledge to help them evaluate the facts of the world, and just like us, they inherited this knowledge from the culture in which they were born. Viewed in this light, the way to understand the events at Rothenbach in 1485 is to become acquainted with the cultural context in which they took place. Such episodes were not absurd. They only appear irrational today because our "given reality" has changed. Some twenty years ago, the seventeenth-century historian David E. Stannard spelt this out:

We do well to remember that the [pre-modern] world . . . was a rational world, in many ways more rational than our own. It is true that it was a world of witches and demons, and of a just and terrible God who made his presence known in the slightest act of nature. But this was the given reality about which most of the decisions and actions of the age, throughout the entire western world, revolved.[6]

The society Stannard described was not only rational but also moral. Then as now, women and men did their best to "do the right thing" in circumstances that were frequently difficult or uncertain. Then as now, their moral judgments reflected the realities accepted by their community. When the Count of Fürstenberg allowed the accused witch to submit to the ordeal, he may well have believed sincerely that this was the fairest way to proceed. At the very least, we should not question the motives behind his decision because we no longer give credence to the beliefs on which it was based. Instead, we need to make ourselves familiar with the mental world in which well-meaning people could take such decisions. This book is an introduction to that world, and this chapter will describe some its defining characteristics.

AUTHORITY AND ANGELS

The great majority of people in pre-modern Europe lived in small rural communities, many containing no more than a few dozen households. Provincial towns could number two or three thousand inhabitants, but even the populations of great cities like Paris and London were only a fraction of the size of a modern metropolis. Contemporaries viewed these great towns as both exceptional and unnatural: one English observer in the 1600s likened the growth of London to a "rickety head". For townsfolk and villagers alike, prosperity depended on the agricultural economy. This was both laborious and insecure: the success of the harvest could never be guaranteed, and a series of poor crops could create intense hardship and even starvation. The exceptionally bad weather between 1560 and 1660 threatened parts of Germany and central Europe with starvation, and a string of disastrous harvests in the 1590s depopulated areas of northern England. The fragility of the harvest was combined with the threat of illness and sporadic outbreaks of epidemic disease. According to the best estimates, the great plague of 1347–8 claimed at least a third of the European population, and the contagion returned intermittently until the late 1600s. By the privileged standards of our own times, infant mortality was shockingly high. Even in the relatively benign conditions of colonial New England, at least one child in four died before the age of ten, at a time when the average family produced eight children. As these figures suggest, pre-modern people felt the presence of death more keenly than us. Not only did parents live with the knowledge that they might bury their children, but death itself was a public event. From the spectacle of the gallows to the vigil of relatives and friends around the deathbed, the end of life was an experience to be shared. It is a token of this fact that guides to the *ars moriendi* – or "art of death" – were available for those who could afford them to make their last moments as gracious as possible.[7]

The fickle nature of human welfare, alongside the near presence of death, was conducive to a profoundly supernatural understanding of the world. The Christianity of the Middle Ages and Renaissance was astonishingly comprehensive and enduring. In the words of R. W. Southern, the medieval church presided over "the most elaborate and thoroughly integrated system of religious thought and practice the world has ever known". This system was disrupted by the emergence of popular heresy from the eleventh century onwards, and the violent split between Catholics and Protestants in the 1500s; but its core beliefs remained intact – and almost universally acknowledged – until the appearance of scientific rationalism in the early decades of the eighteenth century. Within the conceptual landscape of western Christianity, two central features stand out as distinctively pre-modern. The first was a willingness to accept the authority of "reputable" texts to establish the facts of life. The scientific method of testing hypotheses through experiments only became fashionable in the late 1600s. Before this, many propositions were accepted on the word of authoritative sources, usually taken from the ancient world. The second characteristic of pre-modern Christian thinkers was their unshakeable conviction, derived partly from these same authoritative texts, in an "invisible world" of metaphysical beings: God, the Devil, angels and demons. An edifice of rational and consistent belief was constructed within these parameters. This system of thought provided a satisfactory account of all the phenomena of human existence, and offered reasonable options for dealing with all manner of practical situations.[8]

For all pre-modern Christians, the most important and trusted text was the Bible. This contained a treasury of information about this world and the next; and while scholars often differed in their reading of this material, no one disputed that the scriptures, if correctly understood, could offer a reliable description of the universe. Some aspects of this description – such as the existence of a personal afterlife – still enjoy widespread acceptance today. Others have disappeared from the belief system of the modern west, or are now confined to minority groups: these include the power of prophecy, the miraculous intervention of God in the movement of planets, demonic possession and the revival of the dead. The testimony of scripture was supplemented by a body of writings by the great thinkers of the early church, among whom St Augustine was pre-eminent. Alongside these Christian authorities, classical writers such as Plato and Aristotle provided respected commentaries on the physical world. While these authors departed from Christian sources on key points of theology, they confirmed many of the central features of the pre-modern worldview, including the existence of "wonders" that contravened the normal rules of nature.

The evidence of scripture and other ancient texts established the limits of possible belief. However uncommon such events might be, it was impossible to discount phenomena like bodily resurrections or the gift of prophecy. Even the most sceptical observers could not assume a priori that these things could not happen. This did not mean that medieval and Renaissance thinkers expected supernatural interventions to occur every day; on the contrary, they assumed that natural processes determined the outcome of most events, following the "accustomed course of nature". When wonders did take place, their credibility depended largely on the authority of those who reported them. Medieval chroniclers of marvellous episodes were at pains to establish the reliability of their sources. Eyewitness testimonies from trusted individuals were highly valued. Before he described the ghastly events surrounding the resurrection of a witch in twelfth-century England, William of Malmesbury stated that "I am sure that none of my listeners will doubt the story, although they might in fact wonder at it. I heard of these events from a distinguished man who swore he had seen them for himself, and I would be ashamed not to believe him". Likewise, the thirteenth-century German monk Caesarius of Heisterbach prefaced his account of the appearance of demons in the town of Mainz by noting that he heard the story "from a worthy citizen, who assured me that it actually happened in his own time at Mainz". Alternatively, chroniclers accepted accounts of wonders when they were transmitted through a chain of reputable testators, provided that this chain led back to a trusted eyewitness. When this could not be proven, they were inclined to dismiss reports of marvellous events as idle fables.[9]

As this practice suggests, pre-modern writers were perfectly capable of scepticism. But their acceptance of scriptural authority, together with their willingness to credit reports of wonders from suitably reputable contemporary sources, made their criteria for judging the facts of the world different from ours. The sixteenth-century Swiss theologian Ludwig Lavater illustrates this beautifully. In 1569 Lavater published a treatise on apparitions and "forewarnings" of future events. He devoted the first part of his work to disproving false reports of such phenomena. These had their origins, he argued, in various natural causes: faulty eyesight and poor lighting, the sound of beetles knocking in furniture, and the over-heated imaginations of credulous people. He concluded that "there happen daily many things by the ordinary course of nature which diverse men, especially they that are timorous and fearful, suppose to be visions or spirits". Lavater's tone changed, however, when he considered the evidence of scripture. Here he found indisputable proof that apparitions and prodigies had appeared, such as the vision of Samuel conjured by the witch of Endor (1 Kgs. 28). He observed that Augustine, and numerous classical writers such as Virgil and Plato, testified to similar events. This material compelled him to accept that visions and forewarnings could take place. He then adduced contemporary reports of such occurrences, noting only those cases recounted by "respectable" men. This morbid tale is typical:

> There was a certain parish priest, a very honest and godly man, whom I knew well, who in the plague time could tell beforehand when any [person] of his parish should die. For in the night time he heard a noise over his bed, like as if one had thrown down a sack full of corn from his shoulders, which when he heard he would say, "Now another biddeth me farewell". After it was day, he used to enquire who died that night, or who was taken with the plague, so he might comfort and strengthen them, according to the duty of a good pastor.

Supported by scripture, the Church Fathers, and trusted acquaintances like the pastor in this story, Lavater asserted that visions and prodigies did exist, though many reports of them were probably false. While it was foolish to accept accounts of wonders without considering the credibility of their witnesses, and the strong possibility that natural causes may be responsible, it was equally rash "to condemn all things which are avouched by so many and so credible historians and ancient fathers, and other grave men of great authority".[10]

Lavater's work also illustrates the second major feature that distinguished pre-modern thinkers. He acknowledged the existence of good and bad angels that could intervene in human affairs. It was "most sure and certain", he observed, "that God hath given his angels the charge to have regard and care over us". More pessimistically, he also noted the existence of demons who were "hurtful and enemies unto men". During the Middle Ages, many scholars accepted not only the activities of angels and demons, but also the returning dead. Saints could offer guidance and protection to their earthly devotees, and the ghosts of ordinary women and men occasionally visited the living to solicit favours or communicate messages from the afterlife. The reality of angels was abundantly proven in the Bible and the New Testament provided copious evidence of the activity of Satan and lesser demons. The cult of the saints emerged in the early Middle Ages and was gradually integrated into the official life of the church. Medieval sermons and chronicles were often enlivened by tales of ghosts returning briefly to earth. Protestant reformers in the 1500s denied the power of both saints and ghosts, claiming that the Bible sanctioned neither, but their devotion to scripture also forced them to accept the reality of angels and demons. Thus all medieval and Renaissance thinkers accepted that supernatural beings participated in earthly affairs.[11]

At its crudest, the existence of demons meant that humans shared the earth with a race of creatures that were both powerful and hostile. It was widely accepted that demons resided in the bowels of the earth and that on rare occasions unfortunate mortals came into physical contact with them. A "certain godly and learned man" reported an example of this to Lavater. This concerned a silver mine in the Alps that was found to be inhabited by a "spirit or devil". When one of the miners rebuked this creature for disturbing his work, the outcome was predictably unpleasant:

> It chanced upon a time that while the said spirit was too busy intermeddling himself with everything, one of the miners . . . began to rail at him very bitterly, and with terrible, cursing words bid him get him thence in the devil's name. But the spirit caught him by the pate, and so writhed his neck about that his face stood behind his back. Yet notwithstanding, he was not slain but lived a long time after, well known unto diverse of his familiar friends, which yet live at this day, howbeit he died within a few years after.

Lavater was clearly impressed by the credentials of his source, as well as the large number of witnesses who apparently confirmed the man's fate, but he also found it easy to credit the report because the existence of sub-terrestrial demons was generally acknowledged in his culture. As late as the 1670s, the English chemist Robert Boyle interviewed miners to ascertain information about them. He asked his informants if they "meet with any subterraneous demons, and if they do, in what shape and manner they appear; what they portend, and what they do". Such direct encounters with demons were less common than other phenomena involving unclean spirits. Demons could manipulate the human senses, tamper with nature and invade the bodies of humans and other living things. In an unusual demonstration of their capacity to work mischief, the people of Annecy in Savoy were troubled by a possessed apple in 1585:

> On the edge of the Hasli bridge there was seen for two hours an apple from which came so great and confused a noise that people were afraid to pass by there, although it was a much used way. Everybody ran to see this thing, though no one dared to go near to it; until, as is always the case, at last one man more bold than the rest took a long stick and knocked the apple into the Thiou, a canal from the lake of Annecy which passes under the bridge; and after that nothing more was heard.

The French demonologist Henri Boguet recounted this bizarre story. Like Lavater, he had no need to seek alternative explanations for the incident, since it was widely known that demons could manifest themselves in animals and plants. Witches in his region were known to plant unclean spirits in their victims' bodies by means of contaminated food. Moreover, the apple was an obvious vessel for such pollution, as it echoed the original source of human corruption in the Garden of Eden. These considerations led Boguet to a straightforward conclusion. "It cannot be doubted", he wrote, "that this apple was full of devils, and that a witch had been foiled in an attempt to give it to someone".[12]

While the residents of Annecy were troubled by bedevilled fruit, most people could rest safe in the knowledge that physical encounters with demons were very infrequent. For Renaissance intellectuals, the most important consequence of the existence of good and bad angels was to extend the range of possible explanations for earthly phenomena. The work of the Elizabethan nobleman Henry Howard exemplifies this point. In *A Defensative Against the Poison of Supposed Prophecies* (1583), Howard denounced what he regarded as superstitious methods of foretelling the future. Like Lavater, he attributed most supposed prodigies to misunderstandings of "the accustomed course of nature", and offered natural explanations instead. His dismissal of "vulgar signs and wonders" captures his robustly critical turn of mind:

> The vulgar sort are wont to live in fear of civil war upon the sight of
> bloody streams in the air, and again, they look for store of grain and
> plenty of all things when the waters bear a taint or colour, not unlike
> to milk. And yet a good philosopher can put them out of doubt that
> the first proceedeth of a scalding vapour, the second by infusion of
> land water.

Howard's scepticism extended to the published prophecies of alleged seers such as Nostradamus, whose riddling pronouncements are still taken seriously by some people today. According to Howard, these predictions were so "dark, ambiguous and flexible" that they merely reflected back the preconceptions of anyone credulous enough to believe in them. Howard conceded however, that the Bible proved that some forms of prophecy were genuine. Divine foreknowledge could be granted to certain individuals, but the standard of prophecy described in the scriptures was so high that he saw no evidence of the same phenomenon in his own time. More darkly, he observed that it was likely that demons would encourage people to believe in false predictions. With this in mind, he devoted a chapter to fake prophecies "conveyed into the minds of mortal men [through] conference with damned spirits". He used the confessions of witches to illustrate this unpleasant business. These included the claim by one woman, whom Howard himself saw hang in Cambridge, that a spirit had requested a drop of blood from her finger before it divulged false information about the future.[13]

For Howard, Lavater and Boguet, the existence of demons provided a credible explanation for events that modern thinkers would need to interpret in different ways. Reports of familiar spirits, sub-terrestrial creatures and screaming apples were not self-evidently ridiculous, and the facts of the Bible offered a context in which they could be understood. For twenty-first-century readers, however, reports of this kind still prompt a question. What about the *first* person to see the familiar spirit or hear the apple groan? How can their experience be explained? Here it is useful to note the importance of systems of belief in shaping our immediate experience of the world. Our prior expectations often determine what we see and hear, as well as what we make of it. As he grew older and his eyesight started to fail, the historian Christopher Hill reflected on this fact:

> When I walk in the country I can identify colours better than objects. If I see something white where I am expecting to see a signpost, a signpost it becomes; whereas in fact it turns out to be a piece of paper. If I were expecting to see a ghost, it would no doubt have become a ghost. So I can understand how in the seventeenth century old men and women (or indeed the greater number of short-sighted people there must have been) saw armies fighting in the sky, and other portents, at times when they were conditioned to expect them.

Hill's observation can be extended to many other phenomena, and does not apply only to the short-sighted. Even with perfect vision, people often recognise familiar faces from a distance in places where they expect to see them, only to find that their first impression was mistaken. Just as often, we may hear or see things we cannot explain, and then simply think no more about them. Such experiences are meaningless without a frame of reference to make sense of them. Here the context of existing knowledge is crucial. If I notice a strange disturbance on the surface of a local pond, I might consider the matter for a while before letting it pass; if I see the same thing on Loch Ness, my mind will inevitably move in a different direction. Psychologists have noted that we rely on our minds to make sense of what we perceive. We grasp things around us "indirectly, through analysing, interpreting and trying to make sense of sensations". How we do this, in turn, depends on what we already believe, and this knowledge is largely provided by our culture. I would not expect to see a monster in Loch Ness without a popular tradition that one existed.[14]

Once a supernatural event was described, and accepted by others as credible, the original details were incorporated within existing frameworks of belief. In some cases, the initial story was fleshed out in later versions. During a restless night in his castle in Prague, the fourteenth-century emperor Charles IV heard a cup crash inexplicably across his bedchamber. Subsequent accounts confirmed the Emperor's claim that a ghostly visitor was responsible, and filled in the details by depicting a spectral figure standing in his room. More often, secondary writers simply related reports of the supernatural to their wider understanding of the world. When Henry Howard and Ludwig Lavater reported the evidence of ancient texts and trusted contemporary witnesses, they self-consciously placed this material in the context of Christian theology. Their religious view of the world was only one variety of knowledge, however. There were other ways of making sense of things in medieval and Renaissance Europe, and perhaps the most important of these was magic.[15]

MAGIC AND RELIGION

The essential components of magic were described systematically in the pioneering work of the anthropologist James George Frazer. In *The Golden Bough* (1890–1915), Frazer identified two principles that underpinned the magical view of the world: the idea that "like produces like" and the belief that "things which have once been in contact with one another continue to act on each other at a distance". Frazer's definitions are still useful for understanding magic in the pre-modern world. Their relevance can be illustrated by a tale from a Scottish witchcraft pamphlet published in 1591. The provenance of this story is doubtful, but it can nonetheless be taken to reflect the assumptions of its readers. The tale concerns the schoolmaster, John Cunningham, who tried to use sorcery to coerce sexual favours from the sister of one of his charges. Cunningham asked his pupil to obtain hair from his sister's vagina so he could employ it in a love spell. Fortunately for the girl, her mother discovered this plot and replaced the hair from her daughter with some from the equivalent parts of a heifer. This led to a memorable denouement when the boy delivered these to the magician:

> The schoolmaster . . . thinking them indeed to be the maid's hairs,
> went straight and wrought his art upon them. But the doctor had no
> sooner done his intent to them, but presently the heifer or cow
> whose hairs they were indeed came unto the door of the church
> wherein the schoolmaster was, into the which the heifer went and
> made towards the schoolmaster, leaping and dancing upon him, and
> following him forth of the church and to what place so ever he went,
> to the great admiration of all the townsmen . . . and many others
> who did behold the same.

Alongside its comic elements, this story points to Frazer's basic principles of magic. The hair taken from the girl (or cow) was held to exert an influence at a distance, and this influence depended on its original connection to the subject of the spell. It was also necessary to cut this hair from an appropriate part of the subject's body, following the principle that "like produces like". In this case, the magician wanted hair from the genitals because he hoped to affect the sexual feelings of his target. Unfortunately for him, it appears that his magic worked just as well when the material came from the relevant part of a cow.[16]

Frazer also suggested a theoretical distinction between magic and religion. Both magical and religious beliefs, he argued, involve the acceptance of supernatural agents with power over human affairs, but magicians attempt to control these agents for their own purposes, whereas the devotees of religion seek to worship, petition and appease them. The sociologist Max Weber made a similar point when he observed that priests "superintend the worship of the gods, while magicians seek to compel demons". Marcel Mauss later refined this distinction by emphasising the essentially private nature of magical operations. These contrast with the public rites associated with religion, in which whole communities seek to manage their collective relationship with supernatural powers. In the context of the pre-modern world, where the existence of supernatural agents was accepted as a matter of course, magic and religion represented two different ways of dealing with the inhabitants of the "invisible world".[17]

These distinctions are useful, but it is important to realise that magic and religion were not completely separate. For Frazer and Weber, belief in magic was a stage through which societies passed in their intellectual development: "magical" cultures evolved into "religious" ones. In pre-modern communities however, religion and magic existed alongside one another and were often interwined. The words of the Latin mass, and even vernacular translations of the Bible, could be used for ostensibly magical purposes. The text of John 1:1 – "In the beginning was the word, and the word was with God, and the word was God" – was recited to cure sick animals, and in some cases it was written down in the form of a spell to be worn around the neck or even ingested as a defence against illness. Candles blessed in church could be taken home to protect their owners from demons. The widespread belief in magic in pre-modern culture should not be regarded as the remnant of an earlier, declining tradition. On the contrary, it appears that magical ideas were remarkably vital and adaptable, and were at least as enduring as official theology. Nor were magical beliefs confined to the lower ranks of society. Some specialist branches of magic, notably the practice of alchemy, required such expensive materials that they were mainly the preserve of social elites. Many highly educated individuals took an interest in magic. These included the Elizabethan mathematician John Dee as well as Sir Isaac Newton.[18]

The practical uses of magic were innumerable. Unscrupulous medieval students acquainted with the *ars notoria*, a form of magic devoted to the acquisition of academic knowledge, could master arithmetic by performing rituals and meditating on a series of intricately drawn figures. The same method could be used to learn geometry, rhetoric, grammar and astronomy. At a more mundane level, "cunning" men and women offered magical services to ordinary villagers. These included the identification of thieves, finding lost or stolen property, divining the future, healing people and animals, and working counter-magic against suspected witches. Far less reputable were the travelling magicians of northern Europe who persuaded hopeful individuals to hand over valuables in order to appease the spirits who, they claimed, guarded hidden stores of treasure. Such charlatans exploited the general acceptance of magic among the population, but most practitioners appear to have offered sincere advice to help people cope with the problems of daily life. The Oxford antiquarian John Aubrey collected some of this advice in the late 1600s. He recorded how wearing a magical inscription around the neck could prevent ague. More ambitiously, he noted a method "to make a man gun-proof" by inscribing characters on a parchment and carrying this in his clothes. By Aubrey's time, the proliferation of published guides to magic had greatly increased public knowledge of the subject. At the top end of the market, learned texts such as Johannes Wecker's *De Secretis* (1582) introduced readers to the "secrets of natural magic", including the complex art of making precious stones. Cheaper, vernacular texts offered miscellaneous advice about practical magic. The English *New Fortune Book* (1720) included, among other things, a magical cure for toothache and the recipe for "true and false love powder".[19]

While magic and religion co-existed in medieval and Renaissance culture, tensions between them sometimes became apparent. In particular, reforming clerics occasionally voiced hostility to magical practices within the church and society at large. The works of St Augustine provided ammunition for those who championed a thoroughly religious view of the world. For Augustine, even well intentioned uses of magic were suspect because they implied a pact between mortals and "corrupt angels". He declared that the practitioners of "this kind of futile and harmful superstition, and the contracts, as it were, of an untrustworthy and treacherous partnership established by the disastrous alliance of men and devils, must be totally rejected and avoided by the Christian". Later church reformers like the fifteenth-century demonologist Johannes Nider endorsed this hardline view. But the practical integration of religion and magic made it impossible for them to eliminate magic completely. Nor was the practice of magic within a broadly Christian framework without its defenders. The anonymous author of a thirteenth-century text on ritual magic commended the practice of conjuring spirits on the grounds that only the pure in heart could perform such operations. "It is not possible", he claimed, "that a wicked and unclean man could work truly in this art; for men are not bound unto spirits, but spirits are constrained against their will to answer clean men and fulfil their requests". In the sixteenth century, the philosopher Cornelius Agrippa defended "natural magic", though he was careful to distance himself from the practice of conjuration. He proposed that the "wise men" described in Matthew 2:1 were magicians, and that their homage to the infant Christ proved there was nothing wicked in their art.[20]

The most sustained conflict between religion and magic was occasioned by the Protestant Reformation of the sixteenth century. In 1517, an obscure German monk named Martin Luther complained about corruption in the church. His protest rapidly expanded to a wholesale attack on the theology and institutions of medieval Christianity. At the heart of Luther's critique was the charge that the church was contaminated with beliefs that were essentially magical. The mass itself was a glorified magical rite that claimed falsely to deliver salvation through the incantations of a priest. In claiming that the performance of rituals and "good works" could earn people redemption, the church was practising a deadly kind of sorcery. In terms of Frazer's definition of magic, churchmen were attempting to influence God's will through human actions. Luther, in contrast, adopted a thoroughly religious view of the world, insisting that no human acts could ever move or stay the hand of God. In 1535, he likened the sorcery of the church to witchcraft:

> When I was a child there were many witches and sorcerers around
> who bewitched cattle and people, particularly children, and did
> much harm . . . Now [the devil] bewitches people in a worse way
> with spiritual sorcery. Witchcraft is a brand of idolatry. As witches
> used to bewitch cattle and men, so idolaters . . . go around to bewitch
> God and to make Him out as one who justifies [redeems] men not by
> grace through faith in Christ but by the works of men's own
> choosing. They bewitch and deceive themselves. If they continue in
> their wicked thoughts of God they will die in their idolatry.

In regions that embraced the Reformation, governments and local elites adopted Luther's condemnation of ecclesiastical "magic". Catholic churchmen, in turn, defended their faith by trying to draw a clear line between religion and "superstition". This led to an effort on both sides to promote a religious understanding of the world, and to impose this understanding on the population at large.[21]

The results of this enterprise were mixed. Protestants and Catholics drew the line between legitimate beliefs and superstition in different ways. While Protestants denounced popular devotions such as pilgrimage and the cult of the saints, reforming Catholics sought to preserve these activities while divesting them of unacceptably magical trappings. Protestant opinion was also split. Luther himself was prepared to tolerate images in churches, while some followers of the French reformer John Calvin renounced such images entirely. Ostensibly magical practices survived at all levels of society. When the papal legate Cardinal Cajetan was travelling through France in 1590, he heard reports of a plot to ambush his party. Unable to determine the truth of these rumours, he wrote the words "Go" and "Do not go" on two pieces of paper, folded them and dropped them in a communion chalice. He withdrew one of the papers and took its advice not to proceed.[22] Learned magicians like Agrippa and John Dee flourished in the sixteenth century, and occasionally enjoyed the patronage of royal courts. Where they survive, the records of Protestant and Catholic visitors sent to ascertain the religious knowledge of ordinary people suggest that magical beliefs remained widespread. Even the symbols of Protestantism could be used for magic. By the 1600s, many north German villagers adorned their homes with pictures of Luther. These probably expressed their affection for the great reformer, but it was also widely believed that they provided protection from evil spirits and fire.[23]

The intimate connections between religion and magic made it impossible for one to supplant the other. They represented two different responses to the given reality of a world penetrated by supernatural forces. It is only in the context of this world, filled with the power of God, angels and demons, and sustained by the authority of ancient texts, that we can make sense of the events at Rothenbach in 1485.

TRIAL BY FIRE AND WATER

By allowing an alleged witch to be tested by ordeal, the Count of Fürstenberg was contributing to a general revival in the use of such procedures across Europe. This was associated mainly with witchcraft. Both the ordeal of the red-hot iron and the more famous practice of "ducking" suspects to determine their guilt or innocence were practised sporadically in witch trials in the sixteenth century. Regional courts in France occasionally used the water test, though it was condemned by the Paris *parlement* in 1590. In 1597 James VI of Scotland endorsed the ordeal by water in witchcraft cases. He explained that an innocent person would sink in the water, but a witch would float as a divinely ordained sign of her pact with the devil. "It appears that God hath appointed, for a supernatural sign of the monstrous impiety of the witches, that the water shall refuse to receive them in her bosom that have shaken off them the sacred water of baptism, and refused the use of it". In 1647 the English witch-finder Matthew Hopkins quoted this passage approvingly. Hopkins himself submitted alleged witches to the ordeal, though he claimed that evidence obtained in this way was not used in their trials.[24]

The use of the ordeal in cases of witchcraft was not common, but its occasional application was understandable given the nature of the crime. Alleged acts of witchcraft were normally committed in secret, and for this reason the guilt or innocence of the accused could be extremely hard to determine. It was because it was a "secret, unnatural crime", James VI noted, that God had provided the water test to assist mortals in its detection. In cases where an alleged offence was too serious to ignore but too hidden to allow for a confident verdict, judges could appeal to the direct intervention of God to reveal the truth. This was the main purpose of the ordeal during its heyday in the Middle Ages. For this reason, trial by fire or water was never used when other evidence was available. It was most frequently employed in situations where judges had only the word of the accused or their accuser to go by, such as sexual infidelity or suspected heresy. The need for the procedure was illustrated in a heresy trial at Vézelay in France in 1167. According to Hugh of Poitiers, two of the accused appeared to recant their errors, but their conversion was disputed and it was impossible to know if their change of heart was genuine. Trial by ordeal provided the only means to settle the matter:

> The two men who gave the appearance of having recanted were conducted to the judgment by ordeal of water. In everyone's opinion, one of them was acquitted by the water. (Nevertheless, there were some who thought it was a dubious decision.) On the other hand, the second man, when plunged into the water, was declared guilty by nearly unanimous acclaim. Remanded to confinement, since opinion was not unanimous even among the clergy, he again underwent the ordeal of water, at his own request, and was a second time immersed, but the water scarcely received him at all. Thus twice condemned, he was sentenced by all to the fire.

Happily for the accused man, this sentence was commuted to banishment. For the authorities concerned, the ordeal by water provided the only sure method to determine the truthfulness of the men's conversion, since no other evidence could reveal the secrets of their hearts.[25]

Within the Christian worldview of pre-modern Europe, the fact that God could execute such judgments was impossible to deny. In principle, divine interventions could alter the ordinary course of nature, preventing hot irons from burning flesh and water from receiving the bodies of sinners. The Bible provided ample evidence for miracles of this kind, and also testified to the immanent judgment of the Lord. The abandonment of trial by ordeal throughout Europe in the late Middle Ages, and its sparing use in the subsequent prosecution of witches, did not mean that pre-modern thinkers came to find the practice absurd. Indeed, its demise coincided with the appearance of another judicial practice that most modern readers would regard as ridiculous: the criminal trial of animals. The use of ordeals was discouraged for reasons consistent with the beliefs of the age. Opponents of the process pointed out that it was not sanctioned by scripture. The Bible showed that God could issue miraculous judgments when He chose to do so; it did not prove that He would make these judgments whenever mortals asked for them. Nor were there any passages describing the specific rites involved in the judicial ordeal. More seriously, the scriptures appeared to condemn the practice of demanding divine judgments. The book of Deuteronomy warned against "tempting God" (6:16) and Christ quoted this passage in his confrontation with Satan in the Gospels of Matthew and Luke (Matt. 4:7; Luke 4:12). In response to these criticisms, a church council condemned trial by ordeal in 1215. Later in the thirteenth century, St Thomas Aquinas summed up the reasons for this decision: the judicial ordeal was unlawful because it was "not sanctioned by divine authority" and required "a miraculous result from God" in response to human bidding.[26]

In the broader context of pre-modern belief, the rejection of trial by ordeal was another instance of the ongoing tension between religion and magic. For those who opposed the practice, it appeared to command God in much the same way that a magician might try to coerce an angel. Opposition to the ordeal also reflected concerns about the activity of demons. Since the results obtained through trial by fire and water were not guaranteed by God, it was possible for unclean spirits to manipulate them. Aquinas observed that unlawful appeals for divine guidance were "not free from the interference of demons". This warning was especially relevant in cases of witchcraft. Those accused of this crime were often believed to have made pacts with the devil, or to employ evil spirits to cause harm. Since the devil took special delight in mimicking the works of God to hoodwink mortals, the use of the ordeal in such cases was extremely perilous. It was not surprising, then, that the *Malleus Maleficarum* denounced the verdict at Rothenbach. It is one of the ironies of the European witch-hunt that judges were occasionally inclined to use trial by ordeal because of the secret nature of the crime, but the widespread denunciation of this practice meant that other methods were more often employed to elicit the kind of hidden information that might otherwise have been disclosed by the water test or the hot iron. Since the torture of suspects was the main alternative, it is possible that a wider use of the ordeal would have reduced the scale of witch persecutions.[27]

Both the opponents and defenders of trial by ordeal acknowledged that God could, in principle, pronounce miraculous judgments against the secret crimes of women and men. The differences between them concerned the legitimacy of the ordeal itself. Trial by fire and water was not abandoned because people came to regard it as irrational; it ended because church leaders decided it was un-Christian. The idea that God chooses not to intervene directly in human affairs is a relatively recent addition to western thought, developed largely in response to the rise of empirical science. But it is no more rational to believe in a God who does not perform wonders than to believe in one who does. Robert Bartlett, the leading modern historian of trial by ordeal, has summed up the matter neatly:

> An atheist will presume that God was not manifesting judgment in the ordeal and that therefore the men of the Middle Ages, who believed that He was, were wrong in so thinking. He will also admit, however, that if one believes in a just, omnipotent, omniscient, and active deity, it is quite rational to believe that He may manifest His will to men on earth in various ways, including, possibly, trial by ordeal . . . The liberal Christian, not familiar or comfortable with the crass and interfering God of the Middle Ages, may be tempted to dismiss the ordeal as irrational, but does so at the risk of intellectual incoherence.

In a world unfamiliar with the immanence of supernatural forces, and reluctant even to attribute miraculous interventions to God, the trial of the witch of Rothenbach may seem absurd. But this is only because the "full-blooded and coherent" religion of the pre-modern age has disappeared. We may be glad this age has passed, but we cannot claim that its people were less reasonable than we are.[28]

2

Angels on a Pinhead

Are there toilets in heaven? Do angels eat food? How big is a soul? These questions evoke the naivety of childhood. They appear to be innocent and unsophisticated, and few adults would give them serious attention. The same can be said about most speculations concerning the physical nature of heavenly beings and life after death. Do angels have real bodies? How fast can they move? Will everyone be the same age in heaven? These questions seem pointless, but this response should not prevent us from asking why – exactly – they deserve to be treated so lightly. Viewed from a historical perspective, the peculiar nature of modern attitudes towards these matters becomes apparent. Western intellectuals gave serious consideration to all the problems mentioned above from the early Middle Ages to the eve of the Enlightenment. It was only in the eighteenth century that European thinkers began to dismiss such speculations as pointless. In the early 1800s, Isaac D'Israeli, the father of the Victorian British prime minister, summed up this attitude by mocking those scholars who asked "how many angels can dance on the head of a very fine needle, without jostling one another?" Most westerners now share D'Israeli's assumption that such questions are inane. But why?

The simplest reason for dismissing the kind of enquiries that D'Israeli lampooned is because they deal with things that do not exist. An atheist might argue that all speculations about the nature of God, angels, heaven and hell are misplaced: if these things are not real, it is futile to wonder what they may be like. Viewed in this light, our reluctance to study the behaviour of angels or the living conditions in heaven is just one aspect of a general decline in religious belief. But this is only part of the answer. The arguments of atheists may be compelling, but their impact appears to be limited: opinion polls show consistently that a majority of Europeans believe in God and the afterlife. In America, both church attendance and religious belief remain impressively strong. It is reasonable to argue that religion remains a significant feature of many modern societies, but other aspects of contemporary culture tend to discourage the kind of precise metaphysical speculations that were once commonplace. Three major trends stand out. First, empirical science has replaced theology as the normal method for establishing the physical facts of life. Second, there has been a general decline in confidence in the Bible as a source of information. This decline has been challenged to some extent by the rise of Christian fundamentalism, but even in the United States literalist interpretations of scripture are some way from enjoying the status of intellectual orthodoxy. Finally, the acceptance of religious pluralism means that Christianity is no longer treated as a source of universal knowledge. While scientists can legitimately attempt to establish general principles about the cosmos, the statements of theologians are always matters of opinion. Even if Christian scholars successfully calculated the number of souls in heaven, they would not expect their findings to gain support among their Jewish or Muslim fellows.

These characteristics of western culture are relatively new. Before the widespread acceptance of empirical science among intellectuals in the late seventeenth century, theology provided the surest method for discovering the facts of this world and the next. The Bible remained an authoritative source of information until well into the nineteenth century, and religious pluralism emerged only gradually in western societies in the last 200 years. In the very different conditions of the pre-modern world, it was no more absurd for theologians to speculate about the physical dimensions of heaven than it is for modern physicists to contemplate the shape of the universe. Critics could accuse both groups of pursuing knowledge to the point of impractical abstraction. After all, do we really need to know if amputees will regain their limbs in heaven? Or for that matter, whether the universe is expanding or contracting? But in their defence, both modern scientists and medieval scholars could claim that the acquisition of knowledge for its own sake is a virtue. If it is worthwhile for scientists who believe in particles of light to speculate about their composition and behaviour, it is valid for theologians who believe in angels to ask the same kind of questions. Until the comparatively recent past, Christian thinkers enjoyed the confidence to do just this. The results of this enterprise may strike us as bizarre. But we would be arrogant to dismiss them as foolish, and we would be profoundly mistaken to regard them as trivial. On the contrary, these metaphysical conjectures reflect the great seriousness with which religious matters were addressed in the pre-modern world. They also offer a striking indication of the gulf between that world and our own.

ANGELS AND DEMONS

Since the counting of angels on a pinhead is the most common charge made against pre-modern theologians, it is appropriate to begin this tour of the fine points of metaphysical speculation with the study of "angelology". The

existence of good and bad angels was a given in early Christianity. In the
magisterial *City of God*, St Augustine included both humans and the good
angels in the company of the redeemed, and argued that demons would suffer
damnation alongside wicked men and women. The attributes and behaviour
of our celestial companions was the subject of careful analysis in the Middle
Ages, culminating in the painstaking studies of the thirteenth-century
Dominican friar, St Thomas Aquinas. During the Reformation in the 1500s,
both Protestants and Catholics accepted the reality of angels, viewing them as
allies in the pursuit of religious purity and the struggle against confessional
opponents. Throughout this period, the existence of angels was proven by the
unimpeachable testimony of scripture. The Bible contains frequent examples
of angelic interventions in earthly affairs, such as the appearance of two angels
in Sodom to destroy the sinful city and rescue the virtuous Lot (Gen. 19). The
prophetic books of Daniel and Revelation also describe the role of angels in
the events of the Last Judgment. This scriptural evidence was supplemented
by numerous later accounts of human encounters with angels. Bede offered
an engaging instance in his eighth-century biography of St Cuthbert:

> One morning he left the inner monastery buildings to go to the guest
> chamber and found a youth sitting inside. He gave him the usual sort
> of kindly welcome, thinking, naturally, that he was a man. He got
> him water to wash his hands, washed his feet himself, dried them,
> put them in his bosom, and humbly chafed them with his hands. The
> youth was asked to wait till after terce, when a meal would be ready;
> otherwise if he left at once he would faint with hunger in the winter
> cold . . . But the youth said he must leave immediately and hurry to a
> far distant place. Cuthbert asked question after question, and finally
> abjured him in God's name to stay . . . When he came back the youth
> had vanished. The ground was covered with fresh snow but there
> were no footprints to be seen.

Cuthbert noticed a "wonderfully fragrant odour" after his guest had
vanished, and discovered in the storehouse three loaves of bread "such as
cannot be produced on earth, whiter than the lily, sweeter than roses, more
delicious than honey". The saint concluded that his visitor was an angel,
"come not to be fed but to feed".[1]

In meetings such as this, angels appeared to God's children to test their
obedience and demonstrate divine favour. But they could also act as instruments
of wrath. The Bible made it clear that they could visit dreadful retribution on
those who displeased the Lord. The Protestant reformer John Calvin noted in
1554 that "angels are the ministers of God's wrath as well as his grace", and
could "descend with the purpose of executing divine vengeance, and of
inflicting punishment". In popular traditions, this role was described in lurid

tales of criminals destroyed by avenging angels. When the Englishman Gabriel Harding murdered his wife, an angel appeared in his house to announce God's sentence against him and hand him over to Satan, who promptly snapped his neck. A sixteenth-century ballad described the celestial visitor:

> His eyes like to the stars did shine,
> He was clothed in a bright grass green,
> His cheeks were of a crimson red,
> For such a man was seldom seen.

The folklore concerning angels included many fabulous tales of this kind, and educated contemporaries were quick to condemn the more colourful or theologically dubious reports as "vulgar superstition". Nonetheless, the clear evidence of scripture, combined with a wealth of testimonies by reputable witnesses, ensured that even the most sceptical pre-modern thinkers accepted the reality of the angelic host.[2]

So what were angels like? Theologians consistently maintained that they were creatures of enormous power. According to Augustine, they enjoyed "powers surpassing those of all living creatures on earth", as well as the ability to overcome demons. Paradoxically however, this power came at the expense of independent action. It was a measure of their status as the most perfect beings beneath the Lord Himself that their will conformed totally to His own. As a consequence, they acted always as His agents. "Even when His angels listen", Augustine noted, it is God Himself "who listens in them, being in them as in His true temple".[3] The Lord employed angels to perform miracles and communicate with mortals, but these acts were never truly their own. In this respect, humans had more in common with demons than angels, since both had rebelled against God to assert their own will. The angels' fidelity had been rewarded with perfect communion with the Lord, while the demons – and a sizeable part of humankind – were condemned for their disobedience to eternal darkness.

Throughout the medieval and Renaissance period, reports of the earthly activities of angels emphasised their perfect conformity to God's will. Indeed, this was one of the signs that a visitation was truly angelic in character. When a woman from Amsterdam was cured miraculously of lameness in 1676, the published account made it clear that the angel who worked the miracle acted solely as an agent of God:

> Being in bed with her husband, she was three times pulled by her arm, with which she awakened and cried out: "Oh Lord! What may this be?" Hereupon she heard an answer in plain words: "Be not afraid, I come in the name of the Father, Son and Holy Ghost. Your malady, which has for many years been upon you, shall cease, and it

shall be given to you from God almighty to walk again." . . .
Whereupon she cried aloud: "Oh Lord! That I had a light, that I
might know what this is." Then she had this answer: "There needs no
light, the light shall be given you by God". Then came light all over
the room, and she saw a beautiful youth, about ten years of age, with
curled yellow hair, clothed in white to the feet, who went from the
bed's head to the chimney with a light, which a little after vanished.

As the angelic child disappeared, she experienced a gushing sensation in her
legs as feeling returned to the previously dead limbs, and within two days she
could walk again. Like the unnatural light that suffused the room, this act of
healing was accomplished solely through the power of God, with the golden-
haired child apparently serving as the conduit for His will.[4]

While scripture and the Church Fathers offered a clear picture of the
behaviour of angels, there was less agreement about their physical nature.
Augustine was ambivalent on whether they possessed real bodies, though
most other early writers assumed that they did. This derived partly from the
belief that the reprobate angels fell from grace by committing sexual sins, a
view supported by the apocryphal book of Enoch and the passage in Genesis
where the "sons of God", normally taken to be angels, begot children by the
"daughters of men" (Gen. 6:2). Other biblical incidents suggested that angels
had physical bodies, such as Abraham's meeting with three celestial
messengers who accepted his offer of food (Gen. 18). This view was
consistent with the belief that God, as the most perfect being, was the only
entity that could exist in a completely disembodied form. The idea of angelic
bodies persisted into the Middle Ages, but was increasingly challenged by
new opinions. In the twelfth century, Peter Lombard expressed doubts about
the corporeality of angels in his *Sentences*, which became one of the core texts
for theological study in medieval universities. More decisively, Thomas
Aquinas argued that both angels and demons were immaterial beings in his
exhaustive exposition of the Christian faith, the *Summa Theologica*.[5]

This new perspective raised an obvious problem. If angels were immaterial
creatures, how did they interact with humans? Did they appear to mortals in
visions? Or did they assume temporary bodies when they descended to earth?
Aquinas and most subsequent writers took the latter view. As he noted in the
Summa, the Bible recorded instances where angels were seen by large groups
of people, making it unlikely that they were merely projections of the mind.
They also appeared to engage physically with human beings, like the angel
who wrestled with Jacob before revealing his message from God (Gen.
32:24–8). Aquinas concluded that celestial beings took on earthly bodies for
our benefit, since as embodied creatures we could not relate to them in their
natural form. "Angels need an assumed body, not for themselves, but on our
account: that by conversing familiarly with men they may give evidence of that

intellectual companionship which men expect to have with them in the life to come". This solution left open many questions, which the "angelic doctor" pursued with exacting tenacity. Did the "assumed bodies" of angels perform the normal functions of life? Did they need to sleep and eat? Here the evidence of scripture was ambiguous, since angels appeared to share food with the patriarch Abraham (Gen. 18:8). Nonetheless, Aquinas argued that "properly speaking the angels cannot be said to eat, because eating involves the taking of food convertible into the substance of the eater". But when an angel assumed a physical body, it was not "of such a nature that food could be changed into it". Moreover, as immaterial beings they had no need for physical sustenance. It followed that angels only appeared to eat food as a courtesy to their mortal companions, who were thereby able to offer them earthly hospitality.[6]

Could angels have sex? Augustine had raised this prospect when he noted the evidence in scripture "that angels appeared to men in bodies of such a kind that they could not only be seen but also touched". While he rejected the view that the "children of God" who paired with women in Genesis 6:2 were angels, he left open the possibility that "spirits with bodies of air (an element which even when set in motion by a fan is felt by the bodily sense of touch) can experience lust and so can mate, in whatever way they can, with women who feel their embraces". Aquinas followed him in this, but denied that immaterial spirits could ever experience sexual desire. This was impossible because "a spiritual nature cannot be affected by such pleasures as appertain to bodies, but only by such as are in keeping with spiritual things". Thus angels were non-sexual beings. It was possible, nonetheless, for fallen angels to assume physical bodies in order to copulate with humans, but they did so only for the intellectual pleasure of encouraging sin.[7]

As well as the physical properties of angels, Aquinas devoted scrupulous attention to their mental abilities. Could they read minds? Or predict the future? Here he was careful to preserve the special powers of God. While the will of angels was aligned to divine purposes, only the Lord Himself possessed a sure knowledge of human hearts. Nonetheless, the friar observed that telltale signs often revealed the hidden thoughts of men and women, and conjectured that angels were exceptionally good at reading these signs:

> A secret thought can be known . . . in its effect. In this way it can be
> known not only by an angel but by a man . . . For thought is
> sometimes discovered not merely by outward act, but also by change
> of countenance; and doctors can tell some passions of the soul by the
> mere pulse. Much more then can angels, and even demons, the more
> deeply they penetrate those bodily modifications.

If angels were exemplary judges of character, they were also preternaturally skilful at guessing the future. Only God had perfect knowledge of events to come, but many occurrences could be predicted accurately by careful observation of signs in the present, just as accomplished doctors could predict the future health of their patients. Aquinas suggested that angels used the same method, only with better results "as they understand the causes of things both more universally and more perfectly". They would make superb gamblers if their disembodiment did not render them immune to material desires.[8]

Precise speculations of this kind were valid in their own right: they supplied details of the pattern of God's creation and focused attention on some of His most sublime works. But the study of angels also had practical applications. Since celestial beings could appear on earth, angelology offered guidelines on how the recipients of these visits should conduct themselves. This advice was necessary in order to avoid demonic deceptions, since even Satan could appear as "an angel of light" (2 Cor. 11:14). The theological consensus was that men and women should listen humbly to angelic visitors, who would reveal their true nature in their words and deeds. Since they always acted in accordance with the will of God, their pronouncements would be consistent with scripture and their actions would promote true religion. It was prudent, nonetheless, to be cautious. In the sixteenth century, the Swiss Protestant theologian Ludwig Lavater suggested that men and women should avoid all conversations with angels. "Ask them not who they are, or why they have presented themselves to be seen or heard. For if they be good, they will like it well that thou will hear nothing but the word of God; but if they be wicked, they will endeavour to deceive thee with lying." [9]

Advice of this kind assumed that people would not deliberately exploit their contact with angels for illicit purposes. But like all forms of knowledge, the science of celestial spirits could be abused. The medieval church condemned attempts to conjure angels to obtain secret knowledge, but surviving texts on ritual magic suggest that the practice was sometimes attempted. A thirteenth-century work attributed to Honorius of Thebes provides a striking example. This includes a ceremony for obtaining a prophetic vision of "the majesty of God in his glory, and the nine orders of angels, and the company of all blessed spirits". The author claims that this rite was revealed to him through an angelic visitation. A manual of ritual magic from fifteenth-century Germany includes a conjuration to obtain visions of angels in dreams. These will impart their knowledge to the sleeping magician. Such practices reversed the normal relationship between angels and mortals by placing the magician in control of the encounter. From the perspective of orthodox churchmen, they also exposed the unwary to contact with evil spirits disguised as "angels of light".[10]

As these anxieties suggest, the activity of demons necessitated their careful study. Like their angelic counterparts, the existence of demons was confirmed by scripture and the writings of the Church Fathers, as well as contemporary reports by reputable witnesses. The Old Testament contains relatively few references to the fallen angels, though the apocryphal book of Enoch describes their rebellion against God and expulsion from heaven. The New Testament, in contrast, features several encounters between Christ and the devil, as well as numerous descriptions of "unclean spirits". Augustine devoted much of his later work to the study of demons, and the lives of the desert fathers described lurid and often violent encounters with them. St Jerome's fourth-century life of Hilarion includes this dramatic episode:

> One night he started to hear babies crying, sheep bleating, cattle lowing, women weeping, as well as lions roaring and the din of an army. In short, many different terrifying sounds. He was driven back by terror at this noise, rather than anything he could see. He realised that the demons were mocking him, and so he fell down on his knees and made the sign of the cross on his forehead. Armed in this way he fought more bravely as he lay there, but he half-wanted to see what he was terrified to hear, and so he carefully looked around him in every direction. All of a sudden, in the moonlight, he saw a chariot with neighing horses rushing over him; but when he called upon Jesus, the earth opened wide and the whole procession was swallowed up.

As this tale suggests, demons were more varied in their appearance than angels. This was confirmed by a wealth of medieval sightings, in which they assumed the guise of handsome men and women, animals, monsters, and even swarms of bees. St Catherine of Sweden was tormented by demons in the shape of children's dolls. When a demon appeared at the bedside of the fourteenth-century mystic Julian of Norwich, she was able to provide a remarkably detailed description of its face:

> I thought the fiend had me by the throat, putting his face very near mine. It was like a young man's face, and long and extraordinarily lean: I never saw the like. The colour was the red of a tilestone newly fired, and there were black spots like freckles, dirtier than the tilestone. His hair was rust-red, clipped in front, with side-locks hanging over his cheeks. He grinned at me with a sly grimace, thereby revealing white teeth, which made it, I thought, all the more horrible. There was no proper shape to his body or hands, but with his paws he held me by the throat and would have strangled me if he could.

Other sightings presented demons as little more than vermin. Around 1230 the German monk Caesarius of Heisterbach described how a priest from Mainz spotted foul spirits on the skirts of a woman in his congregation. "They were as small as dormice and as black as Ethiopians, grinning and clapping their hands and leaping hither and thither like fish enclosed in a net". The priest abjured the creatures to be still and ordered the poor woman outside, where a crowd gathered to watch him drive them away.[11]

Since they lacked the perfect integrity of angels, the behaviour of demons was much harder to predict. They rejoiced in deception. Demons showed remarkable ingenuity in their efforts to dupe mortals, masquerading as angels and even mimicking the miracles of God. But their intentions were always wicked. Augustine observed that they were "spirits whose only desire is to do us harm, who are completely alien from any kind of justice, swollen with arrogance, livid with envy, and full of crafty deception". This ill will manifested itself in several ways. Demons could physically assault the faithful, as they did St Antony during his years in the wilderness. More subtly, they could terrorise the mind with perverse thoughts and temptations. After their nocturnal assaults on Hilarion were thwarted, the demons turned their attention to his mind: "often naked women would appear to him as he lay resting, often the most splendid banquets would appear to him when he was hungry". Medieval saints faced similar trials. In one memorable episode in fourteenth-century Italy, demons tempted Catherine of Siena with "vile pictures of men and women behaving loosely before her mind, and foul figures before her eyes, and obscene words to her ears, shameless crowds dancing around her, howling and sniggling and inviting her to join them". We can only admire Catherine's fortitude in resisting these advances. In their most complex and successful strategies, demons erected whole systems of false belief in which they were venerated as gods. Early Christians explained the pagan religions of Greece and Rome in these terms and later thinkers applied the same logic to the native cultures of America. In a seventeenth-century manual for priests working among South American tribespeople, Jacinto de la Serna identified medicine men as "ministers of Satan", and explained the local custom of identifying babies with animals "as further evidence of the way in which the devil, by means of his pacts, deceives these miserable people". Back in Europe, demonologists viewed the secret conspiracy of witchcraft as a more explicit means by which demons achieved the same objectives; and both Catholic and Protestant theologians denounced their confessional opponents as "dupes of Satan" during the Reformation.[12]

Given the pervasive involvement of demons in human affairs, theologians were keen to establish the limits of their power. In this they applied similar principles to those used in the study of angels. Like angels, demons were constrained by God-given laws of nature, but unlike their heavenly rivals, they never willingly assisted God in the performance of miracles that involved the temporary suspension of these laws. It followed that the feats performed by demons were always restricted by natural boundaries: they were "wonders" or "marvels", not true miracles. In 1616 the English pastor William Gouge set out the conventional view that evil spirits could only perform acts "in the compass of nature"; they never contravened the laws of the universe, but could exploit these laws to create remarkable effects. In this respect, demons were like modern-day conjurors: they pretended to achieve impossible feats by manipulating objects and gulling their audience. But they were conjurors par excellence. They possessed the same extraordinary knowledge and mental ability as angels, and put these advantages to ruthless use.[13]

One common form of demonic deception was the creation of hallucinations. Augustine noted that demons pretended to effect miracles by tricking the human senses, so that extraordinary feats were performed "merely in respect of appearance". In the *Malleus Maleficarum* (1486), Heinrich Krämer and Jacob Sprenger speculated on the mechanics of this process. They suggested that devils transferred images from the human memory to the organs of sight. As a result, the victim "is compelled to think that he sees with his external eyes" something that exists only in his imagination. Demons employed less subtle manipulations to convince mortals that they could see into the future. Nicolas Rémy suggested in 1595 that their ability in this regard resulted from little more than life experience:

> The longevity of the first men is said to have given them much
> leisure for observation; and out of this rose the science of astrology,
> by which it is thought to be possible to have precognition of the
> overthrow of kingdoms, of wars, the yields of crops, pestilences, and
> such matters. What wonder, then, if having lived continuously,
> without even sleeping, from the beginning of the world, the demons
> with their vigorous memory and unfettered powers of reasoning have
> acquired some faculty for conjecturing the future?

Some demonic prophecies were not even clever guesses. Rémy observed that wicked spirits sometimes exploited the inadequacies of human systems of communication by "predicting" events that had already taken place. He noted how "demons are able to announce, almost at the very moment of its occurrence, that which has happened in remote and distant regions, so that men in the slowness of their perception marvel at it and regard it in the light of a prognostication".[14]

While angels acted as messengers of God, a role that tended to limit their physical contact with humans, demons engaged in various kinds of corporeal relationships. They could assail human bodies with blows, and enter these bodies in cases of possession. As Caesarius of Heisterbach explained, "when the devil is said to be within the body of a man, this must not be understood of the soul but of the body, because he is able to pass into its empty cavities such as the bowels". Given these remarkable abilities, there was much speculation about the physical composition of demons. Most early Christian writers assumed they had real bodies, normally composed of some type of air. Augustine lent credence to this view by speculating that the original, celestial bodies of demons were transformed as a result of their fall. He suggested that they were reconstituted with aerial bodies so they could suffer punishment in the element of fire. This view commanded support throughout the Middle Ages, but in the thirteenth century it was challenged by the rival position that demons, like angels, were immaterial beings. Aquinas denied that demons possessed bodies of their own, but maintained that they assumed an artificial form when they appeared to mortals. Most writers on witchcraft in the Renaissance upheld this view. Whatever their natural state however, the material reality of the "assumed bodies" of demons was never in doubt. Medieval reports of demonic encounters were often violently physical. When a foul spirit appeared to the fourteenth-century saint Peter Olafsson, it hurled stones at his door that left visible marks. The fate of a wicked knight from Cologne was more terrible: Caesarius described how he was snatched up by a demon that "dragged him through the roof so roughly that his bowels were torn out by the broken tiles". Demons were also vulnerable to assaults on their assumed bodies. According to legend, St Dunstan grabbed a devil by its nose with a pair of tongs. In an incident from the 1440s, the friar Simon Granau described how a similar act led to tragic consequences. A carter arrived at the Prussian town of Thorn during a carnival, in which local men dressed up as demons to chase women outside the town walls. Not knowing what was happening, he jumped down from his cart to rescue one of the women, driving an axe through her attacker's head.[15]

While the assumed bodies of demons could suffer physical harm, this had no material effect on the foul spirits themselves. Lacking human flesh, they were incapable of suffering in the same way as mortals. Some medieval writers derived a surprising conclusion from this fact: demons were unable to do penance for their sins, even if they regretted their rebellion against God. They shared with humans the misfortune of living in a fallen state, but they could never atone for their crimes through bodily punishment. A first-hand account of this novel tragedy was provided in thirteenth-century France, when a demon spoke through the mouth of a possessed Dominican friar. The spirit began by talking about the good angels, then declared that "you don't know how sublime they are, but I know – I who fell from the company of them. And since I do not have flesh in which I can do penance, I am not able to climb there anymore". The creature added remorsefully that "if I had as much flesh as is in the human thumb, I would do so much penance in it that I would yet rise to a higher place". Tales of this kind reminded contemporaries that demons, despite their great powers, were irretrievably doomed. As Aquinas noted, they were sorrowful as well as malignant. The fate of the demons also provided an incentive for mortals to practise the repentance they could never perform.[16]

The angels and demons studied by pre-modern academics belonged to a parallel, "invisible" world that occasionally intersected with our own. Their study was part of the general enterprise of understanding the works and purposes of God. Knowledge of angels was important in this light, though relatively few people experienced direct contact with them. But another area of metaphysical speculation dealt with events that would affect everyone, bringing them face to face with the judgments of God and the facts of the invisible world. This was the study of the afterlife.

THINGS TO COME

Pre-modern people embraced two distinct ideas about life after death, both of which derived from the Bible and the Church Fathers. The first was the general resurrection of the dead. This would take place at the end of time, when Christ would restore life to the saved and the damned before consigning them to their eternal fates. St Paul looked forward to this final day, when "the trumpet shall sound and the dead shall be raised incorruptible". They would be restored to life "in a moment, in the twinkling of an eye" (1 Cor. 15: 52). This vision was elaborated in the book of Revelation, which described how the earth and the oceans would yield up the dead for their final reckoning. The resurrected would stand before God to be "judged out of those things which were written in the books, according to their works" (Rev. 20:12). The redeemed would become citizens of a heavenly city that would descend from the sky, and the damned would be tossed into the eternal furnace of hell, which most scholars located beneath the surface of the earth. In the thirteenth century, Gerardesca of Pisa described the luminous habitation of the risen saints, revealed to her in a vision of the world to come:

> She saw a vast plain called the territory of the Holy City of
> Jerusalem. There were castles in amazing numbers and very beautiful
> pleasure-gardens. All the streets of the city-state of Jerusalem were of
> the purest gold and the most precious stones. An avenue was formed
> by golden trees whose branches were resplendent with gold. Their
> blossom remained rich and luxuriant according to their kind, and they
> were more delightful and charming than anything we can see in
> earthly pleasure-gardens. In the middle of this territory lay
> Jerusalem – holy, sublime, very beautiful and ornate.

Today a minority of Christians hold steadfastly to the belief in a future world remade by divine intervention, but most westerners are probably more familiar with the second kind of afterlife envisioned in the pre-modern age. This was the immediate transition of the soul to another place after death. This view was implied in Jesus's parable of the rich man and the beggar Lazarus. When the beggar died he "was carried by the angels into Abraham's bosom", while the rich man was ushered by death to a "place of torment" (Luke 16:22, 28). Psalm 49 echoed this promise: the psalmist rejoiced that "God will redeem my soul from the power of the grave: for he shall receive me" (Ps. 49:15). These two beliefs co-existed in the pre-modern world, with the immediate fate of the soul upon death normally viewed as a preliminary to its eventual state at the end of history.[17]

Both forms of the afterlife raised technical questions. In the case of the general resurrection, one obvious problem concerned the restoration of corpses. Did they need to be intact at the moment of regeneration? What would become of those people whose bodies had been dismembered or burnt to ashes? St Paul offered one solution in his second letter to the Corinthians, where he inferred that when the last trump sounded the blessed would discard their earthly remains to be clothed in "spiritual bodies". This view implied that corpses were merely abandoned husks. Paul's opinion was challenged, however, by the physical resurrections described in the book of Revelation, and the later Church Fathers also insisted on the bodily reconstitution of the dead. Augustine faced the problems this raised squarely in the *City of God*. What would happen to "those bodies that have been consumed by wild beasts, or by fire, or those parts that have disintegrated into dust?" The answer lay in the incomparable power of God. "It is inconceivable", Augustine reasoned, "that any nook or cranny of the natural world, though it may hold those bodies concealed from our detection, could elude the notice or evade the power of the creator of all things". Cannibalism posed a more testing problem. What would happen at the general resurrection to those whose corpses had been eaten by other people? Here he argued that the flesh consumed by the cannibal would be converted back to its original owner, while the cannibal would be restored to the condition he enjoyed before his meal. Peter Lombard restated these arguments in the twelfth century in his standard theological text, the *Sentences*. An encyclopaedia of Christian doctrine compiled in the same period by the abbess Herrad of Hohenbourg contained a picture of beasts, birds and fish regurgitating the bodies of the saved. As the accompanying text explained, the "bodies and members of people once devoured" will be disgorged in this way so the "members of the saints will rise incorrupt". In the thirteenth century, Aquinas agreed that bodies would be restored to their original state when they were raised up for judgment. He also conjectured that minor body parts, such as fingernails and hair, would not be ignored in this process. While these parts were not essential to life, they contributed to the perfection of the human body, and "since man will rise again with all the perfections of his nature, it follows that hair and nails will rise again in him".[18]

As well as the issues raised by the reassembly of dead bodies, the physical nature of the general resurrection presented theologians with a tangle of technical problems. Once the dead were raised, what form would their bodies take? They were, after all, destined for eternal life, and could not be composed of the same perishable flesh worn by men and women before the Last Days. Other questions concerned the life cycle of the resurrected. How old would they be? Would babies be restored in their original bodies, and would they grow up to be adults? Here again, Augustine provided the standard answers. He argued that resurrected bodies would "have the substance of flesh, though never having to experience corruption or lethargy". Just as God furnished men and women with bodies suited to their earthly lives, He would provide them with new flesh fitted "for living in heaven". These renewed bodies would not need to eat or drink, or perform the other functions required for our present existence. There would be no toilets in heaven. On the question of the resurrection of infants, Augustine employed an argument reminiscent of modern genetics. He surmised that all human beings were imprinted at birth with the "pattern" of their future growth:

> All parts of the body are already latent in the seed, although a number of them are still lacking even at birth, the teeth, for instance, and other such details. There is thus, it seems, a kind of pattern already imposed potentially on the material substance of the individual, set out, one might say, like the pattern on a loom; and thus what does not yet exist, or rather what is there but hidden, will come into being . . . in the course of time. And so in respect of this pattern or potentiality an infant can be said to be short or tall in that he is destined to be the one or the other.

It was this pattern that would be realised at the general resurrection, not the physical state of the body at the time of death. Thus infants would "not rise again with the tiny bodies they had when they died"; rather, they would "gain that maturity they would have attained by the slow lapse of time". Peter Lombard endorsed this opinion in the twelfth century. Aquinas confirmed that the "imperfections" of physical immaturity and old age would not afflict the bodies of the redeemed. Men and women would be restored "in the youthful age", when the body was fully formed but not yet touched by signs of physical decline.[19]

Regarding the appearance of the risen bodies, Augustine argued that they would enjoy unblemished skin and physical beauty. "This means that fat people and thin people have no need to fear that at the resurrection they would not be the kind of people they would not have chosen to be in this life, if they had had the chance". As well as physical perfection, the renewed bodies of the elect would possess a lightness and agility unknown in this life. According to Aquinas, this would result from a new harmony between the soul and the body, which would react more quickly to execute its commands. This ability was also consistent with the purposes of God, who wished to enhance the happiness of the blessed. Most medieval and Renaissance scholars endorsed these ideas. In 1692 the English Protestant theologian Thomas Watson described the luminous glory of the risen servants of Christ:

> Though the bodies of the saints shall rot and be loathsome in the grave, yet afterwards they shall be made illustrious and glorious. The bodies of the saints, when they arise, shall be comely and beautiful. The body of a saint in this life may be deformed; those even whose minds are adorned with virtue may have misshapen bodies – as the finest cloth may have the coarsest list; but those deformed bodies shall be [made] amiable and beautiful.

Watson observed that "the bodies of the saints, when they arise, shall be swift and nimble". While our earthly bodies are heavy and unresponsive to the spirit, our "new flesh" will reflect the perfection of the remade world. "Now the body is a clog: in heaven it shall be a wing. We shall be as the angels".[20]

Scholars also pondered the biology of eternal damnation. Would the damned enjoy the same complete and uncorrupted bodies as the blessed? Aquinas noted that this appeared to be unjust, since physical deformities were sometimes "appointed as punishments for sin". This was certainly true of the mutilations imposed on criminals by the law courts of medieval Europe. Would these punishments be erased when sinners were resurrected with perfect bodies? He countered this objection by observing that "the punishments which in this temporal life are inflicted for sin are themselves temporal", whereas a different order of retribution awaited the damned in hell. Medieval scholars agreed that the bonfires of the afterlife would provide the principal torment of the damned. This was confirmed by the book of Revelation, which predicted that sinners "shall have their part in the lake which burneth with fire and brimstone" (Rev. 20:8).[21]

This grim promise raised some interesting physical questions. How could a fire burn forever without consuming the bodies within it? Was the fire of Hell the same as that found on earth? The first problem was resolved by the incorruptible nature of the bodies of the damned. As the Saxon monk Hugh of St Victor argued in the early twelfth century, these bodies were designed to endure everlasting flames. While the immortal flesh of the saved brought them eternal pleasure, the same attribute permitted the condemned to suffer endless agonies. Peter Lombard and Aquinas shared this view. As for hellfire itself, Aquinas conjectured that it was the same as earthly fire except "it needs no kindling, nor is kept alive by fuel". The same arguments were applied to the flames of purgatory, which purified sinful souls as they awaited the Judgment. The effects of earthly bonfires on human remains confirmed their similarity to the purgatorial pyres. Condemned heretics burnt to a cinder because they were utterly riddled with sin. The relics of saints, in contrast, were uncorrupted by earthly flames, and this method was sometimes used to confirm their authenticity.[22]

As well as the physics of the afterlife, scholars addressed questions of location and space in the world to come. Was hell in the centre of the earth? Given the vast numbers who would suffer there – with real bodies no smaller than our own – an enormous space would be needed. "Since the multitude of the damned will be exceeding great", Aquinas noted, "the space containing that fire must be exceeding great". It was therefore reasonable to ask whether there "is so great a hollow within the earth" to contain them all. To resolve this dilemma the friar turned to the book of Proverbs, where hellfire was identified as one of the three things that are "never satisfied" (Prov. 30:15–16). He took this to mean that the pyres of hell would never lack space for the condemned. Moreover, divine power was sufficient to "maintain within the bowels of the earth a hollow great enough to contain all the bodies of the damned". Some later thinkers adopted a more mathematical approach. Italian Jesuits attempted to calculate the precise dimensions of hell in the seventeenth century. Allowing 6,000 years since the world was made, and estimating the number of the damned at between 20 or 30 thousand million, Francisco de Rivera suggested that an area equivalent to the Italian peninsula would be sufficient. Others challenged this calculation. "It is very probable", argued Leonardo Lessio, "that in that place of punishment there is not room for them to stand upright, but rather they are piled on top of one another and heaped together in the same way as wood in a pile". This allowed Lessio to reduce the space needed to a twentieth of Rivera's estimate. His work was challenged in turn by Cornelio a Lapide, who favoured a much larger inferno:

> It does not seem probable that the bodies will be so tightly packed in hell, but rather they will have more space so that the violence of the flames can carry them up high and then plunge them back into the fire, turning them and captivating them in many ways . . . Since it is probable that after the Day of Judgment the demons themselves will be enclosed in bodies in order to be tormented and to suffer the sight of the damned, but since there are so many of these spirits, the space calculated by Lessio would be too small.

Similar calculations allowed the curious to estimate the living space that the risen saints would enjoy. Speculations in this area were assisted by the book of Revelation, which described the dimensions of the heavenly city that would descend to earth following the Last Judgment: "the city lieth foursquare, and the length is as large as the breadth; and he measured the city with the reed, twelve thousand furlongs" (Rev. 21:16). Some medieval and Renaissance scholars followed the specifics in Revelation 21 to produce scale drawings of the celestial city. More ambitiously, others attempted to measure the space required

for the Day of Judgment itself. As late as 1692, the esteemed New England
pastor Samuel Lee suggested the entire event could occur in an area smaller
than the British Isles. This allowed for the world to last 10,000 years, with an
average of a thousand million people in each generation, and assumed that each
resurrected body would require "a place five foot square to stand upon".[23]

The future world described so confidently by Samuel Lee would be the
final abode of all men and women who died. But the fate that awaited the
dead in the years before the Judgment was another matter. The Bible had less
to say on this subject than the Last Days, and St Paul referred to the dead
before the Judgment as merely "sleeping" (1 Cor. 15:6, 20). Augustine held
that God would receive the spirits of the dead in "secret abodes" before they
were reunited with their bodies. In accordance with Jesus's parable of the rich
man and Lazarus however, it was generally assumed that these holding places
involved some form of judgment. At his death the rich man was tormented
with flames, and was separated by a "great gulf" from the redeemed Lazarus.
The nature of this judgment was elaborated in the Middle Ages, so that
Aquinas could declare that "a place is assigned to souls in keeping with their
reward or punishment, as soon as the soul is set free from the body". While
the world remained in its present state, the condition of the dead was
temporary and incomplete. Peter Lombard noted that the souls of the dead
would only find perfect contentment when they were dressed in the new flesh
of their resurrected bodies. Dante expressed the same thought in *The Divine
Comedy*. Here disembodied souls looked forward to the day "when our flesh,
then glorified and holy, is put on us once more". On that day they would "be
in greater perfection, as being complete at last".[24]

While the Bible provided few details about the migration of souls after death,
many later accounts described the process more fully. In the fourth century,
Jerome described how St Antony tramped across the desert to meet Paul of
Thebes, only to discover that the holy man was dead. Antony was forewarned
of this outcome in a vision as he neared the hermit's cave: "he saw Paul among
the hosts of angels, among the choirs of prophets and apostles, shining with a
dazzling whiteness and ascending on high". Rushing on to his destination, he
found Paul's corpse in a kneeling posture with its arms stretched out towards
the skies. Bede recorded a similar incident in his life of St Cuthbert. As
Cuthbert was watching sheep one night, "he suddenly saw light streaming from
the skies, breaking the long night's darkness, and the choirs of the heavenly host
coming down to earth". He watched as the angels gathered up "a human soul,
marvellously bright, and returned to their home above". The next day he heard
that Aidan, the pious bishop of Lindisfarne, had died in the night, and he
immediately resolved to take monastic vows. Other reports of the afterlife were
more direct. Around 1230 Caesarius of Heisterbach recorded the experience of
Gosbert, a monk whose soul passed temporarily into heaven as he lay on his
sickbed. Gosbert offered this first-hand account of his journey:

When I was lately sick and in the greatest pain, something came over
my bed. And having touched first my feet, ascending step by step, it
touched my belly and then my breast, and yet I felt no harm from the
touch. But when my head was touched, at once I expired and was
brought to a very pleasant and most delightful place, where I saw
different kinds of trees and flowers of many colours. There met me
too a youth of great beauty, by whom I was most courteously saluted
and led before Our Lady the queen of heaven, with much joy. A seat
was placed for me at her feet, but as I sat in it in much happiness of
heart, I was ordered to go back to the body.

Before this untimely resurrection, Gosbert was promised that he would
return to his place at Mary's feet in a short while. He died three days later.
Many similar deathbed revelations were reported in medieval and
Renaissance Europe. In an example from Elizabethan England, the puritan
Philip Stubbes described how his wife Katherine received a celestial vision
in the last moment of her life. Katherine exclaimed to the people gathered
at her bedside that she saw "infinite millions of most glorious angels stand
about me, with fiery chariots ready to defend me". She used her final breath
to proclaim that "these ministering spirits are appointed by God to carry my
soul into the kingdom of heaven".[25]

While visions of this kind affirmed the glorious reward awaiting redeemed
souls, other deathbed experiences confirmed the wretched fate of the
damned. As a "notorious usurer" lay dying in Bacheim in thirteenth-century
Germany, she was suddenly beset by a flock of demonic crows. She watched
as these creatures blackened the fields outside her window, then they swooped
down on her body, making her scream that "they are tearing out my breast,
now they are dragging out my soul". On other occasions, the spirits of the
damned were released from their place of punishment to instruct the living.
Around 1125 William of Malmesbury reported an especially grisly episode
of this kind from the French town of Nantes. This concerned two impious
young scholars who were curious to discover the fate of souls after death.
They pledged that the first of them to die would return to the other within
thirty days. When death "came crawling and snatched the last breath from
one of the two friends", the survivor waited anxiously until the appointed
time, when his friend appeared at his bedside from "the sulphurous abyss of
hell". The hideous spectre implored the scholar to mend his ways, and
provided a graphic demonstration of the reality of his pains:

In order that his friend might learn from his countless torments, he
held out a hand dripping with ulcerated sores and said: "See here,
does this seem insubstantial to you?" When his friend replied that
the hand did indeed seem light and lacking in substance, the other

bent his fingers and flicked three drops of pus on to him. Two of them struck his friend on the temple, so that they pierced his skin and flesh like cauterising fire and made a hole the size of a walnut. When the living man gave a great shout of pain, his dead companion said: "This will mark you as long as you live. It will serve as a proof of my suffering and, unless you ignore it, a special reminder of the need to look to your own future health."

Unsurprisingly chastened, the man sold his possessions and joined a monastic order. Caesarius of Heisterbach reported a similar apparition in thirteenth-century Bavaria. The spirit of a corrupt court official appeared in his widow's bedroom, accompanied by the crashing sounds of an earthquake. Driven forward by a demon in the form of a "gigantic black man", the man warned his wife not to perform good deeds merely "for vain glory". He was then called out of the room "and driven on, the whole castle being shaken at his departure and his cries of woe long heard".[26]

The general acceptance that souls were judged at the moment of death, and consigned to an appropriate waiting place before the general resurrection, led medieval academics to ponder the geography of the afterlife. Where exactly did the spirits of the dead reside? The Church Fathers were largely silent on this technical question, but a revival of interest in the scientific theories of Aristotle in the thirteenth century allowed thinkers to map out the abodes of the blessed and the damned. Aquinas accepted the Aristotelian view that the universe was composed of a series of concentric spheres with the earth at the centre. The infernal region of hell was within the earth's core, while the heavenly region, or "empyrean", existed outside the last circle of the visible planets. This provided a home for the spirits of the saved before the Judgment. In the words of the fourteenth-century theologian John Ruusbroec, the empyrean was "the exterior dwelling-place and kingdom of God and of his saints". According to Aquinas, this celestial space would also provide the habitation of the risen saints after the general resurrection. Rejoined with their bodies, the blessed would ascend to the region beyond the stars, leaving the remade universe unpopulated except for the suffering bodies of the damned.[27]

As well as the location of the souls of the dead before the Last Judgment, scholars contemplated the circumstances in which they existed. One ticklish problem concerned the punishment of damned spirits in the inferno. How could disembodied souls feel the fires of hell? Aquinas resolved this question by asserting that immaterial beings could experience "spiritual contact" with material things, just as the human soul enjoyed contact with the body. Moreover, he noted Christ's definitive statement that there was an "everlasting fire prepared for the devil and his angels" (Matt. 25:41). Since he regarded demons as disembodied spirits, he reasoned that it must therefore be possible for immaterial entities – including human souls – to suffer in a material fire. Could the dead return to earth? The Bible implied this was possible, and a host of later sources testified to the appearance of departed spirits in this world. The precise mode of their transportation, and the nature of the bodies in which they appeared, were matters for speculation, but most authorities agreed that the souls of the redeemed enjoyed greater freedom to travel than those of the damned. The medieval cult of the saints encouraged frequent sightings of the glorified dead, who intervened miraculously in human affairs. Appearances of the damned were less common, and were often presented as limited and transient excursions controlled by higher powers. Thus the damned courtier from Bavaria informed his wife that he could not stay long before the demons hauled him away. During the Protestant Reformation of the sixteenth century, Lutheran and Calvinist theologians challenged the medieval consensus by denying that any spirits could leave their abodes before the Day of Judgment. In an effort to explain the continued sightings of spirits in Protestant territories, they argued that all such manifestations were either demons or angels with dispensation from God to appear in the guise of the dead.[28]

The close scrutiny of the afterlife by pre-modern scholars strikes many people today as shockingly "literal-minded". This is a telling phrase. For the great majority of people in pre-industrial Europe, as well as the colonies of seventeenth-century America, there was nothing allegorical about life after death. The heaven they believed in was real. In the same way, modern scientists assume that the objects they examine – atomic particles, chemicals, gases or planets – really exist. They are literal-minded too. What is truly remarkable about medieval thinkers like Aquinas is their complete acceptance of the reality of heaven and hell, angels and demons. Once this belief is granted, the questions they asked can be accepted as rational and important. If human souls survive death, it is reasonable to ask where they go. If the future resurrection of the body is sincerely anticipated, enquiring minds may be expected to ask questions about the physical processes this will involve. It is possible, of course, to argue that some areas of knowledge are in principle off limits to human investigators.[29] This argument was sometimes used in the pre-modern world against "over-precise" theological speculations; it is still employed today by some people who are wary of certain areas of science, such as human genetics. If we accept, however, that the pursuit of knowledge should be unfettered, it is hard to deny that the pre-modern thinkers who pondered the physics of heaven and the biology of angels were engaged in a legitimate activity. In fact, this understates the case. If the reality of the Christian afterlife is accepted, then thinkers like Aquinas were pursuing a project more important than anything attempted in contemporary science: to describe the eternal destiny of the human species. Since most modern westerners still appear to believe in life after death, it is rather strange that we no longer treat this project with the same rigour.

3

They Hang Horses, Don't They?

When five-year-old Jehan Martin was murdered in 1457, the culprits were quickly apprehended, imprisoned and brought to trial. The case followed the normal procedure for such a serious crime, except in one important respect: the accused were pigs. Following the customs of the Burgundian court that dealt with the matter, the pigs' owner was invited to make representations "concerning the punishment and execution of justice" against the animals. He waived this right, and the prosecutor demanded the death penalty. The judgment that followed was unusually tricky, since one of the animals appeared to be more culpable than the others. The child was killed by a sow in the presence of her six piglets. These were stained with blood at the scene of the crime, but there was no "positive proof that they had assisted in mangling the deceased". After consulting with local experts, the judge ruled that the sow should be executed. A hangman was brought from a neighbouring town to hang the beast by its hind legs from an oak tree. The verdict on the piglets was less severe. They could return to their owner if he was prepared to vouch for their future behaviour and present them in court "should further evidence be forthcoming to prove their complicity in their mother's crime". The owner refused these terms, and the pigs were forfeited to a local noblewoman. It appears that their subsequent conduct was blameless, and no further punishments were needed.[1]

The trial and execution of this homicidal pig was not an isolated oddity. From the first recorded case in 1266, the criminal prosecution of animals was a recognised part of legal practice in medieval and Renaissance Europe. The procedure originated in northern France and spread to the Netherlands, Germany and Italy, reaching its peak in the sixteenth and seventeenth centuries. It was only in the 1700s that official prosecutions began to die out, and the "rough justice" of village mobs replaced the deliberations of lawyers in dealing with criminal beasts. During the heyday of the practice, the prosecution of animals involved the careful observance of due procedure. Accused animals were sometimes remanded in prison before their cases were heard; they enjoyed legal representation; and if they were found to be guilty, professional executioners presided over their punishment. Where the court records have been preserved, they indicate the seriousness with which judges presented their rulings. When a pig was convicted of mauling an infant to death near the monastery of St Martin de Laon in 1494, the sentence invoked the full majesty of the law:

> We, in detestation and horror at the said event, and in order to make an example and to guard justice, have said, judged, sentenced, pronounced and appointed that the said pig, being detained prisoner and shut up in the said abbey, will be hanged and strangled by the master of high works on a branched gibbet near and adjoining the place of high justice of the said brothers, being near their farm of Avin.

The same spirit of commitment was evident in other aspects of the trials. Care was taken to ensure that accused animals were correctly identified and efforts were made to determine the guilt of individual beasts in relation to their fellows. When a herd of pigs trampled a young swineherd in Burgundy in 1379, only four of the animals were punished for leading the stampede. The others were set free, "notwithstanding that they had been present at the death of the said swineherd". Once an animal was condemned, its execution was performed with due attention to local custom. Beasts were carted or dragged to their place of execution. When large animals such as horses or bulls were convicted, special apparatus was sometimes constructed for the purpose. On one occasion, it took two days to erect a platform and system of pulleys to hang a felonious bull.[2]

These refinements were possible when big animals – usually pigs, horses or bulls – were accused of crimes against particular persons. In another class of animal trials, large numbers of vermin were arraigned for offences against whole communities. The first documented cases of this kind occurred in Switzerland and the surrounding region in the fifteenth century. From here they spread into France and Germany, and were recorded as far afield as Italy, Spain and Scandinavia. The accused animals included mice, fish, caterpillars and weevils. In one of the best-documented episodes, the townsfolk of Saint-Julien-de-Maurienne in France sued a plague of flies for destroying a vineyard. Their first attempt to prosecute the insects was made in 1545. On this occasion, the court ruled that it was "unbecoming to proceed with rashness and precipitance against the animals". Instead, it enjoined the community to conduct public prayers and other religious exercises, assuming that the infestation was a judgment of God. Some thirty years later, the flies returned and the harvest was lost again. This time the court accepted a formal complaint against the insects, and appointed Antoine Filliol, a distinguished canon lawyer, to conduct their defence. In June 1587 Filliol argued that the plaintiffs were acting unjustly, since his clients – like all living things – were commanded by God to "be fruitful and multiply" (Gen. 1:22). They were entitled to feed on the vineyard by divine law. In response to this claim, the plaintiffs convened a public meeting in the city square. Here the townsfolk acknowledged the insects' right to feed and multiply, and agreed to set aside a piece of land for this purpose outside the vineyards. It is impossible to know if this ingenious legal manoeuvre was successful, as the papers recording the outcome of the trial have been lost. They were apparently destroyed by insects.[3]

Faced with proceedings like these, modern observers are pushed to the very limits of understanding. In the words of Esther Cohen, the foremost modern historian of the trials, "the practice runs counter to all commonly accepted conceptions of justice, humanity and the animal kingdom". It is hardly surprising that many writers on the subject have explained it in terms of ignorance and folly. In a pioneering study of 1906, E. P. Evans attributed the criminal prosecution of animals to "an extremely crude, obtuse, and barbaric sense of justice". More recently, Ervin Bonkalo has suggested that those involved were led astray by "superstitious alarms". These explanations are rendered inadequate, however, by the very facts that make the trials seem so bizarre. Until their decline in the eighteenth century, they were presided over by highly educated lawyers. One of the attorneys involved in the pig trial of 1458 was a counsellor to the Duke of Burgundy. In the sixteenth century the president of the *parlement* of Provence, Bartholomé Chassenée, made his reputation by defending a colony of rats. More generally, the careful and highly technical arguments of the lawyers involved, along with the meticulous efforts of all concerned to ensure the observance of due process, suggest that animal trials were not driven by hysteria. As for the charge of "barbarism", it is hardly consistent with the appointment of attorneys to defend the accused animals, not to mention the relatively high rates of acquittal. However hard it may be to accept, the people involved in these cases were acting rationally. To understand how this was so, we need to consider the intellectual background to the trials and the social circumstances in which they took place.[4]

ANIMALS AND THE LAW

When the courts dealt with animals in the pre-modern world, they did not normally treat them as conscious subjects capable of moral decisions. In the great majority of cases, beasts were recognised as property. Even when animals were implicated in unlawful acts, such as the sow that killed Jehan Martin in 1457, their owners were sometimes named as defendants, though they were not held to be personally responsible for their livestock's conduct. In those cases where courts accepted suits against animals, this did not mean they acknowledged the rationality of the creatures accused. Indeed, it was precisely because they did not that attorneys were appointed to act on their behalf. Likewise, the plaintiffs and their lawyers did not treat rats and beetles as if they were rational beings. When the residents of Saint-Julien-de-Maurienne offered a plot of land to the flies destroying their vineyards, they were not trying to negotiate with the insects: rather, it was a technical move to acknowledge the creatures' God-given right to feed. The interventions of pre-modern courts imposed human-centred laws on the animal kingdom; they did not abolish the distinctions between people and beasts.

There were several contexts in which animals were involved in legal proceedings. Most often, they were at the centre of disputes about ownership or cases of theft. In some instances, their status as human property meant they could be mutilated as part of the punishment of their owners. According to the thirteenth-century lawyer Henry de Bracton, the horses of noblemen convicted of rape could be castrated. There were three other circumstances – each of them uncommon and highly specific – in which animals were subjected to penalties by courts of law. The first of these involved cases of bestiality. Here the beasts themselves were not accused, but they could be executed along with their abusers if the charges were proved. William Bradford described this unpleasant business in a case from New England in 1642, when the condemned man was asked to identify the animals he had violated:

> Whereas some of the sheep could not be so well known by his description of them, others with them were brought before him and he declared which were they and which were not. And accordingly, he was cast by the jury and condemned, and after executed about the 8th of September 1642. A very sad spectacle it was. First the mare, and then the cow and the rest of the lesser cattle were killed before his face . . . and then he himself was executed. The cattle were all cast into a great and large pit that was digged of purpose for them, and no use made of any part of them.

As this account makes clear, the destruction of the animals was not merely symbolic: only those beasts involved in the crime were marked for death. At the same time, the treatment of their bodies emphasised their impurity. The Bible provided the legal basis for such killings. "If a man lie with a beast", declares the book of Leviticus, "he shall surely be put to death: and ye shall slay the beast" (Lev. 20:15). The same principle was applied in 1653, when a man was condemned to death in Edinburgh for committing buggery with a mare. According to a contemporary English newsbook, the judge stipulated that he should be "burned together with the beast, according to the Mosaical law".[5]

In the other two contexts where animals could be punished by courts, they were effectively treated as the perpetrators of crimes. In some secular jurisdictions, large animals could be tried for specific criminal acts, normally involving the death of humans. These proceedings followed as closely as possible the local laws for dealing with human offenders. The customary laws in parts of France, Germany and Italy permitted such trials, and lawyers familiar with these conventions incorporated them into their stock of working knowledge. Handbooks of customary law, or "customals", recorded these local practices and provided guidance on their application. Religious law provided the final context in which animals could face judicial penalties. Alongside the system of secular justice, the church presided over its own courts of "canon" law. It was in these tribunals that collective charges were brought against whole groups of animals: the townspeople of Saint-Julien-de-Maurienne, for example, took their case against the flies to the bishop's court. As befitted such assemblies, the punishments they imposed were spiritual in nature: instead of ordering the physical extermination of pests, they condemned them to anathemas, exorcisms and – in some cases – excommunication.

In the context of both secular and ecclesiastical law, the prosecution of animals was never uncontroversial. Philippe de Beaumanoir, the author of one of the earliest customals to mention the practice, condemned it on the basis that beasts possessed no understanding of right and wrong, and could therefore not be held accountable for their deeds. Beaumanoir's thirteenth-century contemporary, Thomas Aquinas, echoed this view. In his discussion of cursing in the *Summa Theologica*, Aquinas argued that it was "idle and vain" to impose maledictions on irrational beings. Some later jurists pointed out that the prosecution of animals had no place in the laws of the Roman Empire, which provided one of the cornerstones of legal thinking in the pre-modern world. While most people today would accept these objections, it is notable that these early critics – unlike modern observers – did not regard the prosecution of animals as inherently absurd. On the contrary, they knew it could be defended on the basis of generally accepted beliefs. The observation of the philosopher Donald Davidson is relevant here. Davidson points out that it is only possible to have a meaningful disagreement "against a background of shared belief", since people cannot argue about things they regard as nonsensical. "Without a vast common ground, there is no place for disputants to have their quarrel". The common ground of pre-modern belief allowed plenty of space for intelligent people to support the trial and execution of animals.[6]

For a start, there was the compelling evidence of the Bible. In Exodus 21:28, God tells Moses that "if an ox gore a man or a woman that they die, then the ox shall be surely stoned, and his flesh shall not be eaten". The same passage makes it clear that the ox, not its owner, is liable to this penalty. The owner would only be punished if he knew the animal was aggressive but failed to control it. In this case, both farmer and beast would be put to death (Exod. 21:29). For lawyers in regions where custom permitted the execution of animals, this passage appeared to justify the practice. Jean Boutillier invoked Mosaic law to support the judicial killing of beasts in his fourteenth-century customal of the laws of Tournai. This text was extremely influential, and was still widely used in the seventeenth century. For those making such arguments, the objection that an animal was not aware of its actions was irrelevant. As with animals slaughtered in cases of bestiality, the penalty was ordained by God. The view that judicial acts should serve God as well as the human community was widely accepted in Renaissance Europe. The jurist Jean Bodin spelt it out most forcefully in 1580 when he claimed that punishment was the least important reason for executions. The main purpose of the scaffold was not to punish criminals, he wrote, but to serve divine justice and "obtain the blessing of God".[7]

The biblical command to execute homicidal beasts was part of a wider Christian understanding of the relationship between humankind and nature. According the book of Genesis, God placed the brute creation under the control of men and women: they had "dominion over the fish of the sea, and over the fowl of the air, and over every living thing that moveth upon the earth" (Gen. 1:28). For an animal to harm a human was a violation of this natural order. In 1531 Bartholomé Chassenée used this premise to support the criminal trial of animals: creatures could face judicial sanctions, he argued, when they transgressed their natural boundaries to the detriment of humankind. Once again, this argument was untouched by the objection that beasts had no conception of right and wrong. Chassenée did not deny that beasts were irrational; nor did he suggest they were capable of wilful misdeeds. Rather, he argued that when they harmed humans they infringed the natural order of things, and the law should recognise this fact. In making this case, it is clear that Chassenée and other defenders of animal trials were invoking a much grander conception of law than we have today. As Esther Cohen has noted, their view of justice "assumed the proportions of supra-human, universal law, beyond the simple mechanisms of human relationships". This is a foreign concept to us. But the idea of universal, God-given laws underpinned a great deal of legal practice in the pre-modern world: statutes against witchcraft attempted to regulate human relations with demons, and the sentence of excommunication – employed widely by ecclesiastical courts – condemned its victims to punishment in the next life as well as this.[8]

The view that animals were created for the benefit of humankind, and contravened divine law when they did us harm instead of service, raised various theological problems. Scholars who wrote on the subject worked through these difficulties, and their arguments were tested in practice in the church courts. It was frequently noted, for instance, that God could send pestilent creatures as judgments for human sins. In such cases, the appropriate response was repentance instead of legal action. When the people of Sorrento in Italy wished to prosecute some fish that infested their waters, the theologian Martín de Azpilcueta suggested that acts of public penitence were a better remedy. The residents of Saint-Julien-de-Maurienne received the same advice in 1545. More generally, the fact that God provided irrational creatures with instincts to feed and survive implied that they were not transgressing His laws when they consumed human crops. According to Antoine Filliol, the advocate for the flies of Saint-Julien-de-Maurienne in 1587, his clients were actually obeying the laws of nature, "originating in the eternal reason [of God], and resting upon a basis as immutable as that of the divine law of revelation". The prosecution accepted this claim, but maintained that the insects could feed elsewhere without harming their human neighbours.[9]

In their deliberations on the harmful acts of animals, both secular and ecclesiastical courts entertained the possibility that beasts could violate the God-given hierarchy of nature. For the practitioners of church law, the prosecution of animals was justified by an additional consideration: the involvement of the devil. Cohen has shown that the prosecution of animals under canon law coincided with wider concerns about the role of beasts in demonic witchcraft. While animal trials did not involve accusations of witchcraft, they were informed by the awareness that demons could influence the brute creation. In a small number of cases, devils actually possessed the bodies of beasts. The authors of the *Malleus Maleficarum* noted the existence of certain wolves that "sometimes snatch men and children out of their houses and eat them, and run about with such astuteness that by no skill or strength can they be hurt or captured". These creatures, they argued, "are true wolves . . . possessed by devils". In many other instances, demons took the shape of animals to torment good Christians or associate with witches. Around 1120, the abbot Guibert of Nogent reported a badger "who was actually the devil in the shape of a badger". In a series of early witch trials in the French Alps, demons appeared as black crows, cats and dogs. The courts dealt with none of these creatures directly, but in 1474 the authorities at Basle in Switzerland condemned a demonic rooster to the stake. This fowl had revealed its true nature by the "unnatural crime of laying an egg". According to one report, the hangman dissected the bird after the sentence was passed and found a number of eggs inside its body.[10]

While such diabolical animals were believed to exist, it was argued more often that beasts acted merely as the Devil's agents. Thomas Aquinas admitted this possibility in the thirteenth century, though he noted that the creatures themselves should not be condemned. This argument was modified in the 1400s, as churchmen became increasingly anxious about demonic agency in the world. Just as the devil could manipulate his human servants in cases of witchcraft and create harmful effects through subverting natural processes, he could use animals to visit calamities on women and men. Equally, the officers of the church were empowered to deal with such attacks. In 1502, the anonymous author of *Malefactio Animalium* presented an ingenious summation of these ideas. He suggested that God had created all animals in one of two groups: those that were useful or those that were harmful to humankind. The intervention of Satan could cause useful animals to became harmful, and in such cases they could be sentenced by law.[11]

The belief that animals could act as demonic agents was reflected in ecclesiastical remedies for their depredations. In one of the earliest acts of this kind, the ninth-century pope Sixtus VI prepared holy water to extinguish a plague of locusts that was destroying the Roman harvest. The words used to consecrate the water reflected the satanic nature of the pests:

I abjure thee that thou mayst not suffer any imp or phantom to abide in thy substance, that thou mayst be imbued with exorcising power and become a source of salvation, so that when thou art sprinkled on the fruits of the field, on vines, on trees, on human habitations in the city or the country, on stables or on flocks, or if anyone may touch or taste thee, thou shalt become a remedy and relief from the wiles of Satan; that through thee plagues and pestilence may be driven away, that through contact with thee weevils and caterpillars, locusts and moles may be dispersed, and the maliciousness of all visible and invisible powers hostile to man may be brought to nought.

In this instance, the blessed water was meant to work as a kind of holy pesticide, driving the devil's agents from human settlements and crops. Later texts directed the words of exorcism at the vermin themselves. In the fifteenth century, Felix Malleolus commended this practice as the appropriate sentence for pests condemned by ecclesiastical courts. His books became the standard texts on the subject, and stayed in print throughout the 1500s. Surviving manuals of exorcism reveal how the language of the rite for animals closely followed the words used to dispossess humans troubled by unclean spirits. "I adjure thee, beetles", runs one such text, "who dissipate and destroy the food of men in this place, that you should depart henceforth and go where you can harm nobody".[12]

The biblical injunction to execute dangerous beasts, along with wider assumptions about the hierarchy of creation and the power of demons, allowed reasonable people to contemplate the prosecution of animals. But this fact alone does not explain why anyone took the trouble to do so. The trial of pigs, bulls and horses in the secular courts was a difficult business: the animals had to be housed and fed, and their execution was not cheap.

Professional hangmen were required, and their receipts indicate that special equipment and gloves were often needed for the job. When plaintiffs brought cases before the ecclesiastical courts, they had to pay fees and employ advocates to pursue their cause, and the process of justice could be extremely slow. For a small minority of experts, the enunciation of legal principles may have justified the business of the courts. When Bartholomé Chassenée was called to adjudicate on the fate of heretics in 1540, he was reminded that he had previously defended the right of rats to receive a fair hearing. This exemplary precedent encouraged him to petition the King to permit legal representation for the dissenters. It is unlikely, however, that the wish to demonstrate such high principles was the motive behind animal trials. To understand why jurists and plaintiffs were prepared to take part in these events, we need to consider the wider functions of the law in pre-modern culture.[13]

SYMBOLS AND REMEDIES

For the people of medieval and Renaissance Europe, the idea that "justice must be seen to be done" carried greater resonance than it does today. All judicial penalties were public acts, from the shaming of the pillory to death on the scaffold, and these spectacles were normally enacted as close as possible to the place of the original crime. Under canon law, even convicted adulterers were required to confess their sins before an audience of their neighbours. Those guilty of more serious offences were subjected to ritual acts of symbolic mutilation: rogues and vagabonds could be branded with the letter "R", blasphemers had their tongues slit and thieves could have their hands removed. These torments were inflicted in public squares, where the sentence could be witnessed by as many people as possible. When this sentence was death, felons were normally carted or dragged to the scaffold and their last words were delivered to large and expectant crowds. With the advent of print in the late fifteenth century, the "dying speeches" of the condemned became a staple of cheap literature and remained popular in much of Europe until the early 1900s.[14]

One extraordinary aspect of pre-modern justice exemplified the symbolic role of punishment. Not only could animals be condemned: so could the dead. The French monk Adémar of Chabannes recorded an early example in 1022. This concerned a canon of Orléans named Theodatus who, according to Adémar, had "given every appearance of piety during his life". Three years after he died, however, reports emerged that he was a secret heretic. The bishop accepted this claim and had his body exhumed and "thrown out into a waste place". The dead could even be subjected to a form of ritual "execution". Writing in the late 1500s, the Jesuit Martín Del Rio advised judges on the appropriate treatment of convicted witches who died before their sentence could be carried out: "one can at the very least dishonour the dead person's memory, exhume his corpse, and burn his bones". If a person committed suicide before their trial ended, Del Rio insisted that the corpse "must be condemned to the gallows". This practice was common in Franche-Comté, where the judge Henri Boguet witnessed it at first hand:

If the accused wilfully and deliberately kills himself in prison, then he must be entirely denied the rites of burial. In this country it is even the custom to drag such a man on a hurdle through the town to the place of execution, where his body is either burned or hanged according to the gravity of his crime. I have seen this done to a schoolmaster who had hanged himself in prison; for by order of the court his body was dragged on a hurdle through the town to the Tartre, and there hanged on a gibbet.

Boguet defended this practice on the grounds that it prevented others from committing similar offences, since "it is found by experience that the fear of being disgraced after death has deterred many from committing a crime". The ritual execution of the dead also symbolised the power of the law: even in death, the guilty could not escape the reach of earthly justice, though they had already received their final sentence from God. There were some other circumstances in which felons could be "punished" despite evading the direct authority of the courts. In certain jurisdictions, effigies of the condemned were sent to the scaffold. As late as 1772, the magistrates of Marseilles condemned the Marquis de Sade to death by decapitation for the crime of sodomy. As the aristocrat had already fled the country, this sentence was carried out on an effigy in a square at Aix.[15]

As these practices suggest, the physical suffering of the offender was only one of the purposes of public execution. The punishment of felons was important, but the theatre of the scaffold conveyed other messages too. The public execution of animals served these wider functions of the law. This was illustrated in a case from Leons de Chatres in 1606. Here a man named Guillaume Guyart was condemned to death for bestiality with a dog. The judges stipulated that Guyart should be hanged on a gallows which, "for best effect", was to be erected in the town's horse market. The dog would be killed in the same place, and the bodies of both parties burnt to ashes. This sentence was passed in the absence of the accused. If Guyart could not be apprehended, the judge decreed that "the sentence will be executed in effigy in a tableau which will be taken and attached to the said gallows" and that all Guyart's remaining goods would be confiscated. Here the court not only required the hangman to put a beast to death, but provided for this act to be performed in effigy. The public enactment of justice was a prime consideration.

In this particular case, killing the dog – or even an effigy of the dog – was an act of purification to cleanse the stain of a crime "against nature". It also affirmed the community's observance of biblical law.[16]

What messages were conveyed by hanging animals for murder? Henri Boguet's claim that it was necessary to execute the dead to deter others from crimes may be relevant here. No one imagined, of course, that sending a bull to the scaffold would make other cattle think twice before stepping out of line. Rather, the public killing of a beast demonstrated the power of human law. In a perceptive and entertaining essay on the subject, Nicholas Humphrey has pursued this idea:

> Until comparatively recently the execution of human criminals was
> done in public with the explicit intention of reminding people of what
> lay in store for future law-breakers. The effect on impressionable
> human minds was presumably a powerful one. Then why should not
> the sight of a pig on the scaffold for a human crime have had the like
> effect? Perhaps it might have proved doubly effective, for such a
> demonstration that even pigs must pay the penalty for law-breaking
> would surely have given any sensible person pause.

As a public affirmation of justice, the execution of animals reminded the whole community of the penalties for serious crimes. In a more limited sense, it also gave notice to owners of livestock to keep dangerous beasts under control. This purpose was sometimes made explicit. When a court in the French bailiwick of Senlis condemned a sow for murder in 1567, it warned all the inhabitants of the region to keep "good and secure guard" on other potentially violent animals. The public display of executed beasts was a potent reminder of this responsibility, and probably made a deeper impression on the community than the mere confiscation of unruly animals.[17]

As well as sending a warning to potential wrongdoers, the execution of animals affirmed the natural hierarchy of the created world. By making a public spectacle of beasts that killed their human masters, the courts drew attention to a disturbance in the God-given order of things. The maintenance of hierarchy was displayed in other areas of judicial punishment. In many jurisdictions, special forms of execution were reserved for those who murdered their social superiors. Vassals who killed their lords could be hanged upside down. Under English law, servants who killed their masters were guilty of "petty treason" as well as murder. The same principle applied to wives who killed their husbands, who were burnt at the stake to mark the peculiar nature of their transgression. This was the fate of the murderess Anne Beddingfield as late as 1763: she was "first strangled at the stake" before her body was consumed in flames, "agreeable to the practice respecting women who are convicted of the murder of their husbands".

Viewed in this wider context, the execution of animals extended the judicial maintenance of hierarchy into the natural world. It may be relevant that these events coincided with the appearance in popular literature of bestial images of the poor, who were only one rung above animals in the hierarchy of nature. The practice of hanging beasts upside down in some regions also appears to have mirrored the treatment of humans whose crimes undermined the social order. In an interesting variation on this practice, certain types of criminal could be symbolically degraded to the level of animals. Jews convicted of murder were sometimes hanged upside down beside dogs, indicating the bestial nature of their crime. In all these grisly rites, the theatre of the scaffold was used to underline the natural order of creation.[18]

The desire to endorse social values through acts of public justice probably motivated many people who participated in animal trials. Such motives were understandable even if those concerned, including lawyers and judges, did not treat the beasts in question as moral agents responsible for their deeds. It is likely, however, that additional concerns informed the behaviour of others involved in these proceedings. When the secular courts prosecuted pigs and bulls for murder, the communities affected may well have imputed a degree of responsibility onto the accused. Joyce Salisbury has argued that the line between humans and animals became blurred in the late Middle Ages, when semi-human creatures such as werewolves were increasingly prominent in popular literature. This cultural trend, she notes, coincided with the earliest animal trials. There was some tension between learned and popular traditions concerning the attributes of beasts. While churchmen and scholars maintained a clear distinction between humans and brutes, Esther Cohen suggests that "country folk, far from denying animals any human characteristics, consistently attributed to them both reason and will". In the context of these widespread assumptions, the prosecution of animals for murder involved more than the public assertion of good order: it provided an explanation for tragedy.[19]

When a pig devoured the four-month-old daughter of Lyénor and Magdeleine Machieu in 1567, the dreadful event could have been viewed as a senseless calamity. Instead, the sow was held responsible for the infant's death: it was convicted by the provincial court and hanged from a tree. In this and many other cases, the prosecution of an animal probably offered a meagre consolation for the family and the wider community: the death was not arbitrary, it was caused by "the cruelty and ferocity" of a wicked beast. To this explanation was added the possibility of a meaningful response. The sow was surrendered to the authorities and condemned. Justice was seen to be done. It is impossible, of course, to know the psychological effects of such actions, but it seems reasonable to assume that they conferred some limited benefit on the victims of disaster. As Nicholas Humphrey has suggested, animal trials may have helped "to domesticate chaos, to impose order on a

world of accidents – and specifically to make sense of certain seemingly
inexplicable events by redefining them as crimes". In this respect, the
condemnation of criminal animals was similar to accusations of witchcraft:
both provided explanations for exceptional calamities – by conferring blame
on the beast or on the witch – and both offered their victims a judicial
mechanism by which they could respond to their misfortune.[20]

By attaching blame to animals, pre-modern people were not suggesting
they were wholly responsible for their deeds, or capable of the same kind of
moral choices available to humans. A homicidal bull was still a bull. It is
plainly absurd, as Erica Fudge has pointed out, to claim "that people could
not differentiate a pig from a human until the emergence of modernity". But
Renaissance villagers may well have ascribed a *degree* of rationality to beasts
that, while falling short of making them their moral equals, was sufficient to
identify "cruel and ferocious" behaviour. In a culture that permitted the legal
prosecution of animals, such attributions could easily turn into allegations of
crime. A modern parallel is helpful here. In 1993, two ten-year-old boys beat
an infant to death in Liverpool. They were subsequently tried in an adult
court and convicted of murder. In a searching account of these events, Blake
Morrison has likened the treatment of Robert Thompson and Jon Venables
to the prosecution of animals in the pre-modern world. Like these earlier
spectacles, he suggests, their trial involved "retributive savagery". But less
negative parallels can also be made. The trial shows how people can attribute
criminal responsibility to those they would not otherwise regard as moral
agents. Despite newspaper claims that the boys were exceptionally
precocious, few people at the time can have believed they were responsible
for their actions in exactly the same way that an adult would be: they were
children, after all. As Morrison reminds us, many people "do something
terrible" between the ages of eight and fourteen, but these acts are
"performed in a childish, first-time daze". The world of childhood "is a
separate place". This simple observation would be obvious in other contexts,
but it was discarded when Thompson and Venables were found guilty of
murder. Why were they put on trial? The main reason, perhaps, was to
explain a tragedy that was otherwise unbearably senseless: even though the
accused were children themselves, their conviction gave meaning to another
child's death. It does not follow, of course, that the people of contemporary
Britain cannot tell the difference between adults and ten-year-old boys.[21]

The trial of Thompson and Venables also indicates how ideas of
culpability can differ between cultures. It is impossible today for most
westerners to conceive of a pig breaking the law. Equally, it was impossible
for the people of Norway to imagine that children could be guilty of murder
when, just one year after the British trial, two six-year-old boys beat and
stoned an infant to death in the town of Trondheim. Despite marked
similarities to the earlier case, the community responded quite differently.

The press did not portray the boys as murderers. Nor did their neighbours, or even the dead girl's grieving mother. Instead, the children were allowed to return to their school – accompanied by a psychologist – only two weeks after her death. Many factors contributed to this response: as well as the killers' extreme youth, Norwegian culture takes a generally liberal view of the culpability of children: the age of criminal responsibility is fifteen, compared to ten in the United Kingdom. However one explains the reaction of the people of Trondheim, their refusal to condemn the children for the killing shows how the understanding of guilt can vary drastically from place to place, and situation to situation, even in our own time.[22]

If the conviction of individual beasts in the secular courts involved the imputation of guilt, this was not the case when ecclesiastical tribunals condemned large numbers of vermin. Nor were the penalties imposed in these cases intended primarily to communicate messages to the human population – though they undoubtedly expressed the authority of the church. The point of prosecuting pests was to make them go away. In communities dependent on the harvest, the decimation of crops could be a terrible affliction. Villagers sought remedies for their suffering through the anathemas and exorcisms pronounced by the courts. In this way, the prosecution of vermin resembled the accusation of "weather witches" elsewhere in Europe. When whole communities were threatened by exceptional weather that blighted the harvest, groups of witches were arraigned for bringing about their misfortune. By destroying the witches, the crops could be saved. It is notable that the prosecution of vermin coincided with the large-scale witch panics in Germany and central Europe during the sixteenth and seventeenth centuries, when extreme weather patterns probably encouraged fears of *maleficia*.[23]

The prosecution of vermin depended, of course, on the belief that religious sanctions would be effective against them. By the fifteenth century, there was a rich tradition of stories describing the power of holy figures to command dangerous creatures. In one of the most famous examples, St Francis confronted "an enormous wolf, terrible and ferocious", which was terrorising the people of Gubbio. He bid the beast to be still and denounced its crimes:

> Wolf, thou hast done much damage in these parts, and many evil
> deeds, ravaging and killing the creatures of God, without His
> permission; and not only killing and devouring the cattle, but having
> the hardihood to destroy men made in the image of God, for which
> cause thou dost deserve to be hung upon the gallows like a convict,
> as being a thief and the worst of murderers; and all the people cry
> out and murmur because of thee, and the whole neighbourhood is
> hostile to thee.

Francis asked the wolf to end its depredations, and promised in return that the townsfolk "shall pardon thee all past offences". It duly changed its ways. In other accounts, holy men displayed the ability to strike down plagues of unwelcome creatures. Bishop Ebert of Trier cursed a flock of swallows that invaded his cathedral, and they promptly dropped to the ground. A similar fate befell a swarm of flies in the church of Foigny when St Bernard pronounced an anathema against them. This proved so effective that the dead pests had to be thrown from the building in shovels.[24]

These precedents established the right of the church to curse and exorcise vermin, and confirmed the potential effectiveness of such measures. Bartholomé Chassenée used numerous examples of this kind in 1531 to commend the power of anathemas against harmful pests. The stories of saints also set out the arguments used to justify this practice. Francis condemned the wolf because it had transgressed its natural bounds by killing men and women. In a similar vein, St Cuthbert addressed the birds devouring a crop of barley in terms used later in formal proceedings against pests: "If God has given you permission, then do as He bade you; if not, be off with you". The birds departed. In the hands of ecclesiastical courts, the power to curse vermin was held to be similarly effective. In the *Tracté des monitoires* (1668), the Savoyard lawyer Gaspard Bailly described the anathemas pronounced by church courts as a "deadly sword". This sword "cutterth the dry wood and the green, sparing neither the quick nor the dead, and smiting not only rational beings, but turning its edge also against irrational creatures".[25]

For those living under the threat of a disastrously poor harvest, the sword of ecclesiastical justice offered the hope of relief. This grim truth was also acknowledged in Bailly's book. In a putative account of the typical pleas and counter-pleas used by lawyers in the trial of vermin, he dwelt at length on the horrors of starvation. He began one address in language that was probably familiar to courts hearing such cases by the seventeenth century:

> Gentlemen, these poor people, on their knees and with tearful eyes,
> appeal to your sense of justice . . . You have a weapon . . . to save
> these poor suppliants from impending famine produced by the
> ravages of little beasts, which spare neither the corn nor the vine . . .
> You know how great are the evils which famine brings with it, and
> you have too much compassion to permit my clients to be involved in
> such distress.

Viewed in this light, the prosecution of vermin resembled other responses to disaster in a profoundly religious culture. Like the prayers, processions and fasts by which communities sought to appease the Lord in times of natural calamity, it was an attempt to relieve suffering in circumstances where all human efforts had failed. Since public acts of prayer in the face of disaster are still common in the west, these other responses do not strike us as absurd. In a culture that accepted the power of the church to cure illness and protect the vulnerable from demonic forces, the attempt to anathematise life-threatening pests was equally viable.[26]

To modern readers, the legal prosecution of animals inevitably provokes amusement. The execution of a pig is a truly surreal idea, and there is something undeniably comic about putting caterpillars on trial. The comedic value of these proceedings was not lost on some contemporaries. Indeed, Jean Racine produced a humorous play on the subject in the same year that Bailly's book was published.[27] But for those who participated in the prosecutions, the condemnation of murderous beasts and plagues of vermin was a deadly serious affair. The ideas invoked in animal trials could, in theory, be applied to a wide variety of crimes: a beast that transgressed the natural order by committing murder could do so just as easily by committing less serious offences. In practice, however, animals were only tried when lives had been lost or livelihoods were at risk. For us, the treatment of these animals may have the character of farce, but it was much nearer to tragedy for the men and women involved.

4

The Roaming Dead

"The corpses of the dead", wrote the twelfth-century English churchman William of Newburgh, can sometimes "leave their graves and wander around". William illustrated this unpleasant fact by recalling some recent events from Melrose Abbey in Scotland. The monastery had been plagued by nightly visits from the body of a dead priest, which came "groaning and murmuring in an alarming fashion". After repeated incursions by the restless corpse, a team of clerics and "stalwart young men" kept vigil in the graveyard where the man was buried. Nothing stirred until midnight, when three of the company "went off to a nearby house to light a fire to allay the chill of the night", leaving one priest to maintain the watch alone. The events that followed were predictably grim:

> Seeing that the priest was now alone, the demon judged the time right to try to break his robust faith, and rose out of the tomb. Glimpsing the monster at a distance, the man at first froze with fear, but soon his courage returned and, with no prospect of escape, he prepared to resist the attack of the evil creature as it came towards him groaning terribly. He struck at it with the battle-axe he carried in his hand. Groaning still louder, the wounded creature turned round as suddenly as it had come, and retreated while the heroic defender chased it back to its tomb. The tomb opened to offer the creature refuge from its assailant and then closed behind it.

The priest's friends returned to the aftermath of this grisly encounter, and resolved to dig up the "cursed corpse" at daybreak. When they set about this task, they discovered that the earth enclosing the body was stained with "many traces of blood, which had flowed from the wound inflicted on the creature". They removed the cadaver and carried it outside the abbey grounds, where it was burnt and scattered to the wind.[1]

The idea that the spirits of the dead could return to the living was common in medieval and Renaissance culture. Physical resurrections like the "unnatural marvel" at Melrose Abbey were less frequent, but reports of wandering corpses – or "revenants" – appeared occasionally in the British Isles, France and Germany in the pre-industrial age, and were widespread in central Europe as recently as the 1920s. Official responses to these accounts have varied over time and place, from dismissive scepticism to complete acceptance. It appears that William of Newburgh had few doubts about the authenticity of his tale. It was one of a series of resurrection stories contained in his chronicle, and was presented in the same style as the other historical events that were its main concern. The author knew of these marvels from the testimony of well-respected men, including senior figures in the English church, and the incident at Melrose Abbey was reported "by men from the religious community itself". He noted that there were many "other clear examples in our own time" of the activity of revenants. This claim was probably well founded. The reanimation of corpses in England was recorded by William's contemporaries and had been described some fifty years earlier by the monk William of Malmesbury. The physical return of the dead continued to be reported and discussed seriously by European churchmen in the later Middle Ages, and it featured in learned texts in the sixteenth and seventeenth centuries.[2]

What should we make of this? A good starting point, perhaps, is the observation of the historian Christina Larner that in our own society "we sometimes encounter educated persons who believe in the resurrection of the body and the life everlasting". These ideas do not appear to require explanation in the same way as culturally alien concepts like witchcraft. Though some people might question whether Jesus rose physically from the dead, those individuals who believe sincerely that he did are not routinely dismissed as crazy. This is because the supernatural claims of the Christian religion fall within the range of familiar beliefs in our culture. In late medieval and Renaissance Europe, Christian ideas about the bodily resurrection were also widely accepted, but they existed within a rather different set of familiar beliefs about the events expected at the end of history, the power of God and the devil, and the relationship between the living and the dead. In the context of these widely recognised ideas, it was possible for both learned and uneducated people to accept that corpses occasionally walked from their graves.[3]

The resurrection of the dead was a central motif in the religion of the Middle Ages and Renaissance. The general resurrection, when the dead would rise bodily from the earth, was expected at the culmination of human history. This climactic moment would be followed by the Last Judgment of the saved and the damned, when "the dead, small and great, stand before God" for their final reckoning (Rev. 20:12). Equally central, of course, was the resurrection of Christ, a miracle closely linked to the Day of Judgment. St Paul spelt out the absolute primacy of these ideas in his first letter to the Corinthians:

But if there be no resurrection of the dead, then is Christ not risen.
And if Christ be not risen, then is our preaching vain, and your faith
is also vain. Yea, and we are found false witnesses of God, because
we have testified of God that he raised up Christ . . . For since by
man came death, by man came also the resurrection of the dead. For
as in Adam all die, even so in Christ shall all be made alive.

(1 Cor. 15)

The sure knowledge of the general resurrection was a warning to wrongdoers
and an incentive to the pious. In the words of the anonymous English author
of the thirteenth-century *Ancren Riwle*, "it is no marvel if we wretched sinners
suffer pains here, if we would arise joyfully at the day of judgement". As
Chapter 2 of this book points out, the general resurrection also posed practical
questions for the more technically minded. Did the body have to be intact at
the moment of resuscitation? What fate awaited those still living on the Day
of Judgment? As these questions indicate, the resurrection of the dead was
understood in robustly physical terms. The same point was clear in religious
art, which communicated the events of the Last Judgment to a much wider
audience. Over the west door of Autun cathedral in France, a twelfth-century
carving depicts angels supporting the unsteady bodies of the newly risen dead,
while the damned are wrenched from their graves by a monstrous hand. In a
German woodcut from the 1480s, the dead unfold their bodies in their coffins,
lever themselves upright and stretch their limbs like awakening sleepers. Such
images supplied a familiar model for imagining the physical return of the
dead, while the speculations of preachers and theologians about the Last Days
created an intellectual framework in which the revival of corpses could be
seriously debated.[4]

Other ideas about the afterlife also lent credence to tales of the restless
dead. The boundary between life and death was drawn rather differently in
the pre-modern age than it is today, and was considerably more porous. Most
medieval and Renaissance Christians believed that the community of the dead
could intervene in the affairs of the living, though this idea was challenged
to some extent during the Protestant Reformation. This assumption provided
the broad context in which the appearance of revenants made sense.

BETWEEN LIFE AND DEATH

Medieval attitudes towards the afterlife were characterised by the
reciprocal relationship between the living and the dead. This relationship was
maintained at several social levels, and was expressed through a marvellous
variety of official and semi-official practices. The relics of the saints – or the
"holy dead" – provided a focus for pilgrimage and devotion. The most

powerful of these figures could offer comfort and protection for their devotees and even punish the transgressions of wrongdoers. St James of Compostela occasionally visited misfortune on those who worked during his festival or refused hospitality to his pilgrims. At a more humble level, the spirits of ordinary men and women could return to communicate with the living; and this correspondence could bring benefit or peril to both parties. The dead could implore their relatives for spiritual assistance, most often by offering masses or "good works" for their souls in purgatory; more prosaically, they could seek the redress of earthly grievances or the settlement of unpaid debts. Returning spirits could also assist the living by issuing warnings or directives: they instructed mortals to amend particular sins, to embark on pilgrimage, or to prepare for misfortune or death.[5]

The bonds between the living and the dead were recorded vividly in the chronicles of religious communities. In the early thirteenth century, Caesarius of Heisterbach described the apparition of a nine-year-old girl in the convent of Mount St Saviour. The child appeared to another young girl as the sisters gathered in the choir. On hearing about this wonder, the abbess instructed the living girl to address the spirit, which revealed the purpose of its visit:

'I have come here to make redress, for I used to whisper with you in the choir. I have been ordered to make atonement for this in the same place where I used to sin in this way. Unless you take care, you will suffer the same punishment when you die.' When she had made atonement in this way on four separate occasions, she said: 'Now my atonement is complete; from now on you will see me no more.' And so it came about that, as her living companion watched, she went towards the cemetery, passing through the wall by supernatural power.

The abbess was apparently convinced that the spectre was genuine, and reported its appearance to Caesarius as an instance of God's mercy. The spirits described by Bartolomea Riccoboni, the fifteenth-century chronicler of the Venetian convent of Corpus Domini, were less troubled but equally helpful to the living members of the community. Soon after her death in 1406, Sister Margarita Mussolini appeared as a spirit to several of the grieving sisters. In the conversations that followed, "she clarified some things they had wondered about and said that God pays less heed to the exterior act than to interior love". Another spectral visitor boosted the reputation of the prioress:

When one of our sisters was in prayer, one of our dead appeared to her; and the living sister asked the dead one many things, to which she replied. Finally, the living one asked the dead, 'Please tell me, which of the women in this convent is most acceptable to God?' The

dead one replied, 'The prioress'. 'Why?' asked the living one, and
the dead replied, 'For her great humility'.

Riccoboni recorded these apparitions as divine messengers and tokens of
God's favour to her community, as well as a comfort to her sisters that they
would be received into heaven.[6]

Like these pious ghost stories, accounts of revived corpses reflected the
interplay between the living and the dead. The dead could rise from their graves
to perform conventionally accepted services for the living, such as offering
warnings of future events. This was the case in another episode recorded by
Caesarius. In this instance, two scholars from Bonn were sitting in twilight
beside a cemetery "when they saw a human shape leave one of the graves".
They watched the figure wander among the gravestones until it "descended into
another tomb". The purpose of this uncanny appearance was revealed shortly
afterwards, when a priest died "in that church and was put into the very grave
which the creature had entered". In other cases, corpses might terrorise mortals
to rebuke their impious behaviour. A much-repeated tale from Germany
described a drunkard crossing a graveyard one evening when he stumbled on
a human skull. The man swore at the relic, only to provoke the appearance of
a revenant. The creature followed him home and beat at his door. When it was
opened, the man saw "the miserable figure of a dead man, presenting the
terrible spectacle of bones and rotting flesh". This story underlined the duty
of the living to pray for the souls of the dead on passing through a cemetery, an
obligation that was spelt out in contemporary sermons. In many other instances,
the wicked life or "bad death" of an individual was punished by their return as
a roaming cadaver. Writing in the late twelfth century, the English cleric Walter
Map described how a man from Worcestershire "died an atheist in his sins" and
was later seen wandering around "dressed in a hair-shirt". A crowd of his
neighbours chased the man back into his grave, then raised a cross on the spot
to keep him from straying again.[7]

The ties between the mortal world and the afterlife were also explicit in the
most extreme cases of revenant activity, when the restless dead attacked
whole communities. In almost every case of this kind, those who rose from
their graves had led impious lives or died badly. In a twelfth-century case
from Wales, a man who "died irreligiously" returned to his neighbours as a
walking corpse, spreading a pestilence through his village. Likewise, a
revenant described in the thirteenth-century Scottish chronicle was a cleric
"who had lived perversely [and] died in the worst way, being bound by
sentence of excommunication". Dressed as a black monk, he came back to
terrify and assault his neighbours. Three of the revenants reported by
William of Newburgh had apparently led scandalous lives, while a fourth died
before he could receive communion and confess his sins. The bonds between
this world and the next meant that mortals could sometimes intervene to

remedy the earthly sins that caused the dead to rise, just as their prayers could assist souls in purgatory. This happened with one of the revenants in William's chronicle:

> [The bishop of Lincoln] prepared a scroll of absolution and gave it to the archdeacon, with the instructions that the dead man's grave should be opened, the scroll placed on his chest, and the grave closed up again. In this way the dead man might have clear benefit from the actions of the faithful. All was done according to these instructions, and . . . the dead man never wandered again.

In this instance, the depredations of a roaming corpse were acknowledged and remedied within the penitential framework of the church. The actions of the living produced an outcome typical of more conventional ghost stories: the unquiet spirit was released from the burdens it had acquired in life and restored to a state of apparent rest.[8]

One further characteristic of revenants also illustrated the wider relationship between the living and the dead. This was the "unnatural" condition of their bodies. It was widely accepted in late medieval and Renaissance Europe that the corpses of the dead could bear signs of acts committed in life. Thus the cadavers of those sentenced to excommunication were strangely preserved, assuming a "black, offensive and swollen" appearance. The remains of saints were also undecayed, though these were generally pale and fragrant. By the same token, the bodies of the dead could sometimes influence the world of the living. This principle underpinned the idea of pilgrimage, as the intercession of the saints was more likely if one visited their earthly remains. In other circumstances, dead bodies could pass judgment on the living. It was commonly believed that the corpse of a murdered person would bleed in the presence of its killer. King James VI of Scotland affirmed that "in a secret murder, if the dead carcass be at any time thereafter handled by the murderer it will gush out blood, as if the blood were crying to heaven for revenge". The two-way relationship between mortal behaviour and the bodies of the dead was exemplified in tales of revenants. When their corpses were exhumed, they often displayed signs of their unholy condition. In one of the cases described by William of Newburgh, a revenant's body was found to be "grotesque and distended, with a swollen, reddened face". The men who unearthed it "struck at the lifeless corpse, from which . . . a continuous flow of blood gushed and soaked the earth". These signs of "ruddiness" and "fluidity of blood" were observed in many later accounts of the unholy dead. Equally, the proper treatment of the corpse could put an end to its depredations: it could be absolved of sins committed in life, dabbed with holy water, or consigned to the cleansing flames of a bonfire.[9]

HOW WERE THE DEAD REVIVED?

The general understanding of the interaction between the living and the dead allowed people of all ranks to accept the possibility that corpses were sometimes revived. But more technical questions remained. How exactly were dead bodies made to walk? Did they have a will of their own? Christian theology provided several potential answers to these questions, and set the parameters for their discussion by the educated. The understanding of revenants among the wider population is inevitably elusive. From the little we know, it appears that popular ideas about the roaming dead were much less systematic, and sometimes involved unorthodox religious concepts. These ideas were, nonetheless, contained within the broad framework of beliefs and social behaviour that constituted medieval Christianity.

The obvious starting point for understanding revenants was the resurrection of Christ, an act that prefigured the general resurrection. The central importance of these events led medieval thinkers to produce careful definitions of "the raising of the dead". A true resurrection, it was generally agreed, involved the complete restoration to life of a deceased person: not only would their body move but their spiritual essence – or *spiritus* – would be fully recovered. Such events were miraculous, and could only be accomplished by God. The Bible contained examples of both true and false resurrections: Christ's raising of Lazarus and daughter of Jairus (Luke 8: 49–56; John 11) involved the genuine restoration of life, while the apparition of Samuel created by the witch of Endor (1 Sam. 28) was a work of "necromancy", or demonic magic. The performance of such fake wonders reflected the devil's desire to ape the miracles of God. Accordingly, classical texts contained illustrations of fake resurrections accomplished by demons, like the imperfect raising of the dead body of a child by the Roman magician Simon Magus. These ideas about true and false resurrections framed the scholarly discussion of revenants.

True resurrections were the most rare and exquisite of miracles, at least in the age before the Last Judgment. But they were technically possible. Indeed, Christ directed his followers to "raise the dead" in the Gospel of Matthew (10:8), and the ability to do so was regarded as a mark of exceptional sanctity. The eighth-century biographer of St Wilfrid recorded an example from England:

> St Wilfrid was out riding one day, going round on his duties as
> bishop, baptising and confirming. Among the people he baptised . . .
> was a certain woman. Her first-born son had died and she was
> bitterly distressed, moaning with grief and tired with the weight of
> the child – for she had the body with her, wrapped in rags and
> hidden in her bosom . . . Then our holy bishop prayed and laid his

hand on the corpse. The breath of life returned and the boy breathed again. He handed the child back to his mother, baptised him, and commanded her in God's name to give her son back to him at the age of seven for the service of the church.

The woman broke her promise and fled when the time came to hand over her son. He was discovered by one of Wilfrid's servants, however, and spent the rest of his life in the service of God. A more melancholy resurrection was recorded among the miracles worked by the Virgin of Alsenberg in Brabant in 1473. Here a stillborn child was restored to life and baptised "in the presence of sage witnesses". The baby "lived on for the space of sixteen hours and then once more he died".[10]

Not only infants but also adults could be restored to life. An eleventh-century collection of the miracles associated with the shrine of St James of Compostela included an episode of this kind. This concerned a tanner who, while making his annual pilgrimage to the shrine, was deluded by Satan into committing suicide. His life was restored through the intercession of St James and the Virgin, and he went on to complete his journey. A more famous instance was recorded in the life of St Stanislaus, the eleventh-century bishop of Cracow in Poland. The saint purchased an estate for his church from a gentleman named Pierre, who acknowledged the sale with a spoken contract. After his death, however, the man's sons attempted to reclaim the land by declaring falsely that it had not been paid for. Stanislaus spent three days in fasting and prayer before visiting Pierre's grave and lifting its stone. He commanded the body "to come forth and bear witness to the truth". The corpse rose and walked with the bishop to the royal court, where it attested that the estate had been honestly sold. This story served as a lasting exemplar of the miraculous power of faith: as late as 1751 the sceptical Benedictine abbot Augustin Calmet described it as a true resurrection "beyond the severest criticism".[11]

The divine nature of these wonders was evident in their pious outcomes. The infant revived by St Wilfrid lived to serve the church, and the infant resurrected at Brabant was baptised into eternal life. The tanner completed his pilgrimage and Pierre saved the church from its enemies. These miracles also involved the complete restoration of life to the dead. It was not necessary in a true resurrection for the corpse to shed instantly all signs of decay: conventional images of the raising of Lazarus showed onlookers protecting their noses from the stench of putrefaction. But it was expected that the revitalised person would be restored to their former self. The biblical account of Lazarus made this clear, and the same points were stressed in later reports of genuine resurrections. The pilgrim raised by St James was greeted in Compostela by his friends, who had earlier left him for dead; and the man raised by St Stanislaus was offered the possibility of continuing his earthly life, though he chose to return to the grave so he would "not anew expose himself to the danger of sinning". Even the child revitalised at Brabant lived for several hours and displayed normal signs of life. In contrast to these heavenly interventions, the "false resurrections" performed by the devil were incomplete, and their products were often malicious or frightful.[12]

The difference between true and false resurrections was illustrated in two outwardly similar stories recorded around 1230 by Caesarius of Heisterbach. The first episode, which "happened this year at Strasbourg", concerned the death of a wealthy citizen whose "property had been ill-gotten". His corpse suddenly revived as it lay on the funeral bier. The man cried out for help, then addressed a brief speech to his wife: "By the mercy of God I have been brought back and I tell you this: unless we relinquish all we have, we cannot be saved". He lived with his wife for another two days, in which time they disposed of "everything as far as they could for their salvation". He died again when this task was done. Caesarius was clear that this event was a miracle: he noted that the man's "soul returned to his body" so that his life and personality were fully restored, and his brief return from the grave produced pious results. The second incident involved a wicked knight called Everard whose dead body also rose up on the bier. In this case, the sinister circumstances of the resurrection caused Caesarius to ascribe it to Satan: "at midnight the devil by raising his body upright on the bier terrified all who were present. His friends . . . bound the body before the mass and buried it". The revitalisation of the corpse was incomplete and served no pious purpose, and all the spectators could do was strap the cadaver down to prevent a further "outrage by devils". Sadly, evil wonders of this kind were more common than the miracle at Strasbourg.[13]

Perhaps the most infamous and dramatic example of Satan's ability to give apparent life to a corpse was reported by the English monk William of Malmesbury in the early twelfth century. As she lay on her deathbed, a woman confessed to her relatives that her wicked life probably meant that she was destined for hell. She told her children that they could probably not "deflect the true judgment of my soul", but instructed them nonetheless to protect her earthly body from Satan: her corpse was to be sewn inside the hide of a deer and placed in a stone casket sealed with iron, and fifty psalms were to be "sung each night, and masses said each day to lessen the ferocious attacks of my enemies". These wishes were observed, but on the third day of the vigil, the church where she lay was besieged by demons:

> One demonic creature, larger and more terrible than the others,
> threw down the entrance door, which was shattered into fragments.
> The priests stood rigid with dread . . . as the creature approached the
> sarcophagus with an arrogant swagger. The creature called the
> woman by name and ordered her to rise up, to which the reply came

that she was unable to do so because of the chains that bound the sarcophagus. 'By the power of your sins you will be unbound', said the demon, and at once pulled apart the iron chain as though it were no more than a cord of flax. The coffin lid was thrown off, and the woman was seized and dragged out of the church before the horrified gaze of the observers. Outside the portals of the church a fierce black horse stood neighing, with iron barbs protruding along the length of its back. Onto these hooks the woman was placed, and the entire demonic retinue quickly disappeared from sight, although . . . the woman's pleas for mercy could be heard up to four miles away.

William presented this ghastly resurrection as no less real than the historical events that made up the rest of his chronicle. Indeed, he had "heard of these events from a distinguished man who swore he had seen them for himself". The monk was also careful to explain that the revival of the dead woman was not a true resurrection. It was, he affirmed, "not a celestial miracle but an infernal wonder".[14]

The same argument was normally applied to revenants that attacked the living. In these cases, the precise method by which the devil produced false resurrections was a matter of careful speculation. One possibility was the use of "phantasms": perhaps the fiend conjured up "aerial effigies" of the wandering dead, which appeared completely real to those who encountered them. This theory was undermined, however, by the common report that revenants possessed real bodies that could be struck with weapons, receive wounds and inflict injuries on the living. The creature that attacked Melrose Abbey was driven back to its tomb with an axe, and a fourteenth-century English chronicle described how a revenant priest appeared to his former concubine and gouged out her eye. Some accounts of the restless dead also stressed the decayed state of their bodies, noting that this posed a potential threat to public health. According to William of Newburgh, the presence of a roaming cadaver in Berwick caused the more medically informed residents to fear that "the air circulating around the town would become infected by the corpse, and so lead to general sickness and death". In such instances, it appeared that the physical presence of the walking corpse was all too real.[15]

If the false resurrection of revenants was the work of Satan and their bodies really did rise from the grave, the simplest explanation for many scholars was demonic possession. The devil entered the corpse and used it like a grisly mannequin. The capacity of demons to affect the physical behaviour of living victims of possession was well known; equally, their ability to enter and manipulate the soulless bodies of animals was attested by biblical episodes like the possessed swine described by St Luke (8:33). They could exploit the bodies of the dead in the same way. This view was advanced by William of Malmesbury and Gilbert Foliot, the twelfth-century bishop of Hereford. When Foliot was asked for his opinion about a revenant in Wales, he suggested that God had permitted an "evil angel . . . to move about in the dead corpse". The idea that revenants were no more than possessed cadavers was illustrated in a truly horrific tale recorded by Thomas of Cantimpré in the thirteenth century. This concerned a pious virgin from the French town of Nivelles, who rose early each morning to pray in church. One evening "a certain deceased man" was brought to the church without her knowledge. She saw the coffin when she entered the building at night, but unafraid she began her prayers. This devout act provoked a Satanic response:

> When the devil saw this he looked upon her with malice, and entering the dead body he moved it at first in the coffin. The virgin therefore crossed herself and bravely shouted to the devil, 'Lie down! Lie down, you wretch, for you have no power against me!' Suddenly the devil rose up with the corpse and said, 'Truly now I will have power against you, and will revenge myself for the frequent injuries I have received at your hands!' When she saw this, she was thoroughly terrified in her heart, so with both hands she seized a staff topped with a cross, and bringing it down on the head of the dead man she knocked him to the ground. Through such faithful daring she put the demon to flight.

In a brilliant reading of this and similar texts, Nancy Caciola has pointed out how learned accounts of revenants often contrasted the lifelessness of the corpse to the active principle of the possessing spirit. The result was a ghastly – and theologically satisfying – image of the restless dead as animated cadavers jerked stiffly about by invading demons. When these demons were put to flight, the bodies they occupied crumpled into lifeless matter. In a case recorded by Caesarius of Heisterbach, the exorcism of a possessed corpse ended with "the body at once collapsing and becoming putrid". This proved to the witnesses that it had "been abused by the devil".[16]

The principle of demonic possession offered medieval scholars an attractive and wholly convincing explanation for the reanimation of the dead. But this was probably only one of many possible interpretations available in the wider community. Surviving reports of revenants hint at tensions between the "official" explanation and alternative traditions, though the detail of these alternative beliefs can only be guessed at. In theory, the Devil could enter the corpse of any dead person to torment the living; in practice, the wandering dead were normally marked out for their fate by sins committed in life. If a revenant was merely a possessed cadaver, it could be dealt with effectively through the instruments of exorcism: indeed, restless corpses were sometimes disinterred and sprinkled with holy water. But it was more common for their bodies to be dismembered and burnt, as if the source of danger were the corpse itself. When the Bishop of Lincoln was told that the usual way to deal with a revenant was to "dig up the body . . . and cremate it", he condemned the practice as "both unseemly and sacrilegious". In other incidents, it appears that the recommendations of senior churchmen were found to be ineffective by the communities under attack, who resorted to alternative remedies. Around 1150, Gilbert Foliot ruled that a Welsh revenant should be disinterred and sprinkled with holy water, but the restless corpse was only laid to rest when it was chased back to its grave and beheaded. A few years later, the Bishop of Worcester asked for a cross to be placed on the grave of a troublesome corpse. This intervention failed and the creature had to be chased back into its tomb by a mob. These conflicting views about revenants were contained, however, within a broader framework of shared assumptions about the power of demons and the relationship between the living and the dead. Even the practice of burning corpses echoed officially sanctioned rites of purification: the late medieval church used bonfires to purge the contamination of impious books and the bodies of heretics. Despite differences of interpretation, the basic assumption that the dead could sometimes walk from their graves belonged comfortably within the conceptual world of the late Middle Ages.[17]

THE POLITICS OF THE LIVING DEAD

The belief that corpses could rise from their tombs survived in western Europe in the sixteenth and seventeenth centuries. In this later period, however, accounts of the roaming dead were presented in a rather different context. Protestant reformers challenged traditional ideas about the relationship between the living and the dead, and provoked an aggressive response from the defenders of Catholic orthodoxy. As a result, the theology of ghosts and revenants became a battlefield between the two sides. In the same period, both Catholics and Protestants grew increasingly concerned about the spread of satanic magic. This inspired a renewed interest in the power of the devil to manipulate the bodies of the dead. As they grappled with these issues, thinkers from across the religious spectrum drew on medieval assumptions about true and false resurrections.

For Martin Luther and all the major Protestant reformers, the doctrine of purgatory was one of the chief abominations of the Roman church. They attacked the idea of a "third place" between heaven and hell as unscriptural and immoral, since it encouraged the false belief that pilgrimages, relics and the intercession of saints could influence the fate of the faithful in the hereafter. In Protestant propaganda, the myth of purgatory existed solely to enrich the papacy through exploiting the fear of death: in the emotive phrase of Nikolaus Manuel, Roman churchmen were "devourers of the dead". The abolition of purgatory in Protestant lands meant that the traffic between the living and the restless dead – who traditionally resided in the "third place" – was officially renounced. In 1569 Ludwig Lavater exemplified this new outlook in his best-selling treatise on "ghosts and spirits". Lavater acknowledged that apparitions of the dead were often "heard softly going, or spitting or groaning" in the dead of night. These apparitions claimed to be human souls in anguish, which could be relieved "if a certain number of masses were sung for them, or pilgrimages vowed to some saints, or some other like deeds done for their sakes". But they were not what they seemed. In some cases, the supposed ghosts were "priests, or other bold and wicked men" who wished to dupe the innocent into accepting the false claims of Rome. More frequently, they were demons impersonating the dead. Lavater flatly denied that the souls of the dead ever truly came back to earth. God confined their spirits in a resting place before their final entry into heaven or hell; there was no intermediary state from which they could return.[18]

Most educated Protestants shared this view, making them cautious about all reports of the unquiet dead. Ghostly apparitions were particularly suspect. In a small number of cases, angels could assume the shape of deceased Christians to impart pious messages, but more often such visitors were demonic. When the apparition of an old man appeared in a cemetery in Lübeck in 1629, the town's Lutheran clergy dismissed the possibility that it was a good spirit: they ruled that it was either a Catholic fraud, a natural delusion or the work of the devil. Reports of revived corpses were slightly different, since they did not necessarily imply the return of a human soul: a demon could merely take possession of the cadaver for its own ends. Lavater was reluctant to admit that Satan had this power, but other Protestants were less cautious. James VI, the Calvinist king of Scotland, employed a rather alarming example to show that demons could animate the dead: "for if they have assumed a dead body, wherein they lodge themselves, they can easily enough open without din any door or window, and enter in thereat". The king was at pains to point out that the possession of corpses revealed nothing about the lives of those individuals whom "the devil carries . . . out of the grave". Their souls were already in heaven or hell, and even the remains of good Christians could be abused in this way.[19]

Catholic writers were generally less sceptical about the return of the dead. In 1586 Pierre Le Loyer challenged Lavater's claim that the spirits of the dead never appeared on earth: "there are", he affirmed, "spectres of souls as well as spectres of angels and demons". This belief was consistent with human experience and the teaching of the church. As the Jesuit Martín Del Rio confirmed, it was "consistent with the tenets both of the Catholic faith and of genuine philosophy" to teach that "the souls of the dead can . . . appear to the living". In this context, Catholic tales of the restless dead often conveyed a polemical message. In 1608 the Milanese friar Francesco Maria Guazzo presented a series of examples to confound those "heretics who say that the spirits [of the dead] are all held imprisoned until the Day of Judgment". His most arresting case concerned the stirring of a corpse in a place near Pavia in 1601:

> The funeral rites of a certain notary were being performed in the church, when suddenly the corpse rose up in the coffin and, turning to one of his relatives who was attending the funeral, said: "Go quickly to my house and take a certain written instrument [document] and restore it to such a place where it justly belongs. For because I suppressed this instrument, when I died I was sentenced by God's judgement to hell". Having said this, he laid down his head as before. This was permitted by God that mortals should know what heavy punishment awaits such dishonest lawyers who embezzle the legacies of the pious.

This story recalled the medieval tradition of the dead returning physically to interact with the living, and implied strongly that the lawyer's behaviour on earth was responsible for the temporary revival of his corpse. Guazzo's other examples underlined the power of the Roman church to prevent such horrors. In 1590, for instance, a woman returned from the grave after refusing to make a deathbed confession. After the timely intervention of an angel, the woman's assaults on the living finally ended as "the bell was heard ringing for the Angelus". Catholic writers also maintained the medieval tradition that Satan could possess the dead. The French judge Nicolas Rémy affirmed that "a dead corpse" could move "through the agency of a demon which has entered it". Such creatures were merely "automatons", though God sometimes permitted Satan to use their bodies in this way to punish sins committed in life.[20]

The conflict between Catholics and Protestants over the meaning of such events was combined with an effort on both sides to clarify the theology surrounding death. This was followed by the reform of "superstitious" practices that had grown up around the experience of bereavement and the attempt to enforce these new standards in the wider community. Protestant regions abolished most of the rites associated with a "good death", and banned all rituals and objects – such as holy water and crosses – that could be used against evil spirits. Nonetheless, many rituals persisted illegally or in semi-official forms. In a partial concession to traditional attitudes, the reformed churches continued to make separate arrangements for the burial of suicides and excommunicates, individuals who were particularly liable to stray from their graves. Catholic authorities were generally more tolerant of customary practices surrounding death, and continued to accept that a

person's wicked behaviour or "bad death" might lead to a restless afterlife.
In one notorious episode from Orléans in 1534, members of the Franciscan
order offered to exhume and exorcise the body of a woman whose troubled
spirit was apparently haunting a cemetery. They claimed that her Protestant
beliefs, together with her request to be buried without the traditional rites,
made it impossible for her soul to rest.[21]

Within both religious confessions, folkloric ideas about the revival of
the dead continued to mingle with official doctrines and practices. These
traditions were tolerated to a greater or lesser degree according to social
circumstances and the convictions of local elites. In 1653 the Cambridge
philosopher Henry More recorded the depredations of two restless spirits in
the province of Silesia. Neither story involved the resuscitation of a corpse,
but both identified an unnaturally preserved cadaver as the source of
supernatural "stirs and tumults". In the first episode, which occurred at
Breslau in 1591, a shoemaker was buried in consecrated ground after his
widow concealed the fact that he had committed suicide. This deception was
exposed when a ghost "in the exact shape and habit of the deceased" began
to terrorise the town's inhabitants. The man's body was disinterred and
reburied under the gallows. This action did not end the spectral assaults,
however, and the magistrates resorted to a more drastic remedy:

> He was again dug up, and it was observed that he had grown more
> sensibly fleshy since his last interment. To be short, they cut off the
> head, arms, and legs of the corpse, and opening his back, took out his
> heart, which was as fresh and entire as in a calf new killed. These,
> together with his body, they put on a pile of wood and burnt them to
> ashes which, they carefully sweeping together and putting into a
> sack, . . . they poured into the river, after which the *spectrum* was
> never seen more.

Both the reburial of the shoemaker under the gallows and the ritual
destruction of his corpse recalled older methods for dealing with the restless
dead, and owed as much to custom as Christian theology. The same can be
said of the second incident that More reported, which took place some years
later in the town of Pentsch. This concerned a malicious spirit that attacked
the townsfolk following the death of an alderman suspected of witchcraft.
The source for this story was the town's Protestant minister, who suffered
nightly attacks from the "troublesome fiend". The pastor finally succumbed
to a serious illness when the spirit crept up to his bedside and exhaled a "cold
breath of so intolerable, stinking and malignant a scent as is beyond all
imagination". Learning from the earlier incident at Breslau, the authorities
ordered the exhumation of the alderman's body. The corpse was
dismembered, burnt and cast into a stream.[22]

The local religious and judicial authorities apparently endorsed the events that More described. This was not the case in many other episodes that involved the apparent revival of the dead. Unsurprisingly, reports of "true resurrections" provoked the most hostile official reactions. In 1651 the London sectarian John Robins was imprisoned for blasphemy and heresy, including the claim that he could raise the dead. At least one of Robins's followers confirmed that he had this power. Some early Quakers professed the same ability. In one infamous case, a Quaker from Worcester allegedly disinterred the body of an apprentice and "commanded him in the name of the living God to arise and walk". It was fortunate, perhaps, that this exercise proved unsuccessful. More dramatically, the Quaker prophet James Naylor appeared to rouse a woman from death in Bristol gaol in 1656. The beneficiary of this miracle, Dorcas Erbury, later informed the city magistrates that she had indeed returned from the dead. This claim provoked the following exchange:

> How was this done?
> I was dead for two days, and he laid his hands upon my head and said, 'Dorcas arise'. And from that day to this I am alive.
> Where was this done?
> In Exeter gaol.
> Who was witness to this?
> My mother did bear witness of it, she standing by.
> If he has such power, why does he not open the prison doors and come forth?
> When the work of the Lord is done in the prison, the doors shall open before him.

Naylor was sentenced to branding and mutilation for this and other acts of blasphemy. Sadly, little is known of the meaning of these "resurrections" to those who believed in them, but those who did not generally attributed them to fraud or religious mania. The incidents received widespread publicity from the enemies of the Quaker movement, and were used to justify its suppression.[23]

A rather more poignant series of divine "resurrections" were recorded at a shrine in the north Italian village of Trava in 1681. Here the inquisition was informed of some "wicked women who for many years . . . have abused the sacrament of baptism and, taking advantage of the faithful, pretend to resuscitate the dead". The women in question performed a rite of baptism for children who had died before receiving the sacrament. They placed the dead babies between them and knelt in prayer to the Virgin before one of the women declared that the child was sweating and opening its eyes. She then sprinkled the infant with holy water and said "certain words" to baptise it.

This practice continued a tradition that was recorded with local variations in many parts of late medieval and Renaissance Europe, and was tolerated by Catholic churchmen until the 1600s. In this particular instance Antonio Dall'Occhio, the Dominican responsible for the investigation, ruled that the miracles were false. The women were unreliable witnesses for the wonders they claimed. More importantly, the supposed resurrections were incomplete, as the babies showed only the briefest appearance of life. For Dall'Occhio, the bereaved parents who visited the shrine were the victims of a blasphemous deception. From another perspective, however, they can be seen to have displayed a complex and distinctly pre-modern understanding of the boundaries between life and death. Through the intercession of a dead saint they received the temporary resurrection of their child, and through the sacrament of baptism they assured that their child would enjoy eternal life before it slipped back into physical death.[24]

The "false resurrections" at Trava illustrated the tensions that could exist between official belief and popular practice. The need to distinguish between orthodox ideas and folk religion was more pressing in the wake of the religious division of Europe, as both Catholic and Protestant elites sought to defend their communities from heresy. At the same time, both sides were aware of the growing threat of satanic witchcraft, and it was in this context that the revival of corpses was most commonly described.

THE VOICE FROM THE GIBBET

Renaissance demonologists often referred to the physical contact between witches and demons. Evil spirits carried witches through the air; they danced and feasted with them at nightly assemblies; and they appeared as *incubi* and *succubi* to have sex with their human acolytes. These activities raised practical problems, since it was generally agreed that devils did not possess physical bodies. These difficulties were explored in early demonologies like the *Malleus Maleficarum* (1486). The authors concluded that spirits had to acquire artificial bodies in order to interact with mortals, and these could be composed of some "changeable and fluid matter" such as air. An alternative strategy, however, was for demons to perform "the functions of life by means of true natural bodies" co-opted for their purpose. Some sixteenth-century writers raised the possibility that devils sometimes possessed dead bodies when they appeared to witches. Nicolas Rémy noted in 1595 that since "they are foul and unclean spirits, it should not be surprising that, as a pig returns to its wallowing place, they should find their favourite habitation . . . in stinking corpses". Henri Boguet asserted in 1602 that Satan has "sometimes borrowed the body of a man who has been hanged, and this he does chiefly when he wishes to associate with a witch". This view was widely shared in the seventeenth century. It was a common opinion, noted the Italian friar Ludovico Maria Sinistrari in the late 1600s, that "the demon assumes the corpse of another human being" when he copulates with his earthly disciples.[25]

This idea raised some unpleasant questions. By appearing in the borrowed flesh of "stinking corpses", demons were more likely to revolt their human confederates than entice them into further acts of depravity. Martín Del Rio confronted this problem head on. He noted that Satan could not confer to a cadaver "any of the vital characteristics which belong to a living body". These qualities, such as "the softness of flesh, the hardness of bones [and] warmth and gentle heat", could only proceed from the miraculous reintroduction of a soul into the lifeless matter. This was, of course, beyond Satan's power. Del Rio asserted, however, that the devil could counterfeit these effects. He could deceive the "external senses" of the witch to make the corpse appear to be alive. Moreover, he "can so make adjustments to this body (especially one which is not too far decayed) that they can completely deceive the sense of touch". Such effects were mere deceptions, and produced no physical change in the rank flesh that the demon wore. For this reason, as Boguet noted, witches who consorted with the devil in this form were "usually ugly and stinking".[26]

As well as co-opting the dead to provide temporary bodies, demons used false resurrections to display their power to witches. Acts of this kind were to be expected, since Satan loved to imitate and mock the miracles of God. Rémy reported an obscene parody of this kind. This concerned a man from the town of Dalheim who, in 1581, entered a pact with a *succubus* demon that involved the sacrifice of his child:

> His succubus . . . forced him to fulfil his solemn given promise to commit foul murder upon his only son; and when he could not endure his loss, and was driven nearly mad by the thought of the infanticide which he had perpetrated, she promised that – if he implored her with supplication and adoration – she would bring the boy back to life. And accordingly for a whole year she caused him by her magic to appear as if he were living and exercising his natural functions. That this was no more than a deception and illusion was clearly and abundantly shown when, without any previous illness, the boy again died, and immediately began to stink so abominably that it was impossible to look at him except from a distance, and that with the nostrils pressed close together.

Rémy assured his readers that this event was "fully confirmed by the inhabitants of the place, who assured many persons that they had seen with their own eyes the boy recalled to a semblance of life". Since the child appeared to live for a whole year, his false resurrection appeared to stretch the limits of the devil's power. This point was later taken up by the Benedictine abbot Augustin Calmet, who regarded the incident at Dalheim as a unique instance of demonic magic. With the permission of God, Satan had performed "on this occasion what he perhaps had never done, nor ever will again – to possess a body and serve it in some sort as a soul, and give it action and motion whilst he could retain the body without its being too much corrupted".[27]

The practice of witchcraft involved one further type of false resurrection: the conjuration of corpses or body parts to make them impart hidden information. This was the purpose of the fake raising of Samuel by the witch of Endor (1 Sam. 28). In 1437, Johannes Nider condemned magicians "who claim that, by means of superstitious rites, they are able to raise the dead to speak on occult matters". Later demonologists often reported such acts as magical operations performed to gain knowledge of the future. This feat was accomplished, they assumed, by demons taking temporary possession of the dead. In 1580, Jean Bodin reported that "one of the great kings of Christendom" had been involved in this art. He employed a magician to perform the rite of Holy Communion then "had the head cut off a young first-born child of ten years old, and had his head placed on the host". The magician demanded information from the head, only to receive the reply, "Vim patior", or "I suffer". Rémy recounted a similar event that occurred in Paris in 1563. This involved a noblewoman of his acquaintance:

> I went to visit her . . . and found her with two officers of the royal
> household, discussing how they could most easily obtain possession
> of the treasure which they said the King had granted them an
> opportunity of inspecting . . . I heard one of these men telling in all
> seriousness how, not many days before, he had conjured a corpse on
> its gibbet to speak with him on this matter, but that he had been
> unable to elicit anything definite from it, since all its answers were
> ambiguous and perplexing.

The failure of this grisly operation was to be expected, since demons delighted in teasing those who invoked them with false or baffling pronouncements. Nonetheless, Rémy and many of his educated contemporaries lamented that people continued to practise magic of this kind, and witches were occasionally indicted for attempting such violations of the dead.[28]

Throughout the Middle Ages and the Renaissance, reports of the bodily revival of corpses were presented as exceptional events that displayed the miraculous intervention of God or – more often – the malice of Satan. They were extraordinary and rare. Even during the most intense periods of witch persecution, lawyers and demonologists were not greatly concerned by the demonic possession of the dead. These phenomena were, nonetheless, viewed within an intellectual framework that made them credible. Individual episodes could be dismissed – there was always the possibility of fraud or delusion, and reports of "wonders" were often rejected as the products of heresy or superstition. But few people believed in principle that the dead could never walk. When Henry More described the troublesome corpses of Silesia in 1653, he did so as an "antidote to atheism": the truth of his stories was "so plain and evident" that no reasonable person could doubt them. He could argue in this way because there was no prior assumption among his contemporaries that a corpse could never stir. The idea was not mad. Today most western people would probably say that it is, and this reflects, perhaps, a profound shift in our shared assumptions about the boundary between life and death.[29]

5

"A Shipwreck of Souls"

Understanding Witchcraft

In 1836 Nathaniel Hawthorne described a doleful ascent of Gallows Hill in Salem, where nineteen alleged witches were hanged in 1692. He observed that from a distance the hill appeared "absolutely overlaid with gold, or covered with a glory of sunshine, even beneath a clouded sky". This bright prospect was deceptive, however. The hilltop itself was choked in a thick carpet of ugly weeds. In Hawthorne's view, this bleak crop was well suited to the place:

> The curious wanderer on the hill will perceive that all the grass, and everything that should nourish man or beast, has been destroyed by this vile and ineradicable weed: its tufted roots make the soil their own, and permit nothing else to vegetate among them; so that a physical curse may be said to have blasted the spot, where guilt and frenzy consummated the most execrable scene that our history blushes to record. For this was the field where superstition won her darkest triumph; the high place where our fathers set up their shame, to the mournful gaze of generations far remote. The dust of martyrs was beneath our feet.

Nearly 200 years later, the events on Gallows Hill still attract the "mournful gaze" of posterity. Hawthorne's verdict on the execution of the Salem witches was endorsed by later generations, and immortalised in our own time by Arthur Miller's play *The Crucible*. Many observers in the 1690s also believed the trials were a cruel mistake. In October 1692 the Boston pastor Increase Mather denounced the prosecutions and successfully brought them to an end. As the prisons began to empty, the Salem Quaker Thomas Maule lamented the destructive "bustlings and clamorous noises about the devil and witchcraft".[1]

The lasting regret that westerners feel for the events at Salem, and the witch trials that claimed some 50,000 other lives in pre-modern Europe and America, is a welcome acknowledgement of the sufferings of people in the remote past. The women and men who perished on Hawthorne's "haunted height" were as real as us, and it is entirely right that we feel distressed that their lives were taken for reasons that now appear to be profoundly wrong. But we completely miss the point of this tragedy if we see it merely as a miscarriage of justice. Injustices were undoubtedly committed in witch trials, both at Salem and elsewhere, but the prosecution of witches was not inherently unjust in terms of the beliefs and procedures of the pre-modern world. Nor were witch trials the "darkest triumph" of superstition. In fact, Renaissance demonologists were among the first to condemn the "superstition" they perceived among ordinary people. Crucially, the crime of witchcraft was accepted by almost everyone as real. Even Increase Mather and Thomas Maule, along with the great majority of those who condemned the trials of 1692, acknowledged the harm done by witches and the need to punish them by law. "That there are devils and witches", Mather wrote, "the scripture asserts and experience confirms; that they are common enemies of mankind, and set upon mischief, is not to be doubted".[2] The critics of the Salem prosecutions never questioned the reality of witchcraft; they challenged only the evidence by which the accused were condemned.

The real tragedy of witchcraft becomes apparent when we acknowledge this fact. Those involved in the accusation and trial of witches normally believed sincerely that they were doing good. Moreover, this belief was entirely reasonable and wholly consistent with their knowledge of the world. They were neither mad nor bad. This observation applies to most of the prosecutions for which detailed records have survived. Paul Boyer and Stephen Nissenbaum expressed it memorably in their classic study of the incident at Salem:

> By twentieth-century standards, of course, the entire episode was
> simply a matter of "superstition". Undeniably, too, there were
> instances of gross injustice – injustice by the standards of that day as
> well as those of our own. But when all this has been conceded, what
> emerges most strongly from the record is the sense of a society,
> confronted with a tenacious outbreak of a particularly baffling crime
> at a time of severe political and legal disruption, nevertheless striving,
> in an equitable way, to administer justice and to restore order. The
> sober conclusion of the Reverend John Hale, in a work written shortly
> after the episode and in fact sharply critical of some of its legal
> aspects, cannot be ignored: "I observed in the prosecution of these
> affairs that there was in the justices, judges, and others concerned, a
> conscientious endeavour to do the thing that was right."[3]

In their efforts to do what was right, the "wise and good men" of Salem – as Increase Mather described the judges in 1692 – condemned nineteen people to hang and caused one more to be pressed to death. To understand how good intentions could produce such awful results, we need to reconstruct the crime of witchcraft and the evidence on which it was based, as these things were understood in the pre-modern world.

MALEFICIUM

The idea of witchcraft that flourished in the sixteenth and seventeenth centuries combined three related concepts. The first of these was the practice of harmful magic, or *maleficium*. The belief that certain people could use sorcery to hurt their neighbours was the most widely accepted of all witch beliefs, and provided the basis for the great majority of accusations. Rather less common, but still widely reported, was the belief that *maleficium* involved the intervention of demons. At its simplest, this meant the assistance of a "familiar spirit". But for most educated writers on the subject, witchcraft also involved a formal pact between the witch and the Devil, normally consummated through a formal act of blasphemy. The third component of Renaissance witch beliefs was the idea of a secret cult of devil-worshippers. This idea was less common among ordinary people, though it featured prominently in the work of experts in the field. The concept of the sabbat – a nocturnal gathering of witches for collective acts of ritual desecration, *maleficium* and murder – surfaced in large-scale witch persecutions across Europe and America, and contributed to the crisis at Salem. However, it was often absent from the prosecution of individuals or small groups of alleged witches that constituted the bulk of trials.[4]

The Bible provided evidence for these ingredients of witchcraft. Sorcery was one of the "works of the flesh" denounced by St Paul in Galatians 5:20. The book of Deuteronomy condemned witches and enchanters, as well as those who communicated with "familiar spirits" (Deut. 18:10–11). The punishment for such offenders was spelt out in Leviticus 20:27: "A man or woman that hath a familiar spirit, or that is a wizard, shall surely be put to death". Scripture was silent on the collective abominations of the sabbat, but St Paul and the Gospels offered detailed accounts of the Devil's determination to pervert human behaviour. As the apostle observed, Satan contrived to enjoy the devotions of those who "sacrifice to devils and not to God" (1 Cor. 10:20). These ideas were amplified by the Church Fathers. In their commentaries on the magical operations described in Exodus, Tertullian and Origen declared that Pharoah's magicians achieved their effects through demonic assistance. St Augustine confirmed that the effects of magic were all too real, and observed that the "marvels of sorcery are achieved by means of the science taught by demons". He also stressed the devil's wish to establish himself as a figure of veneration among mortals, whom he gulled with "deceitful miracles" into joining his service.[5]

The message of these authoritative texts was especially relevant in the magic-believing culture of pre-modern Europe. The records of ecclesiastical visitations in the sixteenth century confirm that magical practices were widespread: wherever Catholic or Protestant agents investigated the beliefs of ordinary churchgoers, they discovered that spells for healing and protection were rife, as well as the fear of *maleficium*. One generally recognised form of harmful magic involved the making of waxen images. The Jesuit demonologist Martín Del Rio described the process succinctly: "they stick pins in them, or melt them in the fire, or break them in pieces, and this makes sure that those people represented by the images waste away or suffer some other kind of death". In 1566 the English "cunning man" John Walsh described a local variation on this technique. He described how clay images were produced from suitably disagreeable ingredients:

> Their confection is after this manner. They . . . take the earth of a new made grave, the rib bone of a man or woman burned to ashes (if it be for a woman, they take the bone of a woman, if for a man, the bone of a man), and a black spider, with an inner pith of an elder, tempered all in water . . . [When the image is made] they put a prick (that is, a pin or a thorn) in any member where they would have the party grieved; and if the said prick be put to the heart, the party dieth within nine days. Which image they bury in the moistest place they can find.

In 1586 an Italian exorcist, Girolamo Menghi, described his own experience of this kind of image magic. He was called to the bedside of a noblewoman who had apparently contracted "a severe and incurable illness". Once all the available medical treatments had been exhausted, Menghi suggested that her bed should be thoroughly cleaned. This led to the discovery of concealed "instruments of maleficent magic", including "an image made out of feathers extraordinarily like a human being, with head, arms, hands, legs, feet and all the other members". The bewitched woman recovered her health when these artefacts were destroyed.[6]

If this form of *maleficium* belonged to the pagan tradition of "sympathetic magic", many other operations involved Christian elements. The Bible and holy objects could be abused in malicious magic. John Walsh described how magicians recited the Latin version of the Lord's Prayer backwards to bring misfortune on their enemies. In 1590 the French demonologist Jean Bodin recorded a more complex abuse of the Catholic Mass:

> They tried a witch who confessed that she had placed the consecrated host into her handkerchief instead of swallowing it, and put it into a jar where she was feeding a toad, and put it all with other powders . . . beneath the doorway of a sheepfold while uttering

some words, which it is not necessary to write, in order to make the flock die. She was caught in the act, convicted, and burned alive.

In a culture where the division between religion and magic was often blurred, and the sacraments offered a powerful source of supernatural power, it was hardly surprising if such abuses sometimes occurred. As Martín Del Rio observed sadly, magicians "do not hesitate to use sacred things" in *maleficia*. For intellectuals like Bodin and Del Rio, this afforded further proof of the blasphemous nature of sorcery, and echoed St Paul's assertion that "you cannot be partakers of the Lord's table and of the table of devils" (1 Cor. 10:21).[7]

Did *maleficium* work? When its potential victims were aware that magic was being used against them, the answer is probably yes. Anthropological studies from magic-believing cultures have shown that cursing can produce traumatic physical effects. People have been killed by voodoo in Haiti. As recently as 1968, a woman in rural France succumbed to a sudden illness after her neighbours, who suspected her of witchcraft, targeted her with counter-magic. Doctors were unable to explain her condition, while the woman herself repeated constantly, "I am afraid". Incidents of this kind are associated mainly with non-industrial cultures, but it is worth noting that medical studies provide compelling evidence for similar effects in developed societies. A recent article in the *British Medical Journal* found that deaths from heart failure in China and Japan tend to peak on the fourth day of each month. This pattern is not repeated elsewhere. Having considered other possible explanations, the authors explained this pattern by the fact that Chinese and Japanese people regard the number four as unlucky. More positively, numerous studies have demonstrated the power of the "placebo effect" in western medicine. Patients offered fake medication will sometimes recover from illness, and their progress can be measured empirically in improved immune responses. The key factor appears to be belief. If a person accepts that something can affect their well being, and others around them sanction this idea, their health may well change solely as a consequence of this belief.[8]

If witchcraft sometimes produced real sickness, it was probably used more often as an explanation for misfortune and disease. Like any explanation, it was only plausible if the right circumstances were in place. An illness or accident that appeared "strange", and could not be easily explained by natural causes, was one necessary component; another was the presence of a credible suspect. When these circumstances were met, *maleficium* offered a believable account of the evidence available. This process was illustrated in an incident at Boston, Massachusetts, in 1688, four years before the calamity at Salem. The eldest daughter of a mason, John Goodwin, was afflicted with a sudden, convulsive illness. Physicians examined the girl and decided she was not suffering from epilepsy. The illness spread to her younger siblings, whose symptoms were equally traumatic:

Sometimes they would be deaf, sometimes dumb, and sometimes
blind, and often all this at once. One while their tongues would be
drawn down their throats; another while they would be pulled out
upon their chins, to a prodigious length . . . They would at times lie
in a benumbed condition; and be drawn together as those that are
tied neck and heels; and presently be stretched out, yea, drawn
backwards, to such degree that it was feared the very skin of their
bellies would have cracked.

While the medical expects were confounded, the existence of an alleged witch
in the neighbourhood lent credibility to the alternative explanation of
maleficia. The mother of the family's laundress had already acquired a
reputation for witchcraft: she was "an ignorant and scandalous old woman in
the neighbourhood, whose miserable husband, before he died, had sometimes
complained of her that she was undoubtedly a witch, and that whenever his
head was laid she would quickly arrive unto the punishments due to such a
one". The fact that the eldest girl had quarrelled with the woman shortly
before her illness – suggesting a possible motive for *maleficium* – provided
further evidence against her. She was eventually accused of witchcraft and
brought to trial.[9]

In this case and many others, both the witch and her accusers appear to
have accepted the second element of the Renaissance concept of
witchcraft: the involvement of demons in *maleficium*. The accused woman
confessed that the Devil helped her to harm the children. By 1688, this
concept was well established and supported by a wealth of evidence. The
Church Fathers Augustine and Origen had claimed that devils were
responsible for the illusions created by pagan magicians, and Christian
thinkers endorsed this view throughout the Middle Ages and Renaissance.
The existence of "necromancy" – a branch of magic involving explicitly
demonic forces – also contributed to the idea that demons were involved in
sorcery. From the fifteenth century onwards, demonologists pointed to the
activity of necromancers to illustrate the Devil's role in magical operations,
and to argue that *all* magic involved at least an implicit pact with Satan.

In the late medieval and Renaissance age, necromancy was practised
mainly within the "clerical underworld" of minor ecclesiastical office-
holders. Men with knowledge of Latin, and access to manuals of exorcism,
could abuse their position by attempting to compel demons through the ritual
invocations of the church. Surviving ceremonies for the conjuration of devils
appear to be amended versions of the official rite of exorcism, in which the
necromancer sought to compel an unclean spirit to do his bidding instead of
driving it away. Medieval writers on witchcraft, such as Nicholas Eymericus
and Johannes Nider, appear to have been familiar with the literature of
necromancy, and derived the idea that witches offered worship to demons

partly from this source. In his thirteenth-century *Dialogue on Miracles*, the German monk Caesarius of Heisterbach described the activities of a necromancer named Philip who provided a service for people who wished to consult with demons. One of his clients, a knight from Prüm, was taken at noon to a crossroads where the necromancer drew a circle in the ground. As the two men stood inside the circle, Philip instructed the knight not to "put forth any of your limbs outside" or risk being "dragged forth by the demons and torn in pieces". The knight took this advice to heart and survived to describe a troop of hideous spirits that swirled around the enchanted space. Another client was less careful and was killed by the demons. Caesarius noted that "I myself have seen this Philip, who was killed a few years ago by the agency, it is believed, of his master and friend, the Devil".[10]

The necromancy described by Caesarius was a form of learned magic, most often associated with disreputable scholars and priests. This tradition survived throughout the age of witch persecutions. In 1653 the English pastor John Rogers recalled how, as an impoverished student at Cambridge, "the devil did often tempt me to study necromancy". While Rogers resisted this temptation, we may assume that some others occasionally succumbed. The conjuration of spirits was also involved in popular magic. Given the general assumption that the world was populated with supernatural beings that could involve themselves in human affairs, attempts to employ these creatures for practical purposes – both good and ill – were an unsurprising feature of village sorcery. In 1590 Nicolas Rémy noted the common belief that witches could send spirits to harm their enemies. Francesco Maria Guazzo observed that they used the same method to destroy cattle. In English witchcraft, the use of "imps" was particularly well documented, both in allegations of *maleficia* and the confessions of witches. In 1582 Ursula Kemp admitted that she kept four spirits, two of them male and two female. Her testimony explained the division of labour between them: "the two he-spirits were to punish and kill unto death, and the other two were to punish with lameness and other diseases of bodily harm, and also to destroy cattle". Other English witches confessed to using spirits in the form of toads, a practice also recorded widely in mainland Europe. Some of those accused undoubtedly believed they possessed the power to command these creatures: Margaret Moore of Ely, for instance, confessed freely to sending imps to torment her neighbours in 1647. While modern readers are likely to regard such beliefs as delusions, it appears that *maleficia* involving malevolent spirits were widely recognised, and occasionally attempted, in the pre-modern world.[11]

If the existence of these practices was not in doubt, their meaning was open to different interpretations. In the case of necromancy, the magicians themselves assumed they were controlling demons for their own ends. Even when they offered sacrifices to devils, this was not meant as a form of worship: these offerings were used to appease or cajole the spirits they intended to exploit. In the eyes of medieval and Renaissance demonologists, however, all traffic with demons involved an implicit pact with Satan. Since scripture explicitly condemned such activities, and warned that the Devil was always determined to destroy human souls, they assumed that demons were in reality exploiting the necromancers. When they turned their attention to popular magic, the same conclusion seemed unavoidable. It appears that village sorcerers employed a colourful variety of different spirits, including fairies and imps as well as creatures that were recognisably demonic. But the dubious status of these creatures within Christian theology led demonologists to assume they were all demons, particularly when they were used for explicitly harmful purposes. Moreover, if the effects of *maleficia* were real, unlettered villagers unfamiliar with the formulae of ritual magic could hardly compel demons to bring them about. It was much easier to believe that witches were simply obeying the Devil. When Henry Howard reflected on the numerous confessions of English witches concerning "imps" in 1583, he concluded that these were the "damned spirits or familiars" condemned in the book of Deuteronomy. He explained their homely appearance as mice, cats and dogs by observing that familiar spirits "take upon them such strange shapes and forms as may best serve their turn".[12]

For men like Howard, the existence of harmful magic was beyond dispute, and it was a "waste of good time" to prove the activity of wicked spirits. The facts were obvious. Martín Del Rio expressed the same certainty when he introduced the subject of *maleficium* in his *Investigations Into Magic* (1600):

> I am not arguing about whether [harmful magic] exists or not. I take
> for granted that it does. Those who deny this are contradicted by the
> precepts of Holy Scripture, canon and civil law, and by historians,
> poets, common belief, and the testimony of all past ages. No branch
> of magic delights the evil spirit more because . . . the disasters of
> human kind are food and drink to evil spirits.

Maleficium was a given reality. The only area for disagreement among experts was on relatively technical matters: the relationship between witches and the Devil, the limits of demonic power, and the precise methods by which magical effects were created. This allowed plenty of room for discussion – and a good deal of critical analysis, but the fundamentals were not in doubt. When the Essex gentleman Reginald Scot denied the reality of magic in 1584, his work was regarded as so eccentric that it barely merited a refutation. The intellectual foundations for a campaign against *maleficium* were strong. But the persecution of witches would probably have been less severe had not educated people come to believe in the existence of an organised witch cult.[13]

THE HORRIBLE SECT OF WITCHES

The origins of the *sabbat* are obscure. The idea of a secret gathering of sorcerers featured in demonological texts in the early fifteenth century, drawing on fears about collective necromancy. In his influential *Formicarius*, composed between 1436 and 1438, Johannes Nider described reports of the ritual murder of infants in the Simme valley in Switzerland. The infants were killed in their cradles by *maleficia*, and then secretly removed from their graves. They were then "boiled in a cauldron until, with the bones having been torn out, almost all the flesh is turned into a liquid draft". This concoction was used in ritual magic. The fluid was poured into a flask and offered to new members of the sect, who entered the secret community by drinking the foul beverage. Nider claimed that members of the sect renounced their Christian baptism and trampled on the cross. The idea of a witch cult was elaborated in the decades that followed and gradually incorporated elements of folk tradition. These included the flight of witches to the sabbat, often astride marvellous beasts. By the middle years of the sixteenth century, most learned writers on the subject agreed that the witches' gatherings included promiscuous dancing and feasting on disgusting food. They were occasions for collective acts of *maleficia*, as well as the worship of demons and the elaborate desecration of Christian rites.[14]

In 1602 the French judge Henri Boguet described the sabbat in its fully developed form. The witches were carried by demons through the night sky to a secret place. Once they were all gathered, their master, the Devil, received them:

> The witches, then, being assembled in their synagogue, first worship
> Satan, who appears to them now in the shape of a big black man and
> now as a goat; and to do him the greater homage they offer him
> candles, which burn with a blue flame; then they kiss him on the
> shameful parts behind. Some kiss him on the shoulder; and at other
> times he holds up a black image which he requires the witches to
> kiss . . . Following this, they dance; and this they do in a ring back to
> back . . . There are also demons which join in these dances in the
> shape of goats and rams. They are not without pipes for these revels,
> for there are those whose duty it is to provide the dance music. Most
> often Satan plays upon the flute, and at other times the witches are
> content to sing with their voices; but they sing at haphazard and in
> such confusion that one cannot hear the other.

These festivities dissolved into a sexual orgy. The demons coupled with their human servants, and the devil himself assumed the shape of a man to fornicate with female witches and a woman to satisfy the men. The members of the sect also fell on one another with indiscriminate lust: "the son does not spare his mother, nor the brother his sister, nor the father his daughter". The orgy was followed by a great banquet. Here Satan urged his followers to renew their pledge to the cult, and to render accounts of the *maleficia* they had performed. This done, they worked together to create more baleful magic, including the production of hail. The assembly climaxed with the formal mockery of Holy Communion:

> They say mass at the sabbat. But I cannot write without horror of the manner in which it is celebrated; for he who is to say the office is clothed in a black cope with no cross upon it, and after putting the water in the chalice he turns his back to the altar, and then elevates, in place of the host, a round of turnip coloured black; and then the witches all cry aloud: "Master, help us!" And to make holy water, the devil pisses in a hole in the ground, and the worshippers are then sprinkled with his urine by the celebrant.

In a pyrotechnical finale, the Devil resumed the form of a goat and exploded into flames. Once his body was reduced to ashes, his followers gathered up the remains "for use in the performance of their execrable and abominable designs".[15]

It appears that nothing in Boguet's catalogue of atrocities was based on real events. Some witch trials in sixteenth-century Italy were inspired by the activities of a fertility cult whose members, the *benandante*, claimed to travel "in spirit" to fight the enemies of the harvest; and the idea of the sabbat may have derived in part from the popular belief that mortals could sometimes attend gatherings of fairies. But these beliefs had little in common with the devil-worship, orgies and acts of ritual depravity described in accounts of the sabbat. Moreover, there is no substantial evidence for cultic activity of any kind in the majority of documented cases of witchcraft. The witch cult imagined by Boguet and his fellows simply did not exist. Attempts to extinguish this cult had real consequences, however. When judges were convinced that the witch cult was a dreadful reality, allegations of simple *maleficium* could lead to more general accusations of organised diabolism. Suspects were encouraged to confess to attending the sabbat, and to name others who were there. This process could spread the accusations until whole communities were caught up in them, as happened at Trier between 1581 and 1593, and Würzburg in 1629. In the latter case, some 400 individuals were accused at the height of the persecution, including children, priests, councillors, and eventually the Prince-Bishop himself. The idea of a witch cult was also prominent in the persecution at Salem. Here the confession of Tituba, the West Indian slave owned by the village pastor Samuel Parris, encouraged the idea that the community was threatened by a conspiracy of witches who had signed their names in the Devil's book.[16]

How could educated people believe things that were so utterly, disastrously untrue? To answer this question, we must note that there was nothing inherently incredible about the sabbat for pre-modern thinkers, even though it was not mentioned in the Bible or other ancient texts. In other words, the idea of a witch cult was not self-evidently wrong. The importance of this observation can be demonstrated by the fact that most people today do not believe in the sabbat because it appears to involve impossible things. Modern readers of Boguet may accept his claim that "witches sometimes go on foot to the sabbat, and this usually happens when the place of their assembly is not very distant from their homes". They may pause, however, on learning that it was more common for them to make the journey by flight, "sometimes on a goat, sometimes on a horse and sometimes on a broom". Their confidence will evaporate completely when they read that even those witches who confessed to walking to the sabbat also claimed they were "sometimes carried there by the Devil", and generally left their homes through the chimney. For Boguet's seventeenth-century audience, however, none of these feats were impossible. They were all within the known ability of demons, as was amply testified in the New Testament. Not only this, but the idea that the Devil might choose to transport his followers in this way was quite plausible: he was, after all, "the prince of the power of the air" (Eph. 2:2). For the most sceptical of Boguet's original readers, the question was not whether such things could happen, but whether they had truly occurred in the cases he described.[17]

Once we accept this point, we can start to appreciate the impact of the idea of the sabbat. It is impossible for modern readers to suspend their disbelief completely in the face of such apparently outlandish claims, but events from the recent past show that educated people are capable of believing in the core elements of the sabbat once they are shorn of supernatural trappings. In 1980, the Canadian "occult survivor" Michelle Smith published an account of her early childhood experiences in an extended family of devil-worshippers. Among other horrors, she claimed to have witnessed incestuous orgies, the desecration of Christian images and the ritual killing of babies:

> They lit a big fire in a corner of the room . . . They never let it go
> out. Next to the fire they assembled a whole collection of crosses –
> paper ones, wooden ones, crosses made of dead holly. Some they
> ripped apart, some they chopped up. They threw all of them into the
> fire. Michelle saw that they had another dead baby, and she cried out
> for them to stop, but they didn't listen. They nailed its little hands
> and feet to a big wooden cross that they had saved from the fire, and
> then they broke all the bones in its body.

Smith's book was followed by a series of similar disclosures from other adult survivors of "Satanic abuse". These were supplemented by the testimonies

Plate 1   Early illustration of the Devil in a stooping position. © Bettmann/CORBIS

Plate 2 Engraving of cherubs coming to collect the spirit of a dead person by
Pierre Daret, from *Doctrine of Morality* by M. de Gomberville. © Historical Picture
Archive/CORBIS

Plate 3 Animals engaging in criminal acts: a pig devours a baby, a bull gores a man and a dog worries a sheep. Illustration from Joducus Damhouder, *Praxis Rerum Criminalium*, 1562

Plate 4 *The Astrologist and Death* by Abad Angelo Donati. © Archivo Iconografico, SA/CORBIS

Plate 5   Devil's Sabbath at the Blocksberg engraving. © Stapleton Collection/
CORBIS

Plate 6   Werewolf, Lucas Cranach Senr. *c.* 1510. *Source:* The Art Archive

Plate 7 Medieval exorcism. A priest drives out the Devil in a medieval manuscript drawing from Chartres. © Cristel Gerstenberg/CORBIS

Plate 8 Woodcut showing interpretation of Satan and suffering. This is a depiction of the Devil appearing to a fever-stricken man. Woodcut *c.* 1843. © Bettmann/CORBIS

Plate 9 Robert Fleury's great picture of the burning of heretics by the Roman Catholics at an auto-da-fé. © CORBIS

Plate 10 Devils attacking a safe. Advertisement depicting Satan's minions unable to break into a Diebold brand safe. © Corbis (Thomas Brett), 1879

of children taken into care from families suspected of the crime. In 1989, similar allegations were reported in the United Kingdom, leading to a series of high-profile cases that culminated in accusations of devil-worship and child abuse in two families on the Scottish Orkney Islands. After exhaustive police investigations in the United States and Britain, charges of ritual abuse were dropped against all the families concerned. Subsequent research has established that the original testimony of Michelle Smith was false, and the accounts of many other adult survivors have been thoroughly discredited.[18]

The alarm about satanic abuse can be viewed as a secular version of the sabbat myth. While the testimonies of some adult "survivors" and children alleging abuse contained supernatural details – such as the physical reality of the Devil – most professionals who accepted their claims treated them as victims of crimes that were possible within a non-magical view of the world. The professional literature about ritual abuse did not accept the existence of harmful magic, and police investigators did not concern themselves with evidence of demonic manifestations. Rather, the modern witch cult was treated as a deviant underground movement: its members practised the "real" crimes of conspiracy, child abuse and murder. These acts were committed in secret, so the main evidence against them was the testimony of survivors. These circumstances meant that each accusation had to be treated separately, according to the particular merits of the case. Unlike historical accounts of the sabbat, there was no "killer fact" that investigators could point out to disprove *all* the accusations – such as the supposed impossibility of *maleficium* or the witches' flight. Even today, in the absence of any empirical evidence to support the existence of ritual abuse other than the disclosures of alleged survivors, it is impossible to rule out the possibility that it may exist. This presents anyone who confronts the issue with a dilemma. As the counsellor Patrick Casement has observed, "it may be that some accounts which are reputed to be of 'Satanic' abuse are delusional, and the narrators may indeed be psychotic in some cases". Nonetheless, he continues, "we must still face the awful fact that if some of these accounts are true, if we do not have the courage to see the truth that may be there (amidst however much confusion that may also be there), we may tacitly be allowing these practices to continue under the cover of secrecy". This is the moral force behind the idea of the sabbat. Once we accept that the crimes attributed to a secret cult may be real, we are obliged to take them seriously. This applies even when there is no evidence except the word of its alleged members or victims, and when previous accusations have been investigated and disproved.[19]

The same dilemma faced Renaissance judges confronting the witch cult. In fact their position was much worse, since most witches suspected of attending the sabbat were also accused of specific acts of *maleficium*, normally attested by numerous witnesses. Reputations for witchcraft were often established over several years, and small communities could normally provide convincing evidence against those suspected of practising harmful magic. The *Malleus Maleficarum* (1486) drew extensively on rumours of witchcraft circulating in German villages. These rumours were sometimes sufficient to establish the reality of *maleficium*, which in turn confirmed the existence of a demonic pact. Once the idea of a witch cult was widely accepted, convincing reports of *maleficium* supported the presumption that accused men and women belonged to it. In 1645 Matthew Hopkins and John Stearne investigated the "horrible sect of witches" in the eastern counties of England, and encouraged alleged victims of *maleficia* to name likely members of the sect. Many of those named had already acquired local reputations and when they were questioned they tended to identify individuals similar to themselves. In the first major trial at Essex assizes, Rebecca West accused five other women of practising witchcraft, including her own accuser, the beggar Elizabeth Clarke. Twenty-one other witnesses supported these allegations, including three members of the local clergy.[20]

The main evidence for the sabbats themselves derived from the confessions of witches. "If one must speak to experts to learn the truth", wrote Jean Bodin in 1580, "are any more expert than witches themselves?" He noted how members of the cult had divulged "their sacrifices, their dances, their nightly transports, their murders, charms, liaisons, and sorceries, with all they have confessed and continue to confess right up to their deaths". In some instances, individuals appear to have offered this information spontaneously. This was the case with María de Ximildegui, a young woman from the Basque region of Spain, who admitted in 1608 to joining the witch cult during a stay in France. María provided a detailed account of the sabbats she attended and named several others who were there. Her confession encouraged others to come forward with their own testimonies, until a series of public statements confirmed the reality of the sect. María's motives were obscure, but other voluntary confessions were apparently inspired by feelings of guilt. In his classic study of witchcraft in France and Switzerland, William E. Monter found that several of those who confessed to making pacts with the Devil were already troubled by anxieties about secret sexual crimes. In some cases, admissions of witchcraft were even made in the privacy of the Catholic confessional, years before the suspects were formally charged.[21]

Such spontaneous disclosures were less common, however, than those obtained through psychological or physical pressure. Torture was not part of the normal process for dealing with alleged criminals and some contemporaries condemned its use in the questioning of witches. The English sceptic Reginald Scot complained that suspects were bound to make false statements because "flesh and blood is unable to endure such trial". But demonologists justified the use of torture as the only means to obtain secret information about the cult. As Henri Boguet explained, the nature of the crime meant that normal rules for obtaining evidence had to be suspended:

Witchcraft is a crime apart, both on account of its enormity, and because it is usually committed at night and always secretly. Therefore the trial of this crime must be conducted in an extraordinary manner; and the usual legalities and ordinary procedure cannot be strictly observed . . . If the judge can draw no confession from the accused, he must confine him in a very narrow and dark cell; for it has been proved that the hardship of prison very often impels witches to confess . . . If the judge is forced to have recourse to torture, he must consider well whether there are grounds enough for doing so, having regard to the indications, conjectures and presumptions against the accused.

These presumptions included evidence of *maleficia* from other sources, and lies or apparent inconsistencies in the suspect's performance under questioning. Blessed with hindsight, historians have pointed out that the torture of suspects produced false confessions and the naming of other members of the sect. It is tempting to dismiss Boguet and other defenders of the practice as naive, but recent history suggests that their arguments can still hold sway with intelligent people. Indeed, they have been used to justify the "unconventional" interrogation techniques employed with alleged terrorists in our own time. US government guidelines for questioning members of al-Qaeda permit the use of "limited pain or discomfort" during interrogations, including sleep deprivation and extremes of heat and cold. These methods have been endorsed because of the extraordinary nature of the threat these people are believed to represent, and the urgent need to obtain hidden information about possible future crimes.[22]

Faced with the leading questions of their interrogators, alleged witches provided confessions that were fed back into the expert literature on the subject and, since judges themselves had recourse to this literature, the questions were repeated and still more evidence was produced. Demonologists were impressed by the consistency of witches' accounts of the sabbat. Jean Bodin noted how "all those who were burned in Italy, Germany and France agree point by point". For Nicolas Rémy, the "unanimous statements of witches" confirmed both the reality of the sabbat and conventional theories about the nature of demons. "It is a fact", he observed, "that all witches who make a demon free with their bodies . . . are completely in agreement in saying that, if the demon emits any semen, it is so cold that they recoil with horror on receiving it". In the same way, witches "have unanimously testified that, in their wild and disordered orgies, they are lacerated by [demons'] claws". To modern eyes, the bizarre nature of these disclosures makes the folly of such reasoning seem obvious. But we should remember that those who believed in Satanic abuse made the same mistake in the 1980s. Adult "survivors" in therapy and children questioned by social workers, produced remarkably similar accounts of the cult that supposedly abused them. This evidence was used to prove the existence of organised Satanism, and encouraged other supposed victims to produce testimonies in the same mould. It was only when outside investigators looked for corroborating evidence – and failed to find it – that the accusations became incredible.[23]

By the early decades of the seventeenth century, the literature on the witches' sabbat was so extensive that it formed a compelling body of evidence in its own right. This literature was largely self-referential. When Francesco Maria Guazzo composed his *Compendium Maleficarum* in 1608, he could draw on the work of Del Rio, Boguet, Rémy and Bodin, as well as older authorities like the *Malleus Maleficarum* and Johannes Nider's *Formicarius*. A century of repetition and elaboration had created a body of knowledge that few educated people were inclined to dispute. The general acceptance of the witch cult also encouraged the very confessions that sustained the myth. In 1610 Alonso Salazar, the sceptical grand inquisitor of Spain, described the process at first hand:

> I deduce the importance of silence and reserve from the fact that there were neither witches nor bewitched until they were talked and written about. This impressed me recently at Olague, near Pampeluna, where those who confessed stated that the matter started there after Fray Domingo de Sardo came there to preach about such things.

Salazar's point seems obvious now. But most of his contemporaries were impressed by the sheer weight of the documentary evidence for the sabbat. Indeed, this material even convinced many twentieth-century historians that some kind of witch cult must have existed in the pre-modern age, though they assumed it was a pagan fertility religion. It was only when the trial documents were examined in detail in the 1970s that this idea was finally laid to rest.[24]

In a world populated by demons, and characterised by the near universal acceptance of magic, there was little room for the outright denial of witchcraft. This did not mean that no one opposed witch trials, but those who did shared the same core beliefs as the demonologists themselves. The debate between believers and sceptics was not a conflict between reason and superstition. Rather, it involved different interpretations of the same given facts. By the same token, the ending of witch persecutions did not mark the "triumph of reason". This becomes apparent when we consider the arguments of sceptical writers in the pre-modern age.

THE VOICE OF DOUBT

At the height of the terrible witch panic in the cathedral city of Würzburg in 1629, the Chancellor to the Prince-Bishop described the "woe and misery" around him in a letter to a friend. He described the trial and execution of students and clergy, and even of young children who were believed to belong to the witch cult. The trial of "attractive" and respected members of the community appears to have caused him particular distress:

> A week ago a maiden of nineteen was executed, of whom it is
> everywhere said that she was the fairest in the whole city, and was held
> by everyone to be a girl of singular modesty and purity. She will be
> followed by seven or eight of the best and most attractive persons . . .
> And thus many are put to death for renouncing God and being at the
> witch-dances, against whom nobody has ever else spoken a word.

The Chancellor's account conveyed a mixture of wonderment and horror, and implied that he had reservations about some of the trials. It appears that others in the city, who knew the good reputations of many of those accused, shared in these concerns. But the doubtful tone of his text was balanced by his sense that the community really was under threat. He affirmed the awful reality of the witch cult in a postscript to his letter:

> Though there are many wonderful and terrible things happening, it
> is beyond doubt that, at a place called the Fraw-Rengberg, the devil
> in person, with eight thousand of his followers, held an assembly and
> celebrated mass before them all, administering to his audience (that
> is, the witches) turnip-rinds and parings in place of the Holy
> Eucharist. There took place not only foul but most horrible and
> hideous blasphemies, whereof I shudder to write.

Even though dozens of outwardly respectable suspects were under investigation, and some of them may well have been innocent, the chancellor still conceded that the sabbat was real. The collapse of the conventional stereotype of the witch – along with the accusation of senior members of the community – eventually led the city's rulers to end the prosecutions. But this was not because they ceased to believe in witchcraft. Rather, they no longer had confidence that all those accused were guilty as charged.[25]

The acceptance of witchcraft in principle, combined with occasional anxieties about the justice of particular cases, was probably common among pre-modern thinkers. In some instances, critics were so concerned with the problems involved in obtaining sufficient proof that they cautioned against legal proceedings altogether. "To kill men", wrote the French essayist Michel de Montaigne in the late 1500s, "we should have sharp and luminous evidence". Such evidence was rarely forthcoming in cases of witchcraft. Other sceptics were troubled by the suspension of normal legal procedures in witch prosecutions, such as the acceptance of children's testimony and the use of torture. In 1631 the Jesuit Friedrich Spee, who acted as confessor to the witches condemned at Würzburg, published an anonymous attack on the judicial methods used during the persecution. He claimed that the threat of torture encouraged false confessions that were misleadingly presented as voluntary, and condemned those confessions obtained through actual torture as worthless.[26]

While Montaigne and Spee condemned the human errors involved in witch trials, the main concern for other critics was the role of demons. The German doctor Johann Weyer, who published two books against the prosecution of witches in the second half of the sixteenth century, was the most important early opponent of the trials. Weyer completely accepted the power of the Devil. He cited the usual evidence from scripture and the Church Fathers to prove that demons could produce harmful "wonders", including all the phenomena associated with *maleficium*. They could afflict people and animals with strange diseases, take possession of their bodies, and induce terrible disturbances in the weather. More prosaically, he noted that Satan "is also wont to stop the milk of cows and prevent it from solidifying into butter, to produce wine from unexpected sources, [and] to unlock doors". He had first-hand experience of these arts. In 1565 he was called to treat a group of nuns tormented by demons in a convent in Cologne. Among other strange afflictions, the women "were frequently thrown to the ground, and their lower torso was made to thrust up and down in the way usually associated with sexual intercourse". It was common in such cases for victims to attribute their condition to bewitchment. Weyer rejected this explanation, however, because he believed that devils always acted on their own initiative. The victims were truly possessed, but not at the instigation of a witch:

> By whose art does scripture attest that this dreadful calamity crushes
> them? By the demon's art. And with whose co-operation or at whose
> command? Nobody's. The calamity occurs only because of the
> demon's own malicious will and with God's permission, in accordance
> with His hidden plan, so that these persons might be tested or
> chastised or corrected . . . This sly old fox [the Devil] needs no one's
> help, being abundantly capable on his own of mocking men, blinding
> them mentally and physically, torturing them with unnatural maladies,
> striking them with ulcers, and disturbing the air in many ways.

For Weyer, the supernatural effects of *maleficia* were the independent work of Satan. He did not require an army of witches to do his bidding, though he sometimes gulled people into believing they had made pacts with him. Just as insidiously, he caused others to believe falsely that their afflictions were produced through witchcraft, leading them to accuse their neighbours of the crime. The result was a "shipwreck of souls". These tactics were hardly surprising as the Devil delighted in bringing disaster through deception. "It is the principal aim of that blood-thirsty scoundrel", Weyer observed, "to promote strife and devise slaughter".[27]

Weyer's approach followed the same basic assumptions as other demonologists, but his insistence that the Devil acted alone led him to question the need for harsh penalties against supposed witches. The best remedy for those troubled by demons, he argued, was repentance and prayer. Legal action against people suspected of *maleficia* was dangerous, since the Devil could exploit this process for his own ends. In this respect, he was even more convinced of Satan's power than the supporters of persecution, who held that earthly laws could protect mortals from his snares. Weyer's argument was consistent with the given facts of the pre-modern world, but it was also weak in crucial respects. He conceded that many of the feats attributed to witches were theoretically possible: if Satan wished to do so, he could indeed carry people through the air. Equally, he acknowledged that the Devil could trick individuals into believing they had entered his service, or that they possessed magical powers. This left the foundations of witch beliefs intact. The doctor's argument was also open to accusations of inconsistency. If the Devil was really determined to attack humankind, and possessed the ability to do so, why should he not exploit witches in his plans? Was not their willingness to make pacts with him a grave crime in itself? A more robust critique of witch trials was offered by the English gentleman Reginald Scot. In *The Discoverie of Witchcraft* (1584), Scot questioned the ability of demons to intervene in human affairs at all. He argued that most phenomena explained in this way were actually produced by natural causes or trickery. Unlike most Renaissance thinkers, he even explained the wonders performed by biblical magicians as clever fakes. Scot's analysis was more consistent than Weyer's, but his effective denial of all demonic interventions appeared to fly in the face of most respected authorities, and was simply incredible to his contemporaries. James VI of Scotland was typical in dismissing him for reviving "the old error of the Sadducees, in denying of spirits".[28]

Scot's attack on the role of demons was revived by other thinkers in the mid-1600s, and eventually achieved the status of orthodoxy in the early years of the eighteenth century. Following the general acceptance of Isaac Newton's vision of a mechanical universe, where natural causes explained the great majority of earthly phenomena, allegations of witchcraft were no longer credible. But the more conservative stance of thinkers like Weyer probably played a greater role in the decline of witch persecutions in the seventeenth century. It was this brand of sceptical demonology that ended witch trials in colonial America. The key figure in this process was the Boston pastor Increase Mather. Twenty years before the crisis at Salem, the case of Elizabeth Knap alerted Mather to the danger of false accusations in cases of bewitchment. Knap was afflicted with a strange illness that escalated into demonic possession. During one of her seizures, she accused a neighbour of cursing her:

She cried out in some of her fits that a woman appeared to her, and was the cause of her affliction. The person thus accused was a very sincere, holy woman, who did hereupon – with the advice of friends – visit the poor wretch; and though she was in one of her fits, having her eyes shut, when the innocent person impeached by her came in, yet could she . . . declare who was there, and could tell the touch of that woman from any one else. But the gracious party thus accused and abused by a malicious devil, prayed earnestly with and for the possessed creature; after which she confessed that Satan had deluded her, making her believe evil of her good neighbour without any cause.

Mather had no doubt that the possession was genuine. Indeed, his conviction that Satan was behind the accusation was one of his main reasons for doubting its truth. Strikingly, he recalled another case from 1662 in which Ann Cole, a possessed woman from Hartford, also accused one of her neighbours. He believed this allegation was genuine because of the corroborating evidence against the accused. She was "a lewd and ignorant woman" already imprisoned on suspicion of *maleficia*, and she promptly made a full confession. Mather never doubted the reality of witchcraft, but he was careful not to accept the testimony of bewitched individuals unless it could be supported by other sources.[29]

This attitude was to play a decisive role in Salem. In the spring of 1692, Abigail Williams, the niece of the village minister, was struck down by a condition similar to that experienced by Ann Coles. Her apparent bewitchment spread to other members of the pastor's household, who accused their neighbours of causing the affliction. Tituba, one of the minister's West Indian slaves, confessed to attending sabbats in the forests that bordered the settlement, where members of the cult had allegedly signed their names in the Devil's book. The accusations continued throughout the summer. Dozens were imprisoned at the height of the persecution, and nineteen witches were eventually hanged. As contemporaries observed, the judges were faced with "grounds of suspicion" that were impossible to ignore, "yet very intricate, and difficult to draw up right conclusions about them". In June, a group of Boston clergy recommended "a very critical and exquisite caution" in the use of evidence, while pointing out the necessity to punish those guilty of the crime. The initial allegations derived largely from apparitions experienced by the bewitched. Wary of such testimony, the authorities went to great lengths to corroborate this information from other sources, placing particular value on confessions and evidence of the supernatural abilities of the accused. Thus no fewer than seven witnesses attested that George Burroughs, the supposed leader of the cult, could perform acts of telepathy and unnatural strength. The problem of "spectral evidence" continued to haunt the proceedings, however, and eventually brought them to an end. On 3 October Increase Mather voiced the anxieties of local churchmen about the prosecutions in a sermon preached in Cambridge. Within ten days, the governor of Massachusetts proscribed the future imprisonment or trial of any alleged witches.[30]

Mather's sermon was a masterpiece of cautious demonology. He devoted much of his text to demonstrating the power of Satan, based largely on scripture and on the evidence of witch trials in the old world. He affirmed that the Devil could carry people through the air; he could possess their bodies and perform terrible acts of *maleficium*; and he was an expert manipulator of the human senses. "He has perfect skill in optics", the pastor observed, "and can therefore cause that to be visible to one which is not so to another; and things also to appear far otherwise than they are". Crucially, it was this power of deception that made the evidence of bewitched people unsound. The apparitions they witnessed could not be trusted because "the Devil may, by divine permission, appear in the shape of innocent and pious persons". Mather proved this point with numerous biblical and contemporary examples, from the false apparition of Samuel (1 Sam. 28) to Ludwig Lavater's account of the demonic impersonation of a godly citizen in sixteenth-century Geneva. He concluded that to "take away the life of any one merely because a spectre or devil, in a bewitched or possessed person, does accuse them, will bring the guilt of innocent blood on the land". This did not mean, of course, that accusations of witchcraft could never be proven, even when they involved "spectral evidence". Mather attended only one of the Salem trials, at which George Burroughs was sentenced to death. In the postscript to the published version of his sermon, he noted that the case against Burroughs was impressively buttressed by corroborating evidence. "If I had been one of the judges", he reflected, "I could not have acquitted him".[31]

The judicious demonology of Increase Mather marked the end of an extraordinary tradition of learned writing on witchcraft. He spoke for a world in which the Devil was a real presence, and demonic interventions could erupt horribly in everyday life. Within a generation, this view would be challenged by the rise of a more naturalistic understanding of physical processes, and this new model would eventually dominate the thinking of educated people. In a world without magic, where the Devil was merely a malign observer of the inexorable laws of God, Nathaniel Hawthorne could look back on the events at Salem and shudder. But these events were not a "dark triumph" of unreason. As Mather himself understood, they were the tragic outcome of the decisions of well-meaning people, who "acted with all fidelity according to their light". This conclusion may prevent us from condemning the apparent folly of our ancestors and should perhaps encourage us to reflect on the consequences of our own beliefs.

6

Werewolves and Flying Witches

Want to be a werewolf? Then the vampire magazine *Bite Me* may have the information you require. In May 2001 it informed readers of the ten most reliable ways to become a lycanthrope, complete with physical transformation from human into wolf. The methods included several that would have been recognised by Europeans in the pre-industrial age: entering a Satanic pact, having a known werewolf as a relative, wearing a magical belt, or being transformed by a conjuror. Some of the other techniques derived from the various legends that have encrusted the werewolf myth in the past hundred years, particularly in Hollywood films. Thus the piece advised readers "to be bitten by a werewolf", though it offered no practical guidance on how this could be achieved. Such information was unnecessary, however, as the article was plainly meant as a joke. The first line set the tone: "Man to wolf to killing frenzy to man to normal life to full moon to frenzy again? Yes please!"

This light-hearted feature highlights a distinctively modern view of werewolves. Most obviously, it presumes that the transformation of humans into beasts is impossible, and assumes that its audience knows this too. The joke would not be funny if people were really scared of lycanthropes. The same point applies to other entertainments based on the idea: comic movies like *Teen Wolf* would be impossible in a culture that regarded werewolves as a real threat. In the context of *Bite Me* magazine, the fact that lycanthropy is treated as something obviously unreal is particularly striking. The same copy of the magazine featured a serious reference to "psychic vampires", who allegedly feed on the "life force" of ordinary mortals, and the previous edition included an interview with a man who believed sincerely that he possessed this ability. This was not a joke. It appears that the existence of psychic vampires does not offend the conventions of normal thinking in quite the same way as a person turning into a wolf, so the idea is not self-evidently absurd. Belief in werewolves, however, is beyond the pale.[1]

Despite its incredulous tone, the ten–point plan for becoming a werewolf implied that this lifestyle could have something to commend it. This is also

St. Louis Community College

RCODE: 300080003871294
TLE: Close encounters of the third kin
DATE: Nov 16 2007
ATUS:

RCODE: 300080003917110
TLE: Adaptation [videorecording] / Col
DATE: Nov 16 2007
TUS:

CODE: 300080005627214
LE: Strange histories : the trial of
DATE: Nov 30 2007
TUS:

CODE: 300080002789144
LE: The Oxford book of the supernatur
DATE: Nov 30 2007
TUS:

CODE: 300080002621985
E: Unexplained! : 347 strange sighti
DATE: Nov 30 2007
US:

CODE: 300080004378003
E: UFOs and popular culture : an enc
DATE: Nov 30 2007
US:

ODE: 300053562130011
E: The Encyclopedia of UFOs / edited
DATE: Nov 30 2007
US:

typical of modern ideas about lycanthropy. Unlike many other monsters, werewolves are often portrayed in a sympathetic light. Beginning with *The Wolf Man* in 1941, Hollywood films have tended to present lycanthropes as romantic figures who are driven by impulses beyond their control. They do not wish to cause harm, and struggle to tame the beast within them. These films also tap into popular ideas about human evolution: the animal drives of the werewolf reflect the supposedly "primitive" instincts that lie dormant in us all. The release of these instincts is both liberating and fearful. When Jack Nicholson's character in *Wolf* (1994) begins to display suspiciously lupine tendencies, he also feels "so good, more alive, stronger". At the same time, however, he observes darkly that this new-found vitality "will have a price".

These views about werewolves are recent additions to a much older tradition. In medieval and Renaissance Europe, the idea that humans could transform themselves into beasts was widely accepted, and provided a topic for serious philosophical and legal debate. Supposed lycanthropes were not sympathetic figures. Werewolves were malign creatures who took a vicious pleasure in the harm they caused. Instead of expressing bestial impulses that lurk in us all, lycanthropy was associated mainly with magic and the Devil. In 1608 the Milanese friar Francesco Maria Guazzo noted a typical example of the phenomenon:

> The shepherd Petronio, who was tried at Dalheim in 1581, whenever he felt moved with hatred or envy against the shepherds of neighbouring flocks (as is the way with such men), used to change himself into a wolf by the use of certain incantations, and so for a long time escaped all suspicion of being the cause of the mutilation and death of his neighbours' sheep.

In other instances, werewolf attacks could result in human deaths, and their alleged perpetrators were tried for murder. This was the fate of Peter Stumpf from Bedburg in Germany, who confessed in 1589 to killing children in "the likeness of a greedy devouring wolf, strong and mighty, with eyes great and large". Nine years later, a French beggar named Jacques Roulet was executed for the same crime. Renaissance accounts of the murderous attacks of lycanthropes were as grisly as anything in modern werewolf fiction. Jean Bodin, the French lawyer and political theorist, presented the following account of the crimes of Gilles Garnier, who was burned as a werewolf at Lyons in 1573:

> On Saint Michael's day, while in the form of a werewolf, [Garnier] seized a young girl of ten or twelve years old near the Serre woods . . . There he killed her with his paw-like hands and his teeth, and ate the flesh of her thighs and arms, and took some to his wife. And in the

same form a month later, he seized another girl and killed her. He intended to eat her but was prevented by three people, as he confessed. And fifteen days afterward he strangled a young child of ten years old in the vineyard of Gredisans, and ate the flesh of his thighs, legs and abdomen. And later in the form of a man and not of a wolf, he killed another boy of twelve or thirteen years old in the woods of the village of Pérouse, with the intention of eating him, had he not been prevented, as he confessed without force or constraint.

Reports of lycanthropy were most common in mainland Europe, but the phenomenon was also known in the British Isles. The chronicler Gervaise of Tilbury reported encounters with werewolves in the thirteenth century. King James VI of Scotland discussed the existence of "men-wolfs" in 1597. Some twenty years later, the Yorkshire gentleman Edward Fairfax commented on "weary wolves, of whom many wise and worthy persons report great wonders". More generally, it was accepted that English and Scottish witches, in common with their European fellows, could disguise themselves in a marvellous variety of animal forms.[2]

In the two centuries that have passed since these beliefs were relegated to the status of "folklore", various theories have emerged to explain historical reports of lycanthropy in "rational" terms. Sabine Baring-Gould, who is better known as the author of "Onward Christian Soldiers", offered a biological explanation in 1865. He proposed that the symptoms of men like Gilles Garnier arose from bestial desires that were normally hidden in civilised people. These compulsions were ghastly but wholly natural, since "man, in common with other *carnivora*, is actuated by an impulse to kill and by a love of destroying life". Baring-Gould's pessimistic views would probably attract little support today, though the belief that lycanthropy is an expression of dangerous animal urges lives on in popular books and movies. When real murders are committed that involve the kind of mutilation and cannibalism attributed to Garnier, the theory of "sexual sadism" is frequently invoked. Alternatively, the medical diagnosis of schizophrenia can be used to explain the delusions of self-confessed werewolves. As for those men and women who once believed that shape-changing was really possible, the most common explanation remains that advanced by Baring-Gould: the "superstitious" tendencies of the uneducated mind.[3]

At first sight, this opinion appears to be confirmed when one examines the work of those university-trained men who studied cases of lycanthropy among their contemporaries in the pre-modern age. Jean Bodin believed that some men could really turn into wolves, but most of his educated peers disagreed. The majority of Renaissance intellectuals, like most western people today, viewed such beliefs as unfounded. In this they followed St Augustine, who claimed in the *City of God* that "stories of this kind are either untrue or at least so extraordinary that we are justified in withholding credence". Instead of accepting the physical transformation of people into beasts, most Renaissance thinkers explained lycanthropy as a kind of delusion. King James VI was typical:

> To tell you simply my opinion in this, if any such thing has been [as men believing themselves to be wolves], I take it to have proceeded from a natural super-abundance of melancholy which, as we have read, hath made some think themselves horses, and some one kind of beast or another. So I suppose that it hath so [confused] the imagination and memory of some . . . that they have thought themselves very wolves indeed at these times, and so have counterfeited their actions.

This general scepticism among the higher ranks of European society discouraged the trial of supposed lycanthropes, and helped spare the continent from outbreaks of werewolf persecution comparable to witch trials. Bodin lamented that magistrates were reluctant to act in such cases because they found them "unbelievable". Even Francesco Maria Guazzo was a doubter. Though he related the tale of the werewolf of Dalheim, he dismissed the possibility that the shepherd could really change himself into a beast. For Guazzo and most of his educated contemporaries, such ideas typified the "superstition" of ordinary people. Most modern observers would heartily agree.[4]

But here we should be careful. The apparently "modern" opinions of men like James VI and Guazzo were, in fact, nothing of the kind. Instead, they were rooted in an understanding of the world no less foreign to us than the peasant beliefs they disavowed. Renaissance sceptics only appear to be enlightened because their conclusions coincide with our own. This point becomes clear when we reconstruct the thinking that led learned Europeans to reject the claim that people could turn into animals. Their argument was not based on empirical evidence or scientific rationalism; rather, it derived from decidedly pre-modern concerns about the power of the Devil and the nature of miracles. More shockingly, the same ideas that led educated men to reject the existence of werewolves caused them to believe in another phenomenon that seems quite ridiculous today: the ability of witches to fly. The reasoning behind both conclusions is considered here.

THE CASE AGAINST WEREWOLVES

Some of the best discussions of werewolves in pre-modern literature can be found in works on satanic witchcraft. This reflected the popular belief that witches could transform themselves into wolves and other creatures. Witches occasionally confessed to attacking their neighbours in the shape of a wolf, like the woman from Franche-Comté who abducted two children in 1580 while "being like a wolf to the sight". More often, their accusers claimed to have seen them in animal form. In 1576 an artisan from the Italian town of Ferrara described how a woman who bewitched his young son appeared to the child in the form of an unusually large cat. Some French witches also assumed this shape in order to enter their neighbour's houses, and could even savage their enemies in the likeness of "great cats". During a stay in Flanders in the late sixteenth century, the Jesuit Martín Del Rio was informed that a local witch had recently turned herself into a toad. More ambitiously, Hungarian witches appeared as wasps and bumble-bees. Perhaps the most expert practitioner of this art was the English sorceress Anne Bodenham. According to a pamphlet published in 1653, she could change herself "into any shape whatsoever, a dog, a black lion, a white bear, a wolf, a monkey, a horse, a bull and a calf". The belief that witches could accomplish such feats persisted in folklore long after the decline of official prosecutions. It was apparently still common in English rural communities in the early 1800s, when the "peasant poet" John Clare recalled his mother's fireside tales of witches transformed into cats and hares.[5]

Faced with these widespread beliefs, learned writers on witchcraft asked if it was possible for people to turn into animals. At one level, the answer was simple. In the book of Daniel, the Bible appeared to provide a concrete example of such a metamorphosis: when King Nebuchadnezzar was sent into exile, he ate grass like an ox and "his hairs were grown like eagles' feathers, and his nails like birds' claws" (Dan. 4:33). This bewildering makeover proved that the human body could be transformed. The Old Testament king was changed by an act of God, whose ability to intervene in such ways was never questioned. It was another matter, however, to claim that the Devil could achieve the same results. All demonologists agreed that Satan was responsible for the horrors associated with lycanthropy, so the key question was whether he was capable of transforming humans into beasts. A minority of scholars believed that he could. For Jean Bodin, the overwhelming weight of past opinion suggested that the metamorphosis of witches was a physical reality. He found it strange "that many cannot believe it, since all the peoples of the earth and all antiquity agree about it". The English philosopher Henry More agreed. It was a mistake, he argued in 1652, to assume that "changing the species of things were a power too big to be granted the devil". Satan's skill in this area was proved by his ability to change his own shape when he appeared to mortals. Why should he find it harder, More asked, to turn "a man into a wolf than when he transforms himself into the shape of a man"?[6]

These arguments were reasonable enough, but they were overwhelmed by the sceptical opinions of most other writers. The French demonologist Henri

Boguet set out the sceptics' case in 1602. "It has always been my opinion", he declared, "that the metamorphosis of a man into a beast is impossible". For such a transformation to happen, the "soul and power of reason" of the witch would have to reside temporarily in the body of a beast. Alternatively, the soul of the lycanthrope would have to leave its human body for the period in which the person changed into an animal. He rejected the first option out of hand. The bodies of animals were not designed to carry souls, and their brains are too small to contain a human intellect. He was equally scathing about the second possibility. If the witch loses his soul on becoming a wolf, how can he get it back "when he resumes the shape of a man?" The departure of one's soul would normally take place at the moment of death, and its restoration was beyond even the power of Satan. More prosaically, Boguet wondered what the Devil would do with the witch's soul in the meantime:

> Where does Satan put the soul when it is separated from its body?
> Does he cause it to wander in the air, or does he shut it up
> somewhere until the lycanthrope has resumed his human shape?
> Certainly I cannot think that God permits him . . . to play such
> tricks with us. Aristotle was far nearer the truth when he said that
> the soul no more leaves the body than a pilot leaves his ship.

Boguet concluded that the human soul simply could not exist inside an animal's body, or depart and return to its natural home, without the miraculous intervention of God. Since witchcraft was the work of Satan, the physical transformations attributed to witches could not be real.[7]

If this was the case, how did Boguet and other demonologists explain the stories about werewolves that circulated in their communities? More tellingly, how did they account for the confessions of witches who claimed to have turned themselves into animals? For some sceptics, the implausibility of these stories implied that the rest of the witches' testimony should be treated with caution. When he discussed the confession of two German werewolves in 1521, Johann Weyer suggested that their belief in physical transformation rendered the whole of their statements unreliable. Reginald Scot echoed this view in *The Discoverie of Witchcraft* (1584), where he presented such outlandish admissions as evidence of mental illness. From a very different perspective, Jean Bodin was worried that such attitudes could let self-confessed werewolves off the hook. He denounced the opinion "that lycanthropy is an illness of sick men who think they are wolves", and cited cases where this assumption had prevented the legitimate prosecution of witches.[8]

Most modern readers would undoubtedly side with Scot against Bodin. But for Renaissance thinkers, there was also a third possibility. While most

scholars agreed that physical metamorphosis was impossible, this did not
mean that those who confessed to it were necessarily mad. Nor did it mean
the Devil was not involved in their actions. As an expert practitioner of
natural science, Satan could create illusions in the minds of both witches and
their victims so powerful that they witnessed the apparent transformation of
humans into beasts. In 1486, the authors of the *Malleus Maleficarum*
discussed this phenomenon at length, and proposed that several types of
illusion were involved. In some cases, the transformation was produced by
deceiving the senses, and existed "only in the organs and perceptions of him
who sees"; in other instances the effect was a "glamour", in which demons
made "an exterior object . . . seem other than it is". This was normally
achieved through the creation of false bodies composed of air. Many other
writers developed this argument in the sixteenth and seventeenth centuries,
and it is easy to understand its appeal. It explained the accounts of human-
to-animal transformations in the classical texts frequently cited in
demonologies. Satanic deceptions could also account for the widespread
contemporary belief in werewolves, and the evidence of apparently credible
witnesses in trials. As the French judge Nicolas Rémy noted in 1595, it was
"incredible that anyone can truly be changed from a man into a wolf or any
other animal. Yet there must be some foundation for the opinion so
obstinately held by so many". It also made sense of the confessions to
lycanthropy by those witches for whom there was apparently compelling
evidence for other types of harmful magic. If they were already known to
have compacted with Satan, demonic illusions provided the most plausible
explanation for their tales of shape-shifting.[9]

The idea of satanic deception could account for the seeming transformation of people into beasts, but it created other problems for the experts
to solve. Rémy, for instance, accepted from his legal experience that witches
could make themselves appear to their neighbours in the shape of wolves, and
acknowledged that this was sometimes explained by sensory delusion. He was
troubled, nonetheless, by the fact that witches also appeared to possess the
"natural qualities and powers" of real wolves. They acquired "fleetness of
foot, bodily strength, ravenous ferocity [and] the lust of howling". Endowed
with these abilities, they could "kill even the biggest cattle in the fields, and
even devour their raw flesh, when they descend upon them as swiftly as any
wolf or other ferocious beast". Moreover, they appeared to leave physical
traces of their attacks that could not have been made by human beings: claw
and teeth marks on their victims, and paw prints on the ground. He
concluded, therefore, that the physical attacks attributed to werewolves were
genuine, though their bodily transformation was not. It was not the witch
herself who performed these feats. Rather, they were "done through the
agency of the demon, who, by virtue of his immense preternatural powers,
makes their accomplishment possible".[10]

This argument solved one of the problems that faced the sceptics, but a much bigger one remained. It was well known that witches could be injured when they assumed the shape of animals and that these wounds would appear on their human bodies. All the experts on lycanthropy acknowledged this fact. Henri Boguet, for instance, presented this dramatic example from Auvergne in 1588:

One evening a gentleman, standing at the window of his chateau, saw a huntsman whom he knew passing by, and asked him to bring him some of his bag on his return. As the huntsman went his way along a valley, he was attacked by a large wolf and discharged his arquebus at it without hurting it. He was therefore compelled to grapple with the wolf, and caught it by the ears; but at length, growing weary, he let go of the wolf, drew back his big hunting knife, and with it cut off one of the wolf's paws, which he put in his pouch after the wolf had run away. He then returned to the gentleman's chateau, in sight of which he had fought the wolf. The gentleman asked him to give him part of his bag; and the huntsman, wishing to do so, and intending to take the paw from his pouch, drew from it a hand wearing a gold ring on one of its fingers, which the gentleman recognised as belonging to his wife. This caused him to entertain an evil suspicion of her, and going into the kitchen, he found his wife nursing her arm in her apron, which he took away, and found that her hand had been cut off.

Martín Del Rio recounted a similar tale in 1599, which was repeated by Francesco Maria Guazzo a decade later. This concerned a peasant from Flanders who fell into a bitter quarrel with a barmaid over the price of his beer. As he left the alehouse, the barmaid declared that "you will not have the power to reach your house today, or I am not the woman I am!" These words were followed by a remarkable demonstration of malicious magic:

When he reached the stream where he had left his boat . . . neither he nor his son (who was pretty strong), could shift it from the bank, even though they leaned on their poles with all their strength. It was as though it had been nailed down in the mud. Now, it so happened that two or three soldiers were marching past, so the peasant hailed them . . . They answered his call, came along, and pushed as hard as they could; but for a long time they pushed in vain. Then one of them, sweating and gasping for breath, said, 'Why don't we unload all this stuff from the boat? Perhaps we'll find it easier to get it down to the water if it's empty'. So they emptied the boat of its load. But then (mark this!) they saw a huge sallow toad in the bottom of the boat, looking at them with glittering eyes. One of the soldiers, rather than pick up the toad, drilled a hole in it with the point of his sword, as far as its swollen throat, and threw it into the water. There, apparently dead, it rolled over on to its back, belly upwards. The other soldiers wounded it still further while it floated, and suddenly the boat came free.

The peasant took his new friends back to the alehouse to thank them for their help. Here he found that the woman who had cursed him had fallen ill and died, and her body was marked with strange wounds to her stomach and neck. The episode was reported to a magistrate, who concluded that her injuries had "appeared in the very same places where the soldiers had struck the toad".[11]

Boguet, Del Rio and Guazzo accepted the facts in these cases. Indeed, they mentioned them in order to demonstrate the real dangers posed by satanic witchcraft. But they did not regard the marks on the witches' bodies as proof of their physical transformation into animals, since they viewed such transformations as impossible. Instead, they advanced alternative explanations based on the ingenuity of the Devil. Perhaps the supposed lycanthropes were not present at the scene of their crimes at all, but were fooled into thinking they were by satanic delusions. The attacks on their victims were real enough – animals or demons could perform them – but the injuries to the witches' bodies were inflicted separately. As Guazzo explained, "when the witch is not bodily present at all, then the devil wounds her in that part of her absent body corresponding to the wound which he knows to have been received by the beast". On other occasions, the experts acknowledged that the witch was really present when she appeared to her victims as an animal, but her true form was encased by the Devil in an artificial body. Del Rio suggested that Satan sometimes "wraps actual people very tightly in genuine animal skins". It was more common, however, to argue that the Devil enclosed his servants in "effigies of beasts" manufactured from air. Each part of these effigies fitted over the corresponding part of the person's real body. In cases like this, Guazzo noted, it was hardly surprising that witches displayed marks on their bodies where they had been injured in animal form, "for the enveloping air easily yields, and the true body receives the wound".[12]

These ideas were not confined to theoretical texts. Law courts were occasionally obliged to deal with cases of supernatural murder that centred on lycanthropy rather than witchcraft, and in these instances the theological positions adopted by Guazzo and others were tested in practical situations. In 1603, Jean Grenier, a fourteen-year-old shepherd from Saint Antoine in Bordeaux, told his friends that he possessed a magic coat that could turn him into a wolf. Tragically, he made this boast at a time when local children had been attacked and killed by wolves, and anxieties about supposed lycanthropes were prevalent. When he was detained and questioned by officers of the judge of La Roche-Chalais, Grenier confessed freely to attacking the children in the shape of a wolf. He was tried and convicted for these crimes, and his case was passed to the *parlement* of Bordeaux to decide his punishment. Here the court received expert advice from the theologian Jean Filesac, who described the means by which Grenier might have assumed the likeness of an animal. This testimony adopted the conventional view that physical transformation was impossible, since it would require the miraculous intervention of God. Filesac also dismissed the possibility that the boy had suffered a hallucination brought on by "natural" causes, and argued instead that the illusion must have involved the Devil. But how? Did Grenier make a demonic pact to act out his crimes, or was he merely Satan's dupe? The theologian set out the acknowledged methods by which the Devil could create the illusion of lycanthropy: visual and mental trickery and the encasement of the boy's body in an "aerial effigy" of a wolf. He also noted that some authorities held that Satan deceived people into believing they had committed crimes that were actually performed by demons. The judges were left to consider this evidence, though Filesac argued strongly that Grenier had knowingly entered a demonic pact and should therefore be executed. The court disagreed, however, and ordered the boy to be kept in a monastery for the rest of his life.[13]

As this episode shows, the refusal of educated Europeans to accept the physical transformation of werewolves did not make them dismiss the phenomenon entirely. The idea of satanic illusions offered a reasonable account of the available evidence: classical sources and popular belief asserted that lycanthropes really changed into animals, but theological arguments showed that only divine intervention could make this happen. As it was known that the Devil could produce "lying wonders", demonic influence was a plausible explanation for cases such as Jean Grenier. The internal logic of this position can be shown by its application to another problem that faced Renaissance thinkers: could witches really fly? Here they employed similar arguments to reach a very different conclusion.

THE CASE FOR FLYING WITCHES

Most learned writers on witchcraft focused on the Satanic aspects of the crime: they saw witches mainly as rebels against God who cemented their apostasy by making a Satanic pact. Many experts also believed that witches practised devil worship and acts of desecration at nightly gatherings, or "sabbats", usually held in remote places. This raised a problem of transportation. How were large numbers of people conveyed to secret locations that were often miles from their homes? One tradition in popular culture provided a potential answer to this problem: the idea that witches did not travel physically at all, but journeyed "in spirit" as their bodies fell into a trance-like sleep. This belief was recorded across much of Europe, and occasionally surfaced in witchcraft confessions. According to James VI, some witches affirmed that "their spirits will be ravished out of their bodies" as they lay in their beds. They claimed to use "this form of journeying . . . most when they are transported from one country to another". The idea of spirit travel appeared in witchcraft allegations heard by Nicolas Rémy and Henri Boguet in late sixteenth-century France, and was known to the Roman inquisition in the same period. The concept played an interesting role in a witch panic in the German town of Calw in 1683. In this case, a group of children confessed to attending sabbats while they were observed to be sleeping. Their parents responded by keeping them awake at night, fearful that the Devil would return to carry off their souls.[14]

Historians are divided on how to interpret this material. To some, like Carlo Ginzburg, it suggests that the idea of the sabbat derived from cultic traditions based on journeys "in spirit" to another world; others find the evidence for such traditions too fragmentary to support this assertion. Outside academic circles, most readers would probably find the idea of travelling in spirit during sleep more understandable than the alternative possibility: that people were bodily conveyed through the air to the sabbat. For many, this reading would also suggest that those who truly believed they had attended the witches' gatherings were simply dreaming. A few readers might also accept the possibility of "astral projection", the modern version of the belief that one's spirit can leave the body to visit distant places. It is unlikely, however, that they would give the same credence to the claim that witches could fly. In the sixteenth and seventeenth centuries, experts on witchcraft consistently took the opposite view: they rejected the belief that witches could travel in spirit as their bodies slept – even when this was asserted in confessions – and insisted instead that they normally went to the sabbat by physical flight.[15]

To understand why, we need to return to Henri Boguet's comments about werewolves. He believed that only God could permit the human soul to depart from and return to the body, as would have to occur if a person turned into a wolf. The same argument applied to journeys supposedly made "in spirit":

> I have never been able to believe that such a thing is in any way
> possible; for if it is true that when the soul is separated from the body
> death must necessarily follow, how can it be possible for a witch, after
> having been in spirit to the sabbat, to return to life by the help of the
> Devil? This cannot be except by a miracle, which belongs only to God.

In other words, to accept that witches went in spirit to the sabbat was to admit that witchcraft could achieve the greatest miracle of the Christian faith: the resurrection of the dead. James VI spelt out the shocking implications:

The soul's going out of the body is the only definition of natural
death; and [those] who are once dead, God forbid we should think
that it should lie in the power of the devils in hell to restore them to
life again . . . What Christ and the prophets did miraculously [by
bringing the dead to life] cannot in no Christian man's opinion be
made common with the Devil.

This argument was strong enough to overrule folkloric ideas about the "flight
of souls", and to invalidate the statements of some alleged witches that they
travelled at night "in spirit only". Thus when French and Italian judges were
confronted with such claims in the late 1500s they tended to view them as
delusions.[16]

But how else could witches go to the sabbat? The obvious answer to
modern observers is that they never went at all: the event existed only in
the fearful imaginations of those preoccupied with satanic witchcraft.
Scepticism about the witches' assemblies did exist in Renaissance Europe,
and even some demonologists paid little attention to this aspect of the crime.
But as Chapter 5 of this book argues, there were also strong reasons for
educated Europeans to accept the reality of secret devil worship. Those who
did so claimed that witches gathered together in various ways. Not only could
they travel on horseback or foot, but demons could also convey them through
the air. There was some speculation about the means by which such
"transvections" were performed, but it was almost universally acknowledged
that they were permitted by the laws of nature. As a master of natural science,
the Devil possessed the knowledge and skills required to accomplish feats of
this kind. As the authors of the *Malleus* noted, his expertise in this area far
exceeded that of mortals; indeed, "there is none greater among the good
angels in heaven". The Bible, moreover, proved the reality of demonic
transvections. Nicolas Rémy noted in 1595 that Christ himself was "taken
up" by the Devil "and set upon the pinnacle of the temple" (Matt. 4:1–11).
This led to an obvious conclusion:

Although . . . a devout Christian [should not] inquire why this was
done, it would be blasphemous to question that it *was* done, since we
are told of it so plainly in the Holy Gospel. If therefore it once
happened to Him who was the vanquisher and conqueror of Satan to
be carried through the air by him [Satan], why should we be so slow
to believe that men, who are so often vulnerable to his attacks,
especially those who voluntarily surrender themselves into his power,
can at his pleasure be lifted up and borne away through the air?

Jean Bodin cited the same passage to prove the transvection of witches and
confute the blasphemy of those who doubted it. As he noted sharply, "it

would be mocking the Gospel story to call into doubt whether the Devil transports witches from one spot to another". This scriptural evidence was sufficient to convince Protestant writers too. In 1597, James VI asserted that witches were carried "above the earth or above the sea swiftly to the place where they are to meet". For James and most other authorities, this preternatural act was more plausible than the miraculous departure of the witch's spirit from her body.[17]

This argument was so forceful that even sceptical writers on witchcraft accepted it. In 1563 Johann Weyer denounced the prosecution of witches as a tragic folly. He claimed that most witchcraft confessions resulted from satanic delusions or mental illness. Nonetheless, he conceded that there was no reason in principle why witches should not be able to fly. He cited the passage from Matthew to prove that demons could carry bodies through the air, and then speculated at length about the means by which they did so. He concluded that wicked spirits did not need to assume material bodies in order to bear weight, as some demonologists argued: rather, they could transport objects through the air without adopting any visible form. There were many cases, he confirmed, "in which individuals are carried from place to place, over moderate distances, by demons". It was rare for scholars to question the ability of demons to perform this act. Reginald Scot came close to this position in his wholesale denunciation of witch beliefs in 1584. By casting doubt on the physical transvection of witches, however, he was forced to reinterpret key passages of scripture. He presented Christ's ascent to the temple, for example, as a vision. Such rationalisations may seem attractive to readers today, but they placed him outside the mainstream of Renaissance thought.[18]

Given the remarkable nature of the witches' flight, learned writers were keen to discuss the mechanisms involved. Some clues were provided in the confessions of witches, who sometimes claimed that they used a magical ointment to carry them through the air. In 1580 Bodin recorded a dramatic illustration of the apparent power of this substance:

> There was . . . at Lyons a young noblewoman a few years ago, who got up at night and, lighting the candle, took a jar of ointment and spread it over herself. Then with a few words she was transported away. Her lover, who was in bed with her, seeing this mystery enacted, took the candle and looked everywhere. Not finding her, but just the jar of grease, out of curiosity to learn the power of the ointment [he] did as he had seen done, and suddenly he also was transported, and found himself in the region of Lorraine with the coven of witches, where he was terrified. But as soon as he called on God to help him, the whole company disappeared, and he found himself all alone naked. He returned to Lyons where he denounced the witch, who confessed and was condemned to be burned.

Similar lotions were described in confessions from Germany and Italy, and Bodin and Rémy used this fact to illustrate the consistency of accounts of witchcraft across Europe. Some modern writers have taken these references to ointments to indicate that witches used them to induce hallucinatory experiences. Renaissance thinkers were generally more sceptical. Rémy noted that witches' lotions and powders were harmless once their users were imprisoned, and concluded that they possessed no intrinsic power. This point was amplified by Martín Del Rio, who asserted that Satan required no special potions in order to convey his servants through the sky. For various reasons, however, he encouraged his followers to use the ointment and duped them into believing "that its power is very great". Sometimes it served as a psychological prop, since they were too timid to attempt to fly without it. On other occasions, witches were too squeamish to endure the "horrible contact" with the demons that really lifted them through the air. As for the unfortunate man from Lyons, Del Rio explained that God punished such people for their "self-indulgent curiosity" by letting Satan carry them away. For Bodin, the irrelevance of the witches' ointment was proved by the fact that they were "careful not to say the name of God" during their nocturnal flights. He cited cases of witches tumbling from the sky when pious words were uttered, and reasoned that this would not happen if the ointment itself were responsible for their flight.[19]

Since the experts assumed that Satan carried witches bodily to the sabbat, they were left with the problem of explaining the accounts of spirit travel in some witchcraft confessions. In some cases, the belief that such acts were impossible encouraged judges to dismiss them as fantasies or dreams. This was the initial response of the Roman inquisition to reports of spirit travel in the Friuli region of Italy in 1575. Likewise, the authorities that dealt with the children at Calw affirmed that they must have dreamt about their journeys to the sabbat. Georg Heinrich Häberlin, the theologian appointed to the commission that investigated the affair in 1684, suggested that the Devil planted illusions in the minds of the children as they slept. Since there was little other evidence against them, the commission decided they were innocent of witchcraft. This case suggests that official scepticism about journeys made "in spirit" could sometimes prevent the development of witch panics.[20]

In other cases, however, witches' confessions to travelling in spirit did not save them from conviction. It was unusual for such admissions to provide the main evidence against the accused: they normally emerged only after other allegations had been made, often relating to harmful magic or *maleficia*. For French judges like Rémy and Boguet, these statements were troubling details in cases that otherwise appeared to be proven. Their most plausible explanation was satanic delusion. In some instances, Boguet noted, witches imagined that they had attended the sabbat as they slept: Satan sometimes "reveals to them in their sleep what happens . . . so vividly that they think they have been there". James VI used the same argument to explain the "spirit journeys" described by Scottish witches, adding that the Devil sometimes gave identical dreams to several individuals so that they all believed they had been present at the sabbat. On other occasions, according to Boguet, witches travelled physically to the sabbat but deceived their spouses into believing that they stayed in their beds. Lulled into "a profound sleep" by satanic magic, "the husband, who has seen his wife come to bed before he went to sleep, will think in the morning that she has not moved throughout the night". The ability of witches to induce such unnaturally deep sleep was confirmed by the standard texts on *maleficia*. Del Rio, for instance, noted one particularly grisly technique called the "hand of glory". This involved rubbing fat into the fingers of a hand cut from a dead body, then setting them alight. This produced an intense sleep in the victim of the spell, allowing the witch to come and go as she pleased.[21]

Such trickery could explain most cases of supposed spirit travel, but sometimes more elaborate deceptions were required. What of those husbands who actually saw their wives sleeping while their spirits – as they later confessed – were apparently transported to the sabbat? As with cases of alleged lycanthropy, the explanation involved a fake body created by demons. As Rémy explained, witches sometimes left "some dummy in their likeness, which their husbands should, if they happen to awake, imagine to be their wives". Satan endowed these replicas with the power to deceive completely those who looked at them. He developed this point with some concrete illustrations:

> Ella, the wife of an officer at Ottingen, said that she had substituted in her place a child's pillow, and Sinchen May of Speirchen some twigs, after they had invoked the name of their demons; and in this manner they had often deceived their husbands. Maria, the wife of Johann Schneider of Metzerech, used a bundle of straw anointed with her ointment, which used to vanish as soon as she herself had returned to the house. Catharina Ruffa declared that her demon had himself at times taken her place in the bed.

Boguet confirmed the reality of this phenomenon, and noted sadly in 1602 that "a husband very often embraces an illusion instead of his wife". A few years later, Francesco Maria Guazzo affirmed that such "false bodies" explained how witches could be physically present at the sabbat while witnesses believed they were there "in spirit only".[22]

If they are viewed in isolation, and plucked from their historical and intellectual context, these ideas may seem truly bizarre. But the thinking that led Rémy, Boguet and James VI to their alarming conclusions was entirely conventional. If anything, these men displayed a lack of boldness and imagination in repeating the standard academic ideas of their day; they cannot be accused of flights of fancy. Nor, of course, was their rejection of the physical transformation of werewolves in any way "far sighted". It was merely the logical counterpart of the same assumptions that suggested that witches could fly. The works of Henry More neatly illustrate this point: as one of the few seventeenth-century writers to accept the physical metamorphosis of werewolves, More also believed that witches travelled to the sabbat "in spirit". Less adventurous thinkers like James VI were probably right to assert that witches never flew from their houses "in the likeness of beasts or fowls". But the king was equally correct, in his own terms at least, when he affirmed that Satan propelled them through the night sky like "a mighty wind".[23]

7

Raptures and Forbidden Words

In 1653 God spoke to John Gilpin. In fact, the Holy Spirit entered his body "like a dove" as he lay in bed, and then told the astonished prophet that day was about to break. Sure enough, Gilpin looked through his window and saw the first gleam of sunlight outside. From somewhere inside him, the voice announced that it was day. Then it assured him of his calling. "As sure as it is light", the Holy Spirit whispered, "so surely shall Christ give thee light".

That morning John Gilpin began a spiritual odyssey. The voice within him declared that his new life was about to start and calmed his anxieties about the prophetic role that God required of him. It also promised that he would enjoy the Lord's special protection and love:

> "Ask what thou wilt of the Father in my name, and He will give it thee." Then said Gilpin, "What shall I ask?" It was answered, "Ask [for] wisdom in the first place." Then he desired that such things might be given him, as made for God's glory and the good of others. It was answered that his request was granted, and that he should be endowed with the gift of prophecy, and singing praises to God.

The prophet was moved to attend a meeting of Quakers, having joined in their congregation on several previous occasions. He was more deeply affected by this gathering than ever before. As he heard the testimony of one of the members, he was "thrown upon the ground" by the Holy Spirit, which continued to speak to him as he lay in an ecstatic transport. Eventually, the voice commanded him to walk into town and proclaim the Gospel. He was also "compelled to sing forth in a strange manner, and with such a voice as was not his own, he sang diverse phrases of scripture which were given to him". As the symptoms of his transformation grew more extreme, he began to question their true character. These doubts were confirmed when the voice commanding him assumed a shocking new tone:

His wife and family going to bed, he remained alone, when he began to question whether these strange actions were divine or diabolical. Whereupon he trembled, and his hand was forced to take up a knife which lay nearby and to point it to his throat, and the voice said to him, "Open a hole there, and I will give thee eternal life". But he threw away the knife, and his wife coming to him, at her persuasion he went to bed, and all the night after he assured himself that he was possessed by the devil.

From that moment onwards, Gilpin was propelled through a dizzying sequence of mystical experiences. The demon that possessed him was driven from his body, accompanied by a crash of thunder. He was briefly restored to normal, then another spirit appeared and offered a message of reassurance: "it was Satan that had possessed and seduced him hitherto, but now Christ was come, and had cast out Satan". This new voice told him the Devil had inspired everything he had done before; but now the Holy Ghost would truly embrace him. A brief period of rejoicing was followed by fresh doubts. Then the bewildered prophet heard a third voice that claimed to belong to Christ, and denounced the other two as "white devils". After days of spiralling confusion, Gilpin finally recovered his senses. He came to regard all his ecstatic experiences as demonic tricks.[1]

For seventeenth-century readers, the story of John Gilpin was a cautionary tale of the dangers of religious extremism. The English Presbyterian Samuel Clarke included it in his catalogue of the judgments of God, known popularly as *The Book of Examples*, which later became a best-selling text in the colonies of New England. As well as displaying the perceived dangers of Quakerism, the story indicated the ambiguous nature of mystical experiences in general. While there was a huge gulf in theory between prophecy and demonic possession, the line between them in practice could be alarmingly thin. Satan loved to appear as "an angel of light". In the case of a few benighted visionaries like Gilpin, the gift of inspiration could oscillate fearfully with the torments of possession. More often, however, it appears that the social context in which people entered ecstatic states determined how they were understood, and their roles were fairly stable once they were established. This still left room for disagreement. When seventeenth-century Quakers heard the "inner voice" of the spirit, they perceived this as a truly divine experience; for most of their enemies, however, it was an obvious sign of possession.[2]

The acceptance of prophecy and possession offers a striking instance of the power of ideas – and social situations – to shape human perceptions of events. The symptoms of the two conditions were very similar. In both, individuals surrendered their senses to an external power and displayed physical signs of its presence. These often involved the acquisition of special abilities, bodily convulsions or "raptures", the perception of visions and the capacity to speak in a powerful new voice. But the decision to recognise someone as a prophet or as the victim of possession depended to a large extent on the behaviour of those around them. In other circumstances, indeed, the same symptoms could lead to a diagnosis of mental illness or fraud. Historians have noted the cultural contexts in which the gift of prophecy has flourished, such as the late Middle Ages in Italy. By the same token, others have observed how its demonic counterpart was more widely acknowledged in the changed circumstances of the sixteenth century. Even in our own time, the distinction between psychological disorders and possession has depended on the contexts in which individuals have presented their experiences. To a Christian pastor in the charismatic tradition, the involuntary cursing of a member of their congregation during prayers could be a sign of demonic affliction; for a clinical psychologist, the same behaviour in a therapy session might indicate a dissociative disorder.[3]

The experience of possession also illustrates the role of culture in shaping physical illness. While the behaviour of people around the victim – known as a "demoniac" – could influence the specific symptoms associated with their condition, these symptoms were often painfully real. In a small number of cases, physicians found clear evidence of deceit. When a team of Parisian doctors examined the demoniac Marthe Brossier in 1599, they concluded that her symptoms involved "nothing from the spirit, many things simulated, [and] a few things from disease". More often, however, those who witnessed the sufferings of the possessed believed them to be genuine, and the victims themselves appear to have endured real physical distress. Equally, there is no reason to assume that the bodily raptures felt by pre-modern visionaries were a confidence trick. Perhaps the best way to understand these episodes is to view them as a form of social drama. The Spanish theologian Diego Pérez de Valdivia noted the theatrical aspects of possession in 1585: he predicted that demoniacs would disappear when "there are no crowds" to watch them. In his study of charismatic religion in eighteenth-century Europe and America, Clarke Garrett has suggested that all types of possession involve "role play". Anthropologists studying possession cults have made the same observation, noting that charismatic experiences are a kind of "sacred theatre". The part performed by the enraptured person – either as a visionary or a demoniac – has to conform to cultural expectations in order to be convincing. This does not mean they are faking. On the contrary, everyone involved has to believe in the performance for it to work. The bodily symptoms of possession and inspiration, which also conformed to the expectations of the "audience", were an essential part of this drama. The idea that cultural theatre can produce bodily effects should not surprise anyone who has felt better immediately after visiting their doctor, whether or not they have received any medication or started to take it.[4]

If the ecstatic transports of charismatic Christians are a form of sacred theatre, in which a receptive audience accepts the manifestation of the spirit of God, the torments of the possessed can be viewed as the theatre of the Devil. Both kinds of drama conveyed powerful messages to those who took part. They also confirmed the core beliefs of the wider communities in which they occurred and tended to reaffirm the social conventions to which their members were bound. At the same time, however, they offered a temporary opportunity to upend the normal rules of society. Women could speak with the authority of God, commanding the attention and directing the behaviour of their social superiors, and the possessed could utter words and ideas that were otherwise completely forbidden.

THE THEATRE OF GOD

Around 1360 Lucia Tiepolo, the Abbess of the isolated Venetian convent of Sant' Apostolo, became "lost and absorbed in spirit" during her afternoon prayers. She was suddenly presented with a vision of Christ, "all wounded and bloody, with the crown of thorns on his head". As she sat enraptured, the figure placed His hands on her shoulders and commanded her to found a new convent in His name. The Abbess recovered her senses and looked around the room, but saw no trace of the heavenly visitor. But the vision returned on three successive nights. On each occasion, He directed her to "Go and do what I tell you, without delay". Taking the hint, she obtained an audience with the patriarch Francesco Querini and described her experience to him. With the patriarch's blessing, she was able to establish a tiny community of nuns on a deserted spit of land at the perimeter of the city. This struggled to survive for some twenty-five years, though Tiepolo insisted that Christ had promised to make it "famous throughout the world". The little nunnery was eventually transformed through the intervention of the great Dominican preacher Giovanni Dominici. He obtained permission to build the large convent of Corpus Domini on the site, and persuaded dozens of patrician women to join the community.

The prophetic events surrounding the convent of Corpus Domini did not end there. Two Venetian women, Isabetta and Andreola Tomasini, influenced Dominici's decision to establish the convent by revealing it to be God's will. They acquired this knowledge through "some beautiful visions on the subject". Soon after his death in 1419, Dominici himself appeared in a rapturous vision experienced by another nun:

> While one of our sisters was in prayer, praying to the Lord for his
> soul with many tears, she was rapt in spirit and seemed to see a great
> light. In that light she saw and recognised the face of this blessed

father, which seemed to cast rays like the sun, and the whole church
was filled with the faces of little children that hovered in the air
around this light. This sister was utterly amazed, and she pondered
to herself, saying, "My Lord, what do all these children signify?"
She heard a voice that said to her, "Be of good cheer. You should
know that those children are the souls that have been brought back
into the bosom of the holy church by his preaching and his advice,
and that is why you see him in such glory".

The entranced sister looked on Dominici's face and asked him to take her and
her companions under his care. The face appeared to laugh "as if with
pleasure at hearing these words". When she recovered her senses, the sister
was delighted that the convent's earthly protector now "enjoyed life eternal
and great honour in the sight of the Lord".[5]

These visionary events were, in many respects, typical of the raptures
experienced by devout Christians in pre-modern Europe. For a start, women
were especially prone to such experiences. This appears to be a recurring
pattern in human society: the anthropologist I. M. Lewis has noted how in
most spirit-believing cultures women are more likely than men to experience
both divine inspiration and demonic possession. Mary Douglas has explained
this by the exclusion of women from positions of public authority, which
means that charismatic experiences provide one of the few ways for them to
exercise power. This interpretation may be relevant to medieval visionaries
like Lucia Tiepolo. Before she established her little community in Venice,
Tiepolo was desperately unhappy in her role as abbess of Sant' Apostolo. She
had been forced to accept the position by the region's bishop, despite
"arguing as best she could with many words and tears". It was only through
the sanction of her divine experience that she was able to escape this posting
and command the attention of wealthy patrons in the city. Likewise, the
women who persuaded Giovanni Dominici to support the new foundation
could only treat him as an equal on the basis of their visions. More generally,
devout women were excluded from virtually all positions of authority in the
medieval church, and this situation was made worse by the closure of
convents in Protestant regions during the sixteenth century. This meant that
divine revelations provided one of the few opportunities for women to
exercise religious authority.[6]

The prevalence of female mystics in the pre-modern world may also relate
to another characteristic of the prophetic experience. This was its passivity.
The true visionary was a recipient of the word of God, an empty vessel to be
filled with the Holy Spirit. The active quest for religious knowledge was the
business of theologians and teachers; prophets, in contrast, were mere
conduits for God's will. In the words of the English visionary Julian of
Norwich in 1373, "the busier we are about discovering His secrets in this

matter or that, the farther we shall be from their discovery". The attitude of patience and passivity that women were encouraged to cultivate in all aspects of life made them ideal recipients for divine inspiration. Ironically, this meant that female prophets were occasionally permitted to speak with the greatest authority of all. For this to happen, however, the experience of inspiration had to conform to social expectations. The women of Corpus Domini received their revelations in a spirit of humble acceptance. In the case of the vision of Giovanni Dominici, the message also affirmed the "fatherly" care of the convent's great protector: this upheld the conventional view that communities of religious women should be governed by men. More prosaically, the vision provided evidence of the preacher's sanctity at a time when the Dominican order was hoping for his canonisation.[7]

The visionary experiences of the women of Corpus Domini were intensely personal, and the surviving records indicate something of their immediate effects. The sisters were "rapt" or "lost in spirit". After witnessing the appearance of Dominici, the nun "came to herself very joyous". Other accounts of prophetic individuals described their experience in greater detail. The fourteenth-century saint Dorothy of Montau was sometimes so "inebriated" with the Holy Spirit that she appeared to be drunk. This rendered her unable to perform household chores, so she adopted the life of an anchoress instead. Dorothy's contemporary, Henry Suso, left a first-hand account of a rapture he experienced inside a church: he was suffused in a spirit of "joyous delight", and felt that his "wishes were calmed and his desire had died out". He gazed lovingly into a brilliant light, which so filled his mind that he was unsure if it was day or night. Other visionaries described the physical sensation of communion with God. When the spirit entered the seventeenth-century English prophet Eleanor Channel, she felt it as "a blow given her upon her heart". During a prolonged illness in the 1630s, Jane Turner "was in a continual converse and exchanging love with God, as it were lodging and living in the bosom of Christ". In the middle years of the eighteenth century, Ann Lee, the leader of the Shaker movement, recorded her own reception of the Holy Spirit. This commenced with a period of spiritual anguish, in which she neglected to eat until her bones became visible through her skin. Then she experienced a sudden rush of spiritual energy. This renewed her senses and infused her body with vigour, making her feel "like an infant just born into the world".[8]

These dramatic symptoms provoke an unavoidable question. How can the bodily transports, visions and voices described by pre-modern visionaries be explained? The best starting point, perhaps, is to accept that these phenomena have been recorded in all human societies: anthropologists have found versions of them in every living culture, including our own. Working within the rationalist framework of modern medicine, psychologists have noted that lack of food or sleep can induce hallucinations. This research may be relevant to the visions of medieval seers and later charismatics like Ann Lee, who subjected themselves to fasts and sleep deprivation. When these symptoms persist, most western clinical psychologists diagnose their sufferers as schizophrenic. We should note, however, that this explanation is only a recent attempt to classify what appears to be a general human experience. The psychologist Richard Gross has observed how the symptoms of "schizophrenia" have manifested themselves differently over time. When people heard voices in the 1920s, "these were often voices from the radio, in the 1950s they often came from the television, in the '60s it was satellites in space, and in the '70s and '80s spirits were transmitted through microwave ovens". By the same token, the visions of pre-modern prophets reflected the commonplace images of their day: Christ appeared to Lucia Tiepolo in his familiar guise as the "man of sorrows". Not only the content, but also the interpretation of such experiences can vary. Gross notes that people in spirit-believing cultures assume that immaterial voices are "directed by unseen forces under the control of demons". More boldly, other psychologists have challenged the idea of schizophrenia itself. For Thomas Szasz, it is merely a definition for apparently unconventional states of mind, whose real causes are still not properly understood. Viewed in this light, the explanations of clinical psychology are no more substantial than those proposed by the nuns of Corpus Domini. They are simply more believable to us.[9]

However these experiences were caused, it is clear that social circumstances determined their meaning for those whom they touched. This was obvious in the case of charismatic groups like the Quakers, the French "Camisards" and the American Shakers. It was also within these communities that the theatrical aspect of inspiration was most marked. The interplay between inspired individuals and those around them was demonstrated dramatically among the early Quakers. George Fox, the movement's founder, described how the words he spoke "through the immediate opening of the invisible spirit" could move audiences to silence, and inspire some of his hearers to endorse their truth. This experience was sometimes marked by the physical reaction that gave the movement its name. When he preached in Carlisle cathedral in 1653, "the power of the Lord was so dreadful . . . that the people trembled and shook", and some felt the building itself was quaking with the Holy Spirit. Not all audiences were so responsive. Fox was thrown down the steps of York Minster in 1651, but even this harsh treatment won some witnesses to his cause, moved by "the very groans that arose from the weight and oppression of the spirit of God in me". On another occasion, the stirrings of the Holy Spirit produced a more dramatic victory:

> The priest and people coming by the house, I went forth with friends into the yard, and there I spoke to the priest and people. The priest scoffed at us, and called us "Quakers". But the Lord's power was so

over them, and the word of life was declared in such authority and dread to them, that the priest began trembling himself; and one of the people said, "Look how the priest trembles and shakes – he is turned a Quaker also".

Unfortunately for Fox and his companions, this conversion proved to be temporary. Later in the same day, the priest "much abused" the Quakers, and his accusations eventually forced them to appear before the town magistrates.[10]

As the movement built more stable foundations, Quaker meetings developed conventions that shaped the expression of charismatic experiences. Members were encouraged to wait in silence for the promptings of the spirit, so that meetings sometimes passed in silent contemplation. "Rash" speeches were discouraged. The "still and cool" atmosphere of the meetinghouse came to exemplify the "Quakerly" way. On Fox's advice, newcomers were subjected to careful scrutiny, and were only admitted to membership if their temperament was agreeable to those already within the group. These measures tempered the fiery enthusiasm that characterised some early Quaker gatherings, and restrained the excesses of men and women overheated by the Holy Spirit. Equally however, the emergence of routines for the "opening of the spirit", and the mutual policing of these rules by others in the community, created an atmosphere in which divine inspiration became a thoroughly normal activity. Later movements like the Shakers repeated this pattern. They began by reviving the unpredictable thrills of charismatic religion, so their enemies could portray them as a circus of spiritual abandon and "fantastic contortions of the body". In the late 1700s, however, the Shakers also evolved conventions for expressing the Holy Spirit that both quietened and normalised the experience.[11]

Through the careful observances of the meetinghouse, Quakers and Shakers managed to contain the spontaneous work of the spirit within permanent religious communities. This was a surprising achievement. It was only possible at all because divine inspiration was a desirable commodity: as long as it was properly channelled and understood, the message of the Holy Spirit worked for everyone's benefit. Demonic possession was entirely different. The ravings of demoniacs were always a threat. By their very nature, the incursions of unclean spirits were a menace to be resisted; and the words they expressed were necessarily the antithesis of everything believed to be good. This made for a more fearful and explosive kind of drama.

THE THEATRE OF THE DEVIL

During the feast of Corpus Domini in 1725, Maria Salinaro, a lay Carmelite nun, was suddenly aware of a loud noise in her ears and a strange mist that obscured her vision. Unable to see or hear the service, her mind was invaded by terrible words: "Worship me, and not God, for there will be no mercy for you". She prayed to God for assistance but was unable to shake off the voice. That night a demon appeared in her bedroom in the form of a man dressed in black; he returned to her on subsequent evenings and demanded sexual favours. After weeks of these visitations, she finally drove the spirit away by asserting God's power over her soul. "You don't scare me", she exclaimed, "God created me and I belong to God, and God will save me and have pity on my soul".[12]

The affliction suffered by Maria Salinaro was one of various kinds of demonic assault that was recognised in the pre-modern world. It was generally accepted that devils could torment women and men through outward attacks on their senses. They could also menace them physically in acts of "obsession". More insidiously, unclean spirits could whisper in their victims' ears, and could even plant alien thoughts in their minds. The English pastor Robert Bolton described this process in 1634. Unlike natural cognitions, he explained, ideas "injected" by the Devil did not form gradually in the mind: they "rush in violently, forcibly and furiously, they are thrown into our imaginations like a flash of lightning". Such projections provided a novel outlet for otherwise inexpressible ideas; though the individuals to whom they occurred were immediately obliged, like Salinaro, to renounce and resist them. The mental onslaughts of demons were also a private affair. Their sufferers were normally forced to rely on their own spiritual resources to repudiate and overcome the Devil's wiles.[13]

Possession was a more extreme form of demonic attack. Here the Devil not only implanted thoughts in his victim's brain, but assumed control of their mind and body for a temporary period. It was uncommon for those so afflicted to relieve this condition through their own efforts; the intervention of others was normally required to expel the invading spirit. This made possession a public affair. Its symptoms were well known from biblical accounts, such as Mark's description of a man infested with a host of demons in the land of the Gadarenes: "he had been often bound with fetters and chains, and the chains had been plucked asunder by him . . . and always, night and day, he was in the mountains, and in the tombs, crying and cutting himself with stones" (Mark 5:4–5). Pre-modern writers frequently noted the bodily contortions of demoniacs, alongside the peculiar strength that allowed them to break the restraints sometimes applied for their own protection. When he visited the afflicted girls at Salem in 1692, Deodat Lawson observed "that their motions in their fits are preternatural, both as to the manner, which is so strange as a well person could not screw their body into; and as to the violence also, being much beyond the ordinary force of the same person being in their right mind". The seizures of the possessed were accompanied by strange voices, sometimes emitting from the throat, but frequently reported from other parts of the body.[14] These differed strikingly from the victim's normal voice: they were sometimes reedy and thin, but more often emerged as a rasping growl. "Fearful shrieks" often accompanied these foreign voices. During his clandestine ministry in England in the 1580s, the Jesuit William Weston feared that Catholic exorcists might be exposed to the authorities because of the "violent and raucous shrieks" of demoniacs under their care. In 1602 Henri Boguet described how a possessed woman "fell to the ground and began to bark like a dog, rolling her eyes in her head with a frightful and horrifying look". Victims of possession in New England displayed similar symptoms. Increase Mather reported a possessed boy in Newbury in 1679 who "made for a long time together a noise like a dog and like a hen with her chickens, and could not speak rationally".[15]

In Christian communities that practise exorcism today, overt manifestations of the physical presence of demons are often regarded as vulgar. Pre-modern thinkers were generally less squeamish. The appearance of lumps on the victim's body, or their perception that something was moving inside them, was frequently reported. James VI noted that one of the true signs of possession was a swelling in "the patient's breast and belly, with such an unnatural stirring and agitation within them". The demoniac examined by Boguet experienced a demon "like a big lump in her stomach". In 1608 Francesco Maria Guazzo pondered the problem of identifying true cases of possession. It was most easy to detect the telltale signs, he noted, "when the evil spirit moves from one place to another" inside the victim's body:

If something moves about the body like a live thing, so that the possessed feel, as it were, ants crawling under their skin. If the part of the body for which the demon is making is stirred by a sort of palpitation. If the patient is tortured with certain prickings. If it is as though wind descended from his head to his feet, and then again went from his feet to his head . . . If the demon rises so far as the throat and causes it to swell, and brings on a dry cough.

The Catholic exorcisms recorded by William Weston were replete with such phenomena. According to one witness, "you could actually see the devils gliding and moving under the skin. There were immense numbers of them, and they looked just like fishes swimming here, there and everywhere". Bodily symptoms of this kind encouraged a suitably physical response. Medieval demoniacs were occasionally beaten to drive the possessing spirits out of them. Less brutal but equally direct was the method of marking the lumps on the victim's flesh with the sign of the cross, which sometimes caused them to migrate to other body parts. The insertion of communion wafers could produce more explosive results. At the climax of an exorcism at Soissons in 1582, Jean Canart thrust the consecrated host into the mouth of a possessed boy and clamped his jaws shut to prevent the wicked spirit from spitting it out. This induced consternation in the child's body; the demon shrieked "like a pig being stifled or a little dog being flayed" before emerging from the boy's nostril in a plume of smoke.[16]

This episode illustrates another characteristic of the possession experience. Afflicted individuals expressed a physical revulsion to holy objects and words. During the sixteenth and seventeenth centuries, when Europe was divided between warring communities of Catholics and Protestants, this tendency expressed itself in ways that reflected the religious conventions of these different groups. Catholic demoniacs were appalled by the words of the Latin Mass, and winced in pain at the touch of holy water. Late in the seventeenth century, Ludovico Maria Sinistrari described the reaction of possessing spirits to other symbols of the Roman faith:

> At the mere utterance of the most holy names of Jesus or Mary, or
> the recitation of some verses of scripture, at the imposition of relics,
> especially of the wood of the most holy cross, or at the sight of
> pictures and statues of the saints, they roar fearfully from the mouth
> of the possessed person, they gnash, shake, quiver, and display fright
> and terror.

Reactions of this kind allowed priests to test the sincerity of demoniacs. The boy in Soissons was sprinkled with ordinary water, which apparently produced no reaction, while blessed water sent him into violent contractions. Marguerite Obry, another victim of the demons at Soissons, was tested with consecrated and unconsecrated wafers, though the results in her case appear to have been inconclusive. The same methods helped to expose the fraud of Marthe Brossier in 1599. When the Bishop of Orléans gave her blessed water to drink – without divulging its special qualities – she apparently consumed the beverage without any ill effects.[17]

The symptoms of possession in Protestant areas were rather more limited. Some Protestant thinkers were suspicious of bodily manifestations of demons in general, but many others accepted the physical signs of possessing spirits while dismissing the power of Catholic rites and artefacts to disturb them. James VI believed their "raging at holy water [and] their fleeing back from the cross" were silly trifles, and argued that the unnatural strength and convulsions of the possessed were more reliable signs of genuine affliction. These attitudes influenced the "script" for possession. Protestant demoniacs recoiled from the words of scripture, but were generally unmoved by holy water and the consecrated host. During the possession of Edward Dinham of Taunton in 1626, one of his demons reacted violently to the Anglican Book of Common Prayer. In 1688, some possessed children in

Boston, Massachusetts, were tormented by acts of Protestant worship: "all praying to God, and reading of His word, would occasion a very terrible vexation to them: they would stop their ears with their own hands, and roar and shriek and holler, to drown the voice of the devotion". Other demoniacs mocked the "godly" lifestyle encouraged by puritan preachers, expressing delight in gambling, dancing and Sabbath-breaking. These acts underline the importance of the social context of possession. Catholic demoniacs played a slightly different role from their Protestant counterparts, and each had to understand – and internalise – the specifics of this role for the drama to be convincing.[18]

There was no reason in theory why any particular type of person should normally take centre stage in these performances. Theologians agreed that possession was often sent to punish impious individuals, but equally, it could be permitted by God to test the faith of His servants. In practice, however, it appears that women were particularly susceptible. Jean Bodin noted in 1580 that almost all the demoniacs in contemporary Italy were female. Women were also prominent among the possessed in Bodin's native France, where a series of high-profile exorcisms commenced with the case of Nicole Obry in 1566 and culminated in the mass possession of nuns in the convent of Loudon in 1634. The prevalence of female demoniacs can probably be explained by the same factors that made women particularly susceptible to visionary experiences. Since they were excluded from positions of authority, the experience of possession provided a rare opportunity for women to command attention and speak with a powerful voice. Moreover, the peculiar nature of this voice allowed women to exceed the normal rules of acceptable speech, which generally imposed more constraints on them than men. The importance of these factors is indicated, perhaps, by the large number of children who also succumbed to possession: like women of all ages, children were excluded from authority and subjected to strict rules of correct speech. The freedom to speak forbidden words came at a price, however. By accepting that the Devil was responsible for their words and deeds, demoniacs were obliged to renounce their own behaviour and submit themselves to the authority of adult men. For the drama of possession to follow a convincing and acceptable course, it normally had to end in a successful exorcism.[19]

The sensational nature of exorcism ensured that crowds of people would sometimes flock to witness the ritual. The most famous and dramatic such case was the "Miracle of Laon". This centred on Nicole Obry, a fifteen-year-old girl from the French town of Vervin. In November 1565, while visiting her grandfather's grave, Nicole received an extraordinary vision. According to one account, "there rose up, as if coming from the ground, a man wrapped in his shroud, and he said to the young woman that he was her grandfather". Nicole took the spirit at his word, and persuaded her family to practise devotions to release him from purgatory. When these were completed, however, she was seized by the symptoms of demonic possession. The spirit within her revealed its true identity as Beelzebub. There followed a series of exorcisms in Vervin. These were transferred to the nearby cathedral of Laon, the only venue large enough to accommodate hundreds of onlookers. At the height of the spectacle in January 1566, daily processions were organised in the city, and the bishop erected scaffolding in the cathedral for some 10,000 spectators. Augustin Calmet, the eighteenth-century abbot of Senores, was one of dozens of later writers to describe the drama's climax:

> At the last day of possession, everybody being assembled in the afternoon, the bishop began the last conjurations, when many extraordinary things took place. Amongst others, the bishop desiring to put the Holy Eucharist near the lips of this poor woman, the devil in some way seized hold of his arm, and at the same moment raised this woman up, as it were, out of the hands of sixteen men who were holding her. But at last, after much resistance, he came out, and left her perfectly cured.

Nicole's exorcism was unusual in its duration, but as a spectacle it was far from unique. German Jesuits also performed dispossessions before large crowds in the sixteenth century. During one of these rituals, the spirit possessing Anna Bernhauser tossed her body so brutally that onlookers feared for her life. Protestant pastors could also preside over such events. John Foxe, the great Elizabethan martyrologist, assisted in the exorcism of a possessed girl in London in 1574. Fasts and prayers were organised by a group of puritan clergy in Cheshire in 1603 to relieve the sufferings of the demoniac Thomas Harrison. These developed into set-piece opportunities for preaching and worship, drawing crowds of sympathetic layfolk from across the region.[20]

While the theatre of the devil often ended with a successful dispossession, it could also climax in the execution of a witch. Though its origins are obscure, the belief that witches could cast demons into people's bodies was established in popular culture by the sixteenth century. Experts on possession made the same assumption. This meant that demoniacs were often a source of witchcraft allegations. In some cases, they believed the spirit was introduced into their body through food provided by a witch. William Sommers of Nottingham, for instance, was made to eat a piece of contaminated bread by a beggar woman in 1598. This induced bodily convulsions and a "strange and idle kind of gestures", leading to his full-scale possession. In the same year, Françoise Secretain used this method to infect an eight-year-old girl in Burgundy, though the judge in her trial noted that witches most often employed apples for this purpose. Many other victims, like the bedevilled children in Salem, received visions of their human tormenters. The unclean spirit itself could also betray its accomplices. This was demonstrated at Taunton in 1626, when the two spirits that invaded Edward Dinham conducted lengthy conversations between themselves. One of them, whose voice was "deadly and hollow", claimed that Dinham's neighbours, Joan Greedie and Edward Bull, had sent them into his body. A contemporary account reveals the flavour of these exchanges:

> But are these witches?
> Yes, that they are.
> How came they to be so?
> By descent.
> But how by descent?
> From the grandmother to the mother, and from the mother to the children.
> But how were they so?
> They were bound to us, and us to them.

The link between possession and witchcraft offered a remedy for the affliction. If the witch could be correctly identified, he or she might be persuaded to remove the demon from its host. This process probably took place informally in most cases. When the symptoms persisted, however, and no other relief appeared to be available, the accusations of demoniacs could lead to the apprehension of a suspected witch. Since the person accused would frequently have a long-standing reputation for *maleficia*, it was often easy to find other evidence against them. Their conviction sometimes removed the symptoms of possession. When Alice Samuel was hanged at Huntingdon in 1593, the young girls she had allegedly visited with demons recovered their senses. This pattern was repeated in New England. In his *Essay for the Recording of Illustrious Providences* (1684), Increase Mather noted how the demoniac Ann Cole "was restored to health and has continued well for many years" following the execution of a witch in Hartford, Connecticut, in 1662.[21]

It is tempting to view the accusations of demoniacs as malicious. This may be accurate in some cases, especially where the accusers were young children. As William E. Monter has noted, making allegations of witchcraft was "partly a child's game". It would be unduly suspicious, however, to view the majority of accusations in this light. If demonic possession was a form of social theatre, its script imposed certain expectations on its leading players. One of these was the involvement of witches. Demoniacs sometimes responded directly to the suspicions of those around them. This was apparently the case with Thomas Darling, a possessed boy from Burton in Staffordshire, who made allegations of *maleficia* in 1596 after an adult raised the possibility. In many other cases, the atmosphere surrounding the possessed appears to have encouraged and sustained such accusations. The parents of Loyse Mallait, the young girl bedevilled by Françoise Secretain in 1598, seem to have suspected their neighbour of witchcraft before Loyse succumbed to possession. Similar suspicions were circulating in 1679, when evil spirits invaded the home of a family in Newbury, Massachusetts. In an incident reminiscent of *The Exorcist*, young John Stiles complained that "his bedstead leaped up and down" when he was alone. Whatever was causing the disturbance went on to possess the boy's body, which was racked with convulsive spasms and given over to "intolerable ravings". The outcome of this case was determined by the adults, who made a series of accusations and counter-accusations of *maleficia* that led eventually to the conviction of his grandmother. For those enacting the drama of possession in such circumstances, making an allegation of witchcraft was, like submitting to an exorcism, one of the socially accepted ways to escape the affliction.[22]

If the expectations of those around the possessed could channel their behaviour in certain directions, it could also, in some extraordinary instances, transform the experience altogether. In a few cases, patients displaying the signs of possession became convinced they were victims of "melancholy", or other natural conditions, when they came under the care of physicians. More dramatically, demoniacs could slip into states of spiritual rapture and, in a more common scenario, visionaries could succumb to possession. These episodes highlight the affinities between demoniacs and prophets. They also provide a sharp reminder of the power of social expectations to influence the belief – and even the physical health – of individual women and men.

A CONFUSION OF VOICES

The sixteenth century was not a good time for prophets. After the glorious flowering of late medieval mysticism in the years before 1520, the shock of the Protestant Reformation led to a clampdown on most forms of visionary experience. The Catholic Church, fearful of spiritual excesses that could stray into heresy, sought greater control over religious expression: cheap visionary literature was suppressed and the practice of prophecy – especially among the laity – was treated with grave suspicion. When a Lombard peasant named Margherita received a vision of the Virgin Mary in 1560, the authorities investigating her story declared it a "diabolical illusion". Pope Pius IV banned the construction of any building on the site to commemorate the event. This pattern was repeated in Spain. Here, the experience of rapture was redefined as a potential danger to the church, especially when its recipients were outside its control. Lay communities of "holy women", or *beatas*, aroused particular concern. The inquisition tried to police their activities during the 1570s. Their religious ecstasies were denounced as unruly, and one member of the Holy Office, Alonso de la Fuente, came to regard them as signs of a demonic cult. The story was much the same in Protestant Europe. Martin Luther denounced the "false brethren" who placed the direct inspiration of the Holy Spirit alongside the Bible, and most Protestant authorities followed his lead. The fate of prophets in the new dispensation was, perhaps, epitomised by the career of Elizabeth Barton, the "holy maid of Kent", who was moved by a series of visions in the late 1520s to denounce Henry VIII's divorce plans. She died on a scaffold in 1534.[23]

Newly suspicious of charismatic experiences, religious experts sought to explain them within a limited range of possibilities. In a small number of cases, the rapturous visions of pious women and men were accepted as genuine. Teresa of Avila, the reforming Carmelite nun who enjoyed passionate and much-publicised visions of Christ, was acknowledged as a faithful daughter of the church and canonised in 1622. Teresa's mystical experiences, like those of the founder of the Jesuits, Ignatius of Loyola, were channelled safely in the service of the Roman hierarchy. Many other visionaries were condemned as frauds. This was the fate of many Spanish *beatas* and Italian prophets. When rapturous experiences could not be dismissed in this way, demonic possession offered a plausible alternative. On both sides of the religious divide, the perceived excesses of heretical groups were sometimes explained in this way. In 1533 some Anabaptist prisoners were made to drink holy water in an attempt to expel the unclean spirits that held them in thrall. In his commentary on Paul's epistle to the Galatians, Luther observed that many "false brethren" were deceived by satanic dreams and false opinions, which were "a manifest sign that they are bewitched of the devil". More generally, the bitter conflict between Protestants and Catholics raised the profile of Satan, as both sides perceived their opponents to be agents of Antichrist. This heightened awareness of the Devil's power alerted everyone to his physical manifestations on earth.[24]

In this bedevilled atmosphere, potential visionaries had few opportunities to express their gift. The script of "sacred theatre" was effectively torn up: behaviour associated with inspiration was unlikely to find a sympathetic audience, and persistent raptures and visions could only be channelled in a more sinister direction. One casualty of this process was Nicole Obry, the girl exorcised so spectacularly at Laon in 1566. In a sensitive and persuasive study of her case, Moshe Sluhovsky has shown that Nicole exercised some control over her fate: she used her experience as a platform for her opinions and needs, and was not blindly manipulated by the priests who managed her dispossession. Nonetheless, her options were restricted. In the early stages of her enchantment, there is every sign that she perceived the experience as a kind of inspiration. On receiving the vision of her grandfather, she directed her family to undertake conventional good works: these included masses, the distribution of alms and a series of pilgrimages. She confirmed the authenticity of these commands through prophetic deeds: as her male relatives journeyed to local shrines, she received visions of their progress that were subsequently deemed to be accurate. When her family failed to complete the last pilgrimage – an expensive trip to Spain – Nicole was overcome with a convulsive fit. She initially believed this was induced by the spirit of her grandfather, or an angel, to compel them to complete the task. It was only when her family consulted a Dominican friar, who suspected demonic possession, that her condition was reclassified. From this moment onwards, Nicole's plight became the public concern of the church and the wider Catholic community, culminating in her violent exorcism at Laon. The girl – or the spirit within her – negotiated the script of this drama within the limits imposed on her: it was the voice of Beelzebub, for instance, that insisted that her dispossession should be performed by a bishop instead of an ordinary priest. But the core elements of this performance were determined by the failure of her visionary experience and the enthusiasm with which the church embraced her role as a demoniac.[25]

The story of Nicole Obry was repeated, in less spectacular fashion, by other visionary women in Renaissance Europe. In 1621 Edward Fairfax, a Yorkshire gentleman, recorded a particularly intimate and harrowing account of the experiences of his daughters Helen and Elizabeth. Both were afflicted with "deadly trances", in which they lost control of their senses and witnessed visions. Fairfax and his acquaintances suspected witchcraft, but Helen, the eldest daughter, was convinced that some of her experiences were divine. One night she awoke to see a man "attired in white, glistening garments", who took her hand and led her towards the window. She turned back and fell into a trance. Two days later, she was visited by a "man of incomparable beauty", dressed in bright clothes and suffused in gorgeous light. This figure, which she took to be God, assured her of His love and protection and led her through a recitation of the Lord's Prayer. When she described these events to her father, he tried to persuade her the vision was satanic. She resisted this interpretation. It took a whole night for Fairfax to convince her that the Devil had come as an angel of light. Newly armed with this knowledge, Helen resolved to confront the apparition the next time it appeared. This produced a dreadful revelation:

> On Thursday, 17 January, my eldest daughter saw the same glorious apparition again, who said he was now come for her, and therefore willed her to go with him. But she defied him and said, "Thou didst deceive me, and I didst pray to thee (God forgive me for it!), for I know what thou art". Yet he still laboured to persuade her that he was God . . . He desired her to say her prayers after him. She said, "I will say my prayers, but that shall be to thy great sorrow". Then he said he would slay her, and presently she saw many horns begin to

grow out of his head, and his beauty and glorious light were gone, and he changed into a most terrible shape.

Now that it was stripped of its disguise, Helen rebuked the demon for deceiving her and mocked its powerlessness before God. The creature responded by changing "into sundry shapes". In a clinching act of defiance, Helen declared that she would speak to the devil no more. She sat mutely and gestured for it to leave. At this the monster departed, and her normal senses were restored.[26]

For Nicole Obry and Helen Fairfax, the transition from inspiration to demonic possession appears to have been permanent. But just as often, demoniacs were visited by fleeting moments of divine illumination that were submerged in the drama of demonic theatre. Marcy Lewis, one of the afflicted girls at Salem, received a vision of a man dressed in white during one of her fits. He showed her "a glorious place, which had no candles nor sun, yet was full of light and brightness". A company of souls resided there. Dressed in shining white robes, they sang psalms and verses from the book of Revelation. Enraptured by this joyful sight, Marcy asked, "How long shall I stay here? Let me be along with you". She was grieved to discover that she had to leave. According to Deodat Lawson, some of the other girls saw the same angelic figure. These revelations conformed closely to traditional images of Heaven, and would not have been out of place among the divine visions recorded at the convent of Corpus Domini in the fifteenth century. For the possessed girls at Salem, however, they could only be explained as a demonic trick.[27]

While demoniacs were denied the chance to communicate a heavenly message, they sometimes fulfilled a positive role through their public pronouncements. When the possessed children of an English family confronted the woman they accused of bedevilling them in 1593, one witness to the encounter was moved by their pious eloquence. One could not receive greater edification, he remarked, by attending ten sermons. But such directly positive utterances were rare. More frequently, demoniacs delivered good news by presenting it as the mirror image of the Devil's wishes. If preachers were saving souls, the possessed would rave against them; when laws were good, unclean spirits would shrilly demand their repeal. These reversed messages were most obvious when the possessed involved themselves in religious disputes. Through the convulsed body of Nicole Obry, Beelzebub declared himself to be a Protestant sympathiser. Her Catholic exorcists seized on this admission, and the publicity surrounding it continued for generations. In 1608, Francesco Maria Guazzo recalled how Nicole's demon had "mocked at the Calvinists, crying out that he had nothing to fear from them since they were his friends and allies". This fact, he added, was "too well known throughout Picardy for it to be denied". Protestant demoniacs replied in kind.

During the possession of the Englishman Alexander Nynde in 1573, some of the witnesses appeared to pray to the Virgin Mary for his deliverance. The exorcist rebuked them for this Catholic error, but the unclean spirit interrupted him to declare that the practice was perfectly acceptable. He denounced the demon for spreading popish lies, and proved his point by successfully expelling it from Nynde's body.[28]

The same principle applied to methods of exorcism. When Catholic demoniacs recoiled from holy water and tried to vomit consecrated hosts, this affirmed the ability of priests to bless water and the power of the mass. Nicole Obry was finally dispossessed by receiving the Eucharist; the same method worked at Soissons in 1582. During a visit to the possessed convent of Loudon in 1634, the sceptical Earl of Lauderdale described how the afflicted nuns, "after great resistance and squeaking, did on great importunity adore the [consecrated] host, and the Jesuits did desire us to see the power of [their] church". Unimpressed, the Earl dismissed this as blasphemous propaganda. More generally, the success of Catholic or Protestant exorcists confirmed their status as true ministers of Christ. The Gospels described how Jesus commissioned his followers to cast out demons, and their achievements in this field were a testament to their ministry (Matt. 10:8; Mark 3:15). At times when confessional rivalry was particularly fierce, exorcism became a kind of competitive sport between the clergy of rival denominations. Henri Boguet noted a victory for his own side in 1602:

> The son of a Huguenot gentleman was possessed of a devil, and they brought the local minister to conjure it. But this minister had no power against devils, as was at once recognised by the father; who, being more anxious for his son's health than strict in the observance of his own religion, secretly sent for a Catholic priest, who used the accustomed exorcisms of the Roman church with such sincerity that the possessed was soon delivered.

Boguet did not say whether this experience caused the family to convert, but this was certainly the case with some other high-profile victims of possession. During the 1560s, members of the German Fugger family embraced the Catholic faith as Jesuits expelled demons from the bodies of their servants. On a wider scale, the publicity surrounding such incidents actively encouraged Protestants to defect to Rome.[29]

Such propaganda raised a ticklish question. If Catholic exorcisms were false – as all Protestants believed they were – how could the extraordinary physical symptoms of the possessed be explained, and why were these apparently relieved through the intervention of priests? Some hostile observers, like the Earl of Lauderdale, attributed the behaviour of Catholic demoniacs to a combination of natural causes and trickery. The antics of the possessed nuns at Loudon were carnival pranks. When Lauderdale witnessed the horrible belching of some possessed women at Antwerp in 1649, his diagnosis was more pithy: "if those were devils", he observed, "they were windy devils, [and] they were only possessed with a morning's draught of too new beer". Another explanation was possible, however, based on the assumption that demonic possession could really happen. Perhaps Satan was playing a double game. King James VI spelt out this ingenious scenario:

> By experience we find that few, who are possessed indeed, are fully cured by them [Catholic exorcists]; but rather the devil is content to release the bodily hurting of them for a short space, thereby to obtain the perpetual hurt of the souls of so many that by these false miracles may be induced or confirmed in the profession of that erroneous religion.

If the possession of poor souls like Nicole Obry was genuine, their apparent exorcism through the rites of the Roman church was a brilliant flourish of the Devil's art. The same argument explained the physical details of the possession experience. When demons pulsed through a human body in response to the sign of the cross, explained the puritan exorcist John Darrel in 1599, this was a sham to delude their would-be exorcists. Their true purpose was to encourage "their superstitious estimation of the sign".[30]

As these arguments show, the Devil could work in mysterious ways. Instances of possession and exorcism, divine inspiration and alleged fraud depended to a large extent on the eyes of the beholder, and what people beheld was determined by their prior beliefs and the particular circumstances in which they found themselves. This was illustrated neatly in England during the 1640s, when the collapse of the official church allowed the sudden proliferation of prophetic women and men. It was in this extraordinary decade that George Fox, the founder the Quakers, commenced his visionary career. During a visit to Mansfield-Woodhouse, Fox encountered a woman taken with strange fits, whom he decided was the victim of demonic possession:

> There was a distracted woman under a doctor's hand, with her hair loose all about her ears. He was about to bleed her, she being fast bound, and many people being about her, holding her by violence; but he could not get blood from her. I desired them to unbind her; and let her alone, for they could not touch the spirit in her, by which she was tormented. So they unbound her; and I was moved to speak to her, and in the name of the Lord to bid her to be quiet and still; and she was so. The Lord's power settled her mind and she mended; and afterwards she received the truth, and continued in it until her death.

In this single episode, the inspired speech of a prophet quelled the symptoms of a woman invaded by a demon and, if Fox can be believed, the cured demoniac went on to embrace the organised inspiration of Quakerism. At the same time, a physician tried unavailingly to treat her as the victim of a natural illness. The same symptoms had different meanings in the context of different assumptions, and the woman's recovery shows us how, in the words of Roy Porter, afflicted men and women can be treated successfully within the "structures of remedy" available to them. Both divine inspiration and demonic possession were scripts in a cultural drama, but they were utterly real to the individuals concerned. As real, in fact, as the scripts we follow ourselves.[31]

8

Suffering Saints

The man lay on his deathbed and the priest sat at his side, his face pressed to his lips to hear his final words. These came in a halting whisper. "Yes my friend", the penitent said, "I do repent". The priest blessed him and urged him gently to make the best use of his last minutes by confessing all the sins on his mind. "I don't understand", the man replied, "any more than you have understood me". He then told his confessor that he had no faith in God and no expectation of Heaven or Hell. His lone regret was that he had not indulged his appetites more fully while he lived: "I only plucked an occasional flower when I could have gathered an ample harvest of fruit – such are the just grounds for the regrets I have". But the priest's advice was not entirely ignored. Determined to make the most of his last moments of life, the man resolved to die in the arms of "six women lovelier than the light of day". In a final act of effrontery, he invited the priest to "partake of the feast" with him.

The Marquis de Sade wrote this hedonistic parable in 1782. His point was simple: if no pleasures or torments await us in a life to come, we should devote ourselves to enjoying the one we have. Sade proclaimed this idea for the rest of his life, and elaborated its more frightful implications with such vigour that he was incarcerated as a threat to public morality in 1801. It is perhaps an indication of the secular nature of western culture that few people today would be shocked by Sade's claim that the afterlife may not exist. Equally, few would deny that the pursuit of earthly pleasures is legitimate, though this view is often qualified by the need to respect the rights of others. Even those who accept a Christian view of Heaven are unlikely to argue that personal happiness should be deferred until after death. The desire for happiness on earth is assumed to be natural. Those who fail to achieve it are deemed unlucky; those who cannot experience it are diagnosed as "depressed". To sacrifice one's own enjoyment for the sake of others is normally perceived as a virtue. On the other hand, to embrace unhappiness for its own sake seems pathological or simply absurd.[1]

But the assumptions behind Sade's tale remain valid. Belief in an afterlife can radically affect one's expectations and behaviour. If there really is no Heaven to reward the virtuous or Hell to punish the wicked, the actions of the dying man are quite rational. Conversely, a sincere belief that acts committed on earth will be punished after death might encourage men and women to abstain from those acts, however pleasurable they may be. For committed believers, the reality of the hereafter allows for a range of calculations unavailable to atheists. A brief pleasure on earth might result in unending torments in Hell, while the finite experience of earthly pain may be compensated by limitless joys in Heaven. This perspective also permits a drastic reformulation of common assumptions about the relationship between God and humankind. Does the Lord even expect us to be happy on earth? Perhaps He prefers to let us suffer here so we can be rewarded in the world to come. Many modern Christians would instinctively reject such views, but they were once widely embraced, and their neglect in our own time perhaps reflects the relative affluence of western societies. In the pre-modern age, the idea of the afterlife underpinned a very different attitude towards earthly suffering and in some cases it even encouraged the belief that misery was a goal to be actively pursued.

THE BREAD OF ADVERSITY

If the Bible promises spiritual riches to God's children, it is also unambiguous about the material hardship they will have to endure. In the Old Testament, this suffering comes mainly at the hands of earthly persecutors, but it is also part of the divine plan for humankind. Isaiah warns that the Lord will nourish his children with "the bread of adversity and the water of affliction" (Isa. 31:20). Their faith will be refined "in the furnace of affliction" (Isa. 48:10). "Many are the afflictions of the righteous", the Psalmist confirms, and the Lord "hast shewed me great and sore troubles" (Ps. 34:19, 71:20). The theme of patient suffering was amplified in the New Testament. Jesus told his disciples that they "must through much tribulation enter into the kingdom of God" (Acts 15:22). St Paul described Christians as "partakers of the afflictions of the Gospel", and enjoined the believer to "endure hardness as a good soldier of Jesus Christ" (2 Tim. 1:8, 2:3). The sufferings of the faithful would increase as the Last Judgment approached. The words of Jesus made this abundantly clear:

> For nation shall rise against nation, and kingdom against kingdom:
> and there shall be famines, and pestilences, and earthquakes, in divers
> places. All these are the beginning of sorrows. Then shall they deliver
> you up to be afflicted, and shall kill you: and ye shall be hated of all

nations for my name's sake . . . For then shall be great tribulation, such as was not since the beginning of the world.

(Matt. 24:7–9, 21)

St Paul pressed the message home. God's people could expect "perilous times" as the Judgment drew close: "false accusers" and "despisers" would assail them, and "all that will live godly in Christ shall suffer persecution" (2 Tim. 3: 12).

In the light of this scriptural tradition, it was hardly surprising that Christians occasionally embraced suffering as a virtue. Paul himself encouraged this attitude by inviting believers to "glory in tribulations" (Rom. 6:3). In times of persecution or religious conflict, earthly enemies provided frequent opportunities to suffer for the cause of Christ, but God's children could also expect to contend with spiritual foes. In the fourth and fifth centuries, the desert fathers provided a model of Christian suffering at the hands of demons. The torments of St Antony were particularly severe:

There was a sudden noise which caused the place to shake violently.
Holes opened up in the walls and a horde of different kinds of
demons poured out. They took on the shapes of wild animals and
snakes and instantly filled the whole place with spectres in the form
of lions, bulls, wolves, vipers, serpents, scorpions and even leopards
and bears too . . . The face of each of them bore a savage expression
and the sound of their fierce voices was terrifying. Anthony, beaten
and mauled, experienced atrocious pains in his body but remained
unafraid.

These physical attacks were less testing for Antony than were the Devil's assaults on his mind. The fiend appeared to him at night in "the attractive form of a beautiful woman, omitting no detail that might provoke lascivious thoughts". He only resisted this temptation by meditating on "the fiery punishment of hell and the torment inflicted by worms". To protect himself from these snares, he tried to subdue his senses through a regime of fasting and continual prayer. He slept on the bare earth and ate nothing but bread and salt. This programme of self-punishment inspired a succession of later ascetics, who refined the art of pious suffering to an astonishing degree. Macarius the Younger sat naked in a mosquito-infested marsh for six months. When he returned to his home, he was so swollen with bites that his friends recognised him only by his voice. St Jerome spent decades alone in the desert as "the comrade of scorpions and wild beasts". These exploits shaped a tradition of saintly mortification that permeated the Middle Ages and survived well into the nineteenth century. For the small band of determined ascetics, as well as the much larger community of Christians who accepted suffering as a necessary part of their faith, the calculation was simple: they measured pains in this world against rewards in the next. The promise was vouchsafed in scripture. As John affirmed, "in the world ye shall have tribulation: but be of good cheer; I have overcome the world" (John 17:33).[2]

The virtue of suffering was institutionalised in monastic life. The pious biographers of nuns and monks routinely presented the endurance of hardship as a noble pursuit. In fifteenth-century Venice, Bartolomea Riccoboni recorded the extreme mortification of nuns in the convent of Corpus Domini with heartfelt admiration. Sister Franceschina da Naole, for instance, led her life as "a constant round of prayers, vigils, flagellation, fasts, and other holy deeds, such that she fell ill and consumed that body, which did not have the appearance of a living thing". Sometimes the practice of deliberate suffering was prompted by remorse for sins committed in youth. The story of Sister Onesta Dei Marchesi, who devoted her early years to "worldly and vivacious" pleasures, served as an edifying exemplar:

> Once she entered the convent, God's grace entered her and she
> became so conscious of her sins that day and night she lamented the
> period of her vanities. She likewise afflicted her body, wearing a hair
> shirt for a long time and fasting and keeping vigil with very great
> prayers and tears. When she received communion, she wept with so
> many tears and sighs that she seemed about to burst . . . She did the
> cooking for as long as she could, and she tended the sick and
> performed many demeaning chores; she served the sisters with great
> charity and held herself in such contempt that she seemed to retain
> no memory of her former condition. She even told me that she
> wanted to go mad in order to wreak vengeance on her body for
> having so offended its creator. The Lord granted her wish, so that
> for several years she bore many stinking sores with great patience.

If this story strikes modern readers as tragic, other accounts of self-inflicted misery now appear faintly comical. In *The Play of St Theodora*, composed around 1500 by another Italian nun, Antonia Pulci, two characters quarrel about which of them should be martyred at the hands of a Syrian tyrant. The tyrant helpfully resolves their "pious war" by condemning them both to death.[3]

As Pulci's drama suggests, the prospect of exchanging earthly torments for celestial joys could offer comfort to communities facing violent suppression. This was the case for the early Christians addressed by Paul, and for later generations of believers under the persecuting regimes of Valerian and Diocletian. The same comfort was available to Christian heretics in the Middle Ages, when even orthodox observers remarked that dissenters convicted by the inquisition often went steadfastly to their deaths. Indeed, the normal practice of sparing the lives of heretics who renounced their beliefs meant that those who refused to do so were choosing a painful death in return for the prospect of eternal life. In the sixteenth century, this next-worldly perspective was captured in the hymns of the Anabaptists, the most persecuted religious group of the Reformation era. The Dutch Anabaptist leader Menno Simons probably composed these words around 1540:

> I'd rather chose the sorrow sore,
> And suffer as of God the child,
> Than have from Pharoah all his store,
> To revel in for one brief while.
> The realm of Pharoah cannot last,
> Christ keeps His kingdom sure and fast;
> Around His child His arm He casts.
>
> In this world, ye saints, you'll be defamed,
> Let this be cause for pious glee;
> Christ Jesus too was much disdained;
> Whereby he wrought to set us free;
> He took away of sin the bill
> Held by the foe. Now if you will
> You too may enter heaven still!

Religion involved the constant threat of violent death for Simons and his companions. Protestant and Catholic authorities executed thousands of Anabaptists from the 1520s onwards, and many of those who survived lived in perpetual risk of discovery. Their "pious glee" in the face of such violence was a grim necessity, and probably strengthened their identification with the first generation of suffering Christians. St Paul himself claimed to "take pleasure in infirmities, in reproaches, in necessities, in persecutions" (2 Cor. 13:10). In this way the cycle of torment was self-perpetuating. Persecution confirmed the Anabaptists' perception that they were children of God, and their persistence in this belief inspired their enemies to further acts of intolerance.[4]

This pattern of patient endurance was unsurprising in times of real persecution, but it could also flourish in much less threatening circumstances. Some Anabaptists clung to the ethic of suffering Christianity in the seventeenth and eighteenth centuries, long after the threat of organised suppression had passed. The puritans of seventeenth-century England and America provide a more famous example of Christians feasting on the bread of adversity despite apparent good fortune. The word "puritan" is now synonymous with the denial of pleasure and a censorious attitude towards sex. This is only partly justified. The puritan experience was far more variegated than this caricature suggests, and some Puritans were notably relaxed in their opinions about sexual behaviour, at least within marriage. Nonetheless, the modern view echoes a perception of Puritanism that has always accompanied the movement. The name "puritan" was coined as an insult in the 1560s; its targets were seen as "busy controllers" who condemned the pleasures of others. This perception was based on experience. While there was far more to puritanism than a distrust of earthly enjoyments, puritan writers and preachers did develop a system of belief that presented suffering in a remarkably positive light.[5]

The puritan mentality emerged from the peculiar circumstances of sixteenth-century England. The Protestant religion was imposed from above on a largely unenthusiastic population, and Catholics probably outnumbered Protestants until the last decades of the 1500s. The Protestant clergy were entrusted by the regime with the introduction of reformed Christianity in the regions. The result was a piecemeal series of "parish reformations". These frequently divided communities into a minority of true believers and a much larger group of nominal Protestants, who nonetheless attended the services of the new church as prescribed by law. While this outcome was acceptable to the crown and much of the church hierarchy, it was barely adequate for the devout vanguard of "godly" Christians who wished to see a thorough reformation of the kingdom. By the turn of the century, these "hot gospellers" were frequently in conflict with their less zealous neighbours. To take one arresting example, Hugh Clarke, the puritan vicar of Wolston near Coventry, started wearing a knife in the 1590s to protect himself from parishioners unimpressed by his "powerful and searching" ministry. Personal experiences of this kind were framed in the wider context of national danger. No English Protestant familiar with John Foxe's *Book of Martyrs* could doubt the constant threat to God's people from a host of foreign and domestic enemies: "grievous afflictions and bloody persecutions" had engulfed the kingdom under the Catholic queen Mary Tudor, and fears of an invasion or domestic insurrection to restore the Roman church survived long into the seventeenth century. Thus English puritans felt besieged by hostile forces at home and abroad. In the words of John Gough in 1561, they were "Christ's soldiers living in the camp of the world".[6]

Faced with these circumstances, puritans found comfort and justification in the rich tradition of suffering Christianity. They embraced the world's disdain as a sign of their calling, and this attitude in turn ensured that they met further hostility from their neighbours. Why did people mock them? Because God tested their faith through the malice of worldly men. Why did foreign princes seek to destroy Christ's church? Because the Devil and his allies would rouse themselves horribly as the Last Judgment neared. At a more basic level, the puritans' plight reflected the fate of all God-fearing people in a world drenched in sin: to be "strangers and pilgrims on the earth"

(Heb. 11:13). In the words of the Oxfordshire preacher Robert Harris, the Gospel and the world "can no better agree than light and darkness, fire and water". The small company of the saved would always find troubles in a hostile land. They could not even trust their own minds, since these were perverted by original sin. Puritan catechisms amplified this doctrine. "The will of man", wrote William Perkins in 1597, "only willeth and lusteth after evil". Only the power of God could overcome this inclination: the Lord confronted believers with a knowledge of their sins and the appalling fate they justly deserved, then "stirred up a longing and a lusting after heavenly things, with sighs and groans for God's favour". This process was described luridly by the London pastor Thomas Goodwin, who likened his unre-generate soul to "the filth of a dungeon, where by a clear light and piercing eye I discerned millions of crawling, living things in the midst of that sink of liquid corruption". Such experiences set Christians at odds with the rest of society, since most people continued to wallow in their natural desires. "Because God will not have his children love the world", Richard Sibbes noted sadly in 1634, "he suffers the world to hate them". In a more aggressive vein, the London pastor Samuel Clarke asserted in 1642 that a "war with the world procureth peace with God". This public conflict was inseparable from the inner struggle to overcome sin, since both pitched the Christian against the fallen state of the world.[7]

It was a small step from these beliefs to assert that misery was a necessary experience on the pathway to heaven. John Calvin implied as much in the *Institutes of the Christian Religion* (1536) by denying that believers could "have consolation enough in God unless we have already experienced desolation in ourselves". This view was embraced by William Perkins, perhaps the most influential of all puritan theologians. Perkins claimed that despair in the face of God was a vital step towards true faith. The journals of the lawyer Richard Newdigate indicate the influence of this idea in the first half of the seventeenth century. Newdigate filled a dozen notebooks between 1626 and 1642 with the insights he gleaned from puritan sermons in London and the parishes around his Warwickshire home. In November 1626 he noted that "without repentance we all perish, [and] without weeping and mourning we cannot repent". Mortification was essential to salvation, and "no member of soul or body [can be] mortified without pain". A few weeks later, he recorded the observation of one of his favourite preachers, John Malin, that "none can have a dram of joy without a pound of grief". The same pastor affirmed in 1630 that "the more we wash our souls with tears of repentance the more pure shall they be in the eyes of God". Newdigate was probably comforted by these sentiments. The prayers appended to his notebooks suggest that he meditated darkly on his own sins: he started one typical composition in 1626 by lamenting that he was "miserably crushed and pressed with the weight of my transgressions".[8]

Why would anyone embrace this melancholy creed? For Newdigate and his fellows, the answer lay in the world to come. The threat of Hell provided a negative incentive, since a comfortable life on Earth would probably have a dreadful sequel. The physical torments awaiting the damned were spelt out memorably by Philip Stubbes in 1583:

> Remember we not that there is a God that will judge us righteously? That there is a Devil who shall torment us after this life unspeakably, if we repent not? At that day the wicked shall find that there is a material hell, a place of all kinds of tortures, wherein they shall be punished in fire and brimstone amongst the terrible company of ugglesome devils, world without end, however light they make account of it in this world.

This message rang out in the sermons that Newdigate heard. "If we weep not here", the lawyer noted in 1626, "we shall gnash our teeth hereafter – too late". The horrors of damnation were balanced by the promise of heaven. A few pages later, he noted that God "hath promised us fullness of joy at His right hand for evermore". It appears that the delights of the saved would include an element of *schadenfreude*. It would be a "comfort for the godly", declared a preacher at Nuneaton, to see "their enemies punished by God in his fit time". Alongside these personal inducements, the collective experience of the suffering people of God could be read as a sign of the coming judgment, when those who endured to the end would receive their just reward. The approach of the Last Days was also a recurring theme in Newdigate's notebooks; this was signalled by the dreadful ascendancy of Christ's enemies at home and abroad, but would eventually culminate in their fall.[9]

While the pleasures of the next life would compensate for earthly pains, few people could hold their focus indefinitely on the world to come. Unlike the desert fathers or medieval ascetics, puritans engaged fully with the world around them, and they drew comfort from signs in this life that their hardships would be rewarded. As Newdigate noted optimistically in 1631, "the Lord is a sun and shield, and no good thing shall be withheld from them that live a godly life". This hope was expressed in the idea of providence. In its most positive form, this involved God's daily oversight of His children and occasional interventions to keep them from harm. Such episodes were reported frequently during the English civil war, and were compiled by puritan propagandists to demonstrate the justice of their cause. This tale is typical:

> Since the beginning of these civil wars, forty honest men from Cornwall were condemned to be hanged by . . . Sir Richard Greenville for not assisting him against the parliament; and when they came to be executed, the sixth man broke a new halter [noose],

wherewith he should have been hanged; and after that another, and after that two twisted together, which miracle of God's mercy did so astonish the adversaries that they let him and all the rest depart in safety.

The hand that protected the good could also smite the wicked. God pronounced providential "judgments" against the various enemies of the Gospel, and in the process He often revealed a macabre sense of humour. Blasphemers were struck dumb and drunkards choked to death on their beer. Those unwise enough to swear by the Devil were liable to vanish in the company of a stranger. Such stories provided a warning to sinners and a reassurance to the faithful that the wicked would perish in this world as well as the next. The following event was reported in a parliamentarian newsbook in 1654:

> One [man] hearing perjury condemned by a godly preacher, and how it never escaped unpunished, said in a bravery: "I have often foreswore myself, and yet my right hand is no shorter than my left"; which words he had scarce uttered, when such an inflammation arose in the hand that he was forced to go to the chyrurgion, and cut it off, lest it should have infected his whole body, whereby it became much shorter than the other.

Dramatic tales of this kind served an obvious public purpose. But the private writings of godly Protestants show that the idea of providence held a central role in their daily lives. In 1601 Lady Margaret Hoby recorded her grim satisfaction at the news that a man in her Yorkshire neighbourhood had been severely injured in a fight. "This judgment is worth noting", she wrote, as the man was "exceedingly profane". He had once caused "a horse to be brought into the church of God, and there christening him with a name, which horrible blasphemy the Lord did not leave unrevenged, even in this world, as an example to the others". More positively, Richard Newdigate ended a prayer in 1626 by thanking God for "thy favour in that part of my life I have already enjoyed", and for "protecting me in dangers, preserving me from Satan's tyranny [and] from the malice of my enemies".[10]

The comforts of providence were limited, however. The doctrine assured the faithful that God would supervise earthly affairs according to His will, but it provided no guarantee of His precise intentions. It was abundantly clear that the Lord sometimes allowed his servants to suffer on earth in order to reward them in heaven. This was, perhaps, the fate of the five men hanged in Cornwall before their companions were reprieved by the divine hand. Moreover, God could even intervene *to permit* the earthly suffering of his servants. In 1633 the puritan lawyer William Prynne published a compendious attack on the theatre.

This included a violent condemnation of female actors, which coincided with the appearance of the Queen in a court masque. Prynne was prosecuted for seditious libel and sentenced to have his ears cut off. Four years later, the lawyer was convicted for a second offence after publishing pamphlets against the bishops; this time he was sentenced to have his nose slit, his face branded, and his ears cut off again. Prynne's modern biographer, William Lamont, takes up the problem raised by this punishment:

> How can ears be cut off twice? The reader has to steer between two interpretations here. Prynne's version is that his ears were cut off on the first occasion, and God by a miracle made them grow again. This is not how his opponents saw it. According to them, his ears were only lightly cropped the first time, but Prynne gave the executioner not the customary ten shillings' tip, but only five shillings . . . Alas, the *same* executioner was on call in 1637; as a contemporary noted, "now the hangman was quit with him".

Whichever version we believe, there is no denying that Prynne's story involves a striking appraisal of the purposes of God. Not only did He cause the lawyer to lose his ears once; He restored them miraculously so they could be hacked off again! Such a God could hardly be expected to protect His people from all material dangers. At best, the idea of providence assured its adherents that God would ultimately preserve His servants and punish their enemies. But while they knew this could happen in this world as well as the Hereafter, they also understood that they would have to endure earthly hardship as part of the divine plan.[11]

Ultimately, the only comfort available to puritans was the belief that God was on their side. This belief rested on the twin doctrines of election and assurance. The first held that God had reserved places in Heaven for a community of faithful Christians, or the "elect", from the beginning of time. He would never abandon these people. According to the doctrine of assurance, it was possible for members of the elect to know their own status. In theory at least, the elect could be sure of eternal bliss despite their earthly trials. As William Perkins noted in 1597, the fact that the smallest measure of God's grace was enough to ensure a passage to Heaven was "the very foundation of true comfort unto all troubled and touched consciences". But there was a catch. How could one know that this grace was real? As Perkins noted, "the wickedness of man's nature is such . . . that a man may easily transform himself into the counterfeit and resemblance of any grace of God". This was a deadly deceit. Arthur Hildersam summed up the dilemma starkly in 1629: "as true assurance of God's favour is a comfortable thing, so a false peace and assurance is one of the most grievous judgments that can befall a man". So how could one tell true grace from the "false peace" of the damned? The answer was to look for continual signs of spiritual regeneration, since these indicated the presence of God's favour. One sign was a simmering anxiety about one's true status. According to Hildersam, the truly elect "are often troubled with doubts and fears" about their salvation, while "they that have this false assurance are most confident, and never have any doubts". For Perkins, "to see and feel in ourselves the want of any grace pertaining to salvation, and to be grieved therefore, is the grace itself". Those who belonged in the company of the saved would also display a heartfelt conviction that they were unworthy. They would "renew their repentance" through constant meditation on their sins. Here was a paradox of puritan faith: it held out the comfort of certain knowledge of salvation, but reserved this comfort for those who were convinced they did not deserve it.[12]

Unsurprisingly, the quest for assurance could be a distressing experience. Even while he was preaching to his London congregation in the 1640s, Vavasor Powell was consumed with anxieties about the fate of his own soul:

> I had been about four years in constant doubts and great fears as to my eternal condition, being oftentimes tempted by Satan to destroy myself; and preaching also to others shaking and terrifying doctrines . . . At that time, for a month's space or above, I was very sad, melancholy and much troubled; neglecting to eat, drink or sleep, and this was occasioned principally through the apprehension I had of that distance which I saw between Christ and my soul.

A line in the Gospel of Luke inspired the "shaking and terrifying doctrines" that Powell preached, and captured starkly his fear that the signs of election he detected in himself were false: "Take heed therefore that the light which is in thee be not darkness" (Luke 11:35). In 1653 another puritan preacher, John Rogers, described his despair at the thought of his own damnation. He imagined demons gathered around him and "heard the damned swearing and raving, and saw them (as t'were) roasting, and their frisking and frying in everlasting torments". Modern readers may observe in these experiences not the signs of religious faith, but mental illness. Contemporaries also considered this option. Rogers himself described his condition as an "inward malady". In 1661 the puritan pastor James Nalton attributed a period of agonising doubts about his salvation to "the effect of melancholy". But we should resist the temptation to explain the mental afflictions experienced by puritans in terms of modern psychopathology. For a start, these experiences emerged within an ideology that viewed moments of despair in a positive light. Second, puritans drew the line between a healthy mind and a "depressed" one rather differently to us. It is hard to imagine a self-help book in the twenty-first century offering the advice tendered by William

Perkins in 1597: "Labour to be displeased with thyself . . . and let this practice take such place with thee, that if thou be demanded what in thine estimation is the vilest of the creatures upon earth, thine heart and conscience may answer in a loud voice: 'I, even I, by reason of mine own sins'".[13]

For the men and women who embraced this view of the world, the search for signs of election was like the alchemist's pursuit of the philosopher's stone. They sought an object of inestimable value that could be theirs if only they observed the correct methods. Whatever pains they had to endure, the prize was too wonderful to be abandoned. The onerous quest for the symptoms of God's favour was elaborated into an empirical system in Elizabethan England, but it was in seventeenth-century America that this system was applied with the utmost rigour, providing the basis for an extraordinary social experiment.

NEW WORLDS OF SORROW

The "great migration" of English puritans to America was impelled by a desire to escape the sinful conditions of the old world and create a truly Christian community across the Atlantic ocean. The settlers saw in this mission the fulfilment of a divine plan, and perceived the hand of God in the adventures and setbacks that accompanied it. The voyage itself was a test of faith. As William Bradford observed in his account of the establishment of the Plymouth colony in the 1620s, even the preliminary voyage from England to Holland could involve divine trials and deliverance:

> [They] endured a fearful storm at sea, being fourteen days or more
> before they arrived at their port, in seven whereof they neither saw
> sun, moon, nor stars, and were driven near the coast of Norway; the
> mariners themselves often despairing of life, and once with shrieks
> and cries gave over all, as if the ship had been foundered in the sea
> and they were sinking without recovery. But when man's hope and
> help wholly failed, the Lord's power and mercy appeared in their
> recovery; for the ship rose again and gave the mariners courage again
> to manage her.

Such episodes were signs of divine favour, but they also warned the colonists of their utter dependence on God. In 1629 a terrible storm assailed another ship and then abated, leaving one of its passengers to note ruefully that the Lord "showed us what he could have done with us, if it had pleased him". In the case of individual sinners, divine justice could be swift and grim. Bradford told this story about one of the less pious seafarers who accompanied the pilgrims:

There was a proud and very profane young man, one of the
seamen, of a lusty, able body, which made him the more haughty.
He would always be condemning the poor people in their sickness,
and cursing them daily with grievous execrations; and [would] tell
them that he hoped to help cast half of them overboard before they
came to their journey's end, and to make merry with what they
had . . . But it pleased God before they came half seas over, to smite
this young man with a grievous disease, of which he died in a
desperate manner, and so was himself the first that was thrown
overboard.

For those who survived the journey, judgment tales of this kind became a
staple of colonial life: as well as providing a gory sub-genre of popular
fiction, they supplied preachers with cautionary tales for their flocks. In 1693
Increase Mather described how a "most wicked person" planned to assault
his minister with a knife, but was frustrated when the victim was not at
home. Soon afterwards, the Devil appeared to him "in the shape of that
minister, with a knife in his hand, exhorting self-murder". This punishment
was, as Mather informed his audience, well tailored for the man's particular
sins.[14]

While the threat of personal judgments kept the faithful on their mettle,
the whole community was aware of the special mission with which God had
entrusted them. Like the Jews delivered from Egypt in the book of Exodus,
their calling involved both the special favour of God and afflictions to test and
purify their faith. In the striking phrase of the emigrant pastor Thomas
Shepard, the pilgrims were exposed to "the Lord's wonderful terror and
mercy". This sense was encouraged by the collective nature of the colonists'
experiences, alongside the relatively brief duration of the "great migration"
itself. The main wave of emigration began in 1629 and ended abruptly in
1640. As a consequence, the settlers enjoyed a unique sense of belonging to
a chosen generation, and their achievement was later held up as an exemplar
of Christian trial and fortitude for others to emulate.[15]

The colonists' status as a special people also required them to establish
the model of a God-fearing society, with a closer felicity to divine
commandments than was found elsewhere. This duty was given concrete
expression in law. In 1648 the preface to *The Book of the General Lawes and
Libertyes* of Massachusetts noted that "among other privileges which the
Lord bestowed upon his peculiar people, these he calls them specially to
consider of, that God was nearer to them and their laws were more righteous
than other nations". With this principle in sight, the lawmakers of
Massachusetts imposed harsh penalties on "frivolous" pastimes that
contravened the injunctions of scripture. Gaming and drunkenness were
prohibited, even in properties licensed to serve alcohol. As a special measure

against drinking on the sabbath, constables were authorised to search out offenders "throughout the limits of their towns". Blasphemy and adultery were made capital crimes in accordance with the books of Leviticus and Deuteronomy. Colonial lawyers adopted a similar approach to matters of public dress. Many years after the laws regulating costume had been abolished in England, the Massachusetts general court introduced statutes against gaudy and "immoderate" clothing. Once again, the lawmakers noted the special obligations of a community blessed with God's special protection: it was their duty "to commend unto all sorts of persons the sober and moderate use of those blessings which, beyond expectation, the Lord has been pleased to afford us in this wilderness".[16]

While the peculiar status of the colonists exposed them to purifying hardships and laws, the nature of puritan theology ensured that their spiritual experiences were equally testing. In England, the arduous search for signs of election was confined to a minority of "hot gospellers"; in the colonies of New England it was accepted as the social norm. The clergy led the way. Ephraim Huitt, the pastor of Windsor, Connecticut, was typical in maintaining that doubts about salvation were a necessary "sickness of the soul". This sickness derived from "a blessed uncertainty, arising from the sense of our own unworthiness"; but its eventual outcome was the "recovery of health". His words were echoed by Thomas Hooker, one of the founders of Connecticut: "The word and means of grace do work good if they make thee more sensible of thy hardness and deadness . . . That physic works most kindly that makes the party sick before it works". This message was not lost on the lay community. In a brilliant reconstruction of popular religion in early New England, David Hall has shown how puritan divines influenced ordinary people in their search for assurance of salvation. Richard Eccles, a farmer from Cambridge, Massachusetts, described how "by Mr Perkins' *Exposition of the Creed* I saw my condition [was] bad". A member of the same congregation confessed that some godly sermons had "tended more to his misery than his comfort". When Peter Pratt from Connecticut read Thomas Shepard's *Sincere Convert* (1641), he found the author "so exceedingly searching, that he . . . brought me many a time to my wit's end".[17]

In an unprecedented religious experiment, the New England communities gave the personal torments involved in puritan spirituality an institutional role. The first generation of settlers attempted to build a church composed entirely of "visible saints", whose probable membership of the elect could be demonstrated by the early signs of God's grace. Since these signs included despair in the face of God's judgment, this effectively made a period of misery a requirement for church membership. This had political as well as religious implications. In Massachusetts, only church members were entitled to vote and hold positions in the civil government. This meant that civil rights were theoretically determined by the will of God, and could be acquired only through a sincere demonstration of unhappiness. Another remarkable consequence of this policy was that anyone who aspired to these rights had to display a genuine belief that they did not deserve them, since an over-confident assertion of one's own election indicated a "false peace of mind". In theory at least, only those who felt unworthy of membership were allowed to join. To paraphrase Groucho Marx, no one who belonged in the club felt they ought to be members.

The surviving papers of New England clergy, church elders and candidates for membership shed some light on the practicalities of this extraordinary system. Typically, applicants appear to have delayed their attempt to join the communion until their late twenties, permitting plenty of time for the signs of "saving grace" to be convincingly assessed. When they presented themselves to the congregation, they would offer a testimony of their spiritual progress to date. This normally conformed to the pattern of conversion spelt out by theologians like Perkins and Hildersam: a period of superficial faith, or "false awakening", would be followed by the dreadful realisation of the depths of their corruption; indications of genuine faith would finally appear, accompanied by frightening incursions of doubt about the true condition of their soul. Church members could question the candidate about aspects of their narrative. In 1641, John Cotton summarised some of the questions frequently addressed to candidates in his Boston church: "How it pleased God to work in them, to bring them home to Christ, whether the law hath convinced them of sin, how the Lord hath won them to deny themselves their own righteousness". The intensity of this scrutiny depended largely on the character of the congregation and its minister's scruples. Thomas Hooker complained in the 1640s that some of his flock in Hartford, Connecticut, focused excessively on "niceties" when they examined prospective members. The careful scrutiny of applicants reflected the desire in many congregations to preserve their communion from the "Antichristian remnants" of the outside world. This ideal was also expressed in some of the covenants that new members were asked to endorse. The covenant of Waterford, Massachusetts, for example, affirmed that church members had "through God's mercy escaped out of the pollutions of the world, and been taken into the society of his people".[18]

The religion of New Englanders rested ultimately on the belief that this life was less important than the next. This conviction allowed the faithful to profess a creed that was, in the words of Ephraim Huitt, "a continual warfare, a daily fighting with inward fears and outward troubles". The imminent presence of death and judgment was spelt out in sermons, books of instruction and the elementary reading the colonists prepared for their children. The *New England Primer* (1690) included this child's prayer:

> Tho' I am young yet I may die,
> And hasten to eternity:
> There is a dreadful fiery hell,
> Where wicked ones must always dwell:
> There is a heaven full of joy,
> Where godly ones must always stay:
> To one of these my soul must fly,
> As in a moment when I die.

This pre-eminent fact pressed on every member of the community. For children, the horrors of Hell were combined with the knowledge that they would be eternally separated from their parents if the latter were numbered among the saved; indeed, the parents of the damned would joyfully abandon them on the day of judgment. For adults, the prospect of heavenly bliss or the "racking torments" of Hell invested their quest for signs of grace with understandable urgency. The transitory pleasures of this life were trivial besides the eternal judgments of the next. John Cotton pressed this point home in his *Dialogue Between Christ, Youth and the Devil*, a lively poem attached to his catechism in the *New England Primer*. At one point the youth protests against the rigours of a Christian life, exclaiming that "I cannot find 'tis good for me to set my mind on ways whence many sorrows spring". Christ's rebuke is stinging and final:

> Unto thyself then I'll thee leave,
> That Satan may thee wholly have:
> Thy heart in sin shall harden'd be,
> And blinded in iniquity.
> And then in wrath I'll cut thee down,
> Like of the grass and flowers mown;
> And to thy woe thy shall espy
> Childhood and youth are vanity;
> For all such things I'll make thee know,
> To judgment thou shall come also.
> In hell at last thy soul shall burn,
> When thou thy sinful race hast run.
> Consider this, think on thy end
> Lest God do thee in pieces rend.

Duly enlightened, the youth decides that the burdens of Christianity may be worthwhile after all. But his new resolve is too feeble to overcome his inborn sinfulness, and he is cast prematurely into Hell. For Cotton and his readers the message was stark: the truly elect would embrace the sorrows of a God-fearing life above the temporary pleasures of a "world-loving" existence, and the pains that attended this life were nothing compared to the torments awaiting the damned.[19]

By insisting that earthly pleasures were less important than eternal judgments, the puritan settlers of New England set standards of self-denial that were extremely hard to meet. Many fell short of these ideals, and even those who embraced them zealously were never entirely sure that their commitment would be rewarded. Puritan churchmen and educators were keenly aware that the burdens of religion could be oppressive: this explains their constant attempts to make ordinary churchgoers "think on thy end", and to recall committed believers to the contemplation of "final things". The fact that so many succeeded in practising the godly life says much about the capacity of human minds to accept the afterlife as a concrete and pressing reality. It also reminds us that people in the pre-modern age, when many parents could expect to witness the death of at least one of their children, were more exposed of the fragility of human existence than us. But even in the relatively comfortable context of our own world, it is worth considering the logic of the puritan claim that the "day of death" is more important than the day of birth. It is hard for anyone who believes in an eternal afterlife to dispute this claim; and if the pains of this life are temporary while the rewards of the next are boundless, it is only sensible to exchange one for the other. On the other hand, anyone who doubts the existence of an afterlife must give serious thought to the arguments of the Marquis de Sade: if the only pleasures we can have are those available in this world, should we not devote ourselves to gathering an "ample harvest" of this rare fruit? [20]

9

The Case for Killing Heretics

It is refreshing to read some really bad verse from the "golden age" of English poetry. Here are some lines from Sir Henry Goodyear's celebration of Prince Charles's visit to Madrid to court the Spanish princess Doña María Ana in 1623:

> The Protestant divines that greatest be,
> For number, knowledge, and for sanctity,
> Retain more knowledge than to presume
> So far to say, the present Church of Rome
> Is not part of God's church, or to deny
> A way to heaven to all that therin die.
> They only say that it should be reformed
> Since it is sickly, mangled and deformed.

The heir to a ruined estate in Warwickshire, Goodyear penned this unfortunate work as part of his campaign to ease his financial troubles by obtaining minor positions in the Jacobean court. These efforts were largely unrewarded, and he died amid mounting debts in 1628. Goodyear is mainly remembered today as a close friend of John Donne, whose work he occasionally tried to pass off as his own. But he was also notable for holding apparently far-sighted opinions on religious toleration. Goodyear believed that both Catholics and Protestants were true Christians, and felt that attempts at religious persecution were counter-productive. He spelt this out in thudding couplets:

> Twas never seen that persecution
> In cause of conscience and religion,
> Did ever conduce unto the public peace,
> But did their number and their heat increase.
> It did th'afflicted part the more unite,
> Were their profession wrong, or were it right.

Goodyear's opinions were not unique, but only a minority of his peers shared them. It was much more common to regard religious toleration as crass and dangerous. On at least one occasion, John Donne warned his friend to express his views less freely as they were likely to cause scandal at court. Anti-Catholic sentiments were, if anything, more intense among the English population at large. The occasion for Goodyear's poem was a proposed marriage alliance between the English and Spanish crowns; the collapse of this plan in October 1623 was greeted by celebratory bonfires across the south of England. Even the most zealous Protestant churchmen, who were generally disdainful of the "lukewarmness" of their flocks, acknowledged that hatred of Catholicism was ingrained in "the common sort of Christians". As the puritan pastor Samuel Clarke noted in 1646, "almost every child" in England knew "that Rome is Babylon and the pope is Antichrist".[1]

Such attitudes were not, of course, confined to Stuart England. Religious intolerance was the social and judicial norm throughout western Europe: William Monter has estimated that some 3,000 people were executed for heresy between 1520 and 1565, and many more lost their lives in the religious wars that were fought into the middle years of the seventeenth century. These deaths were a crude measure of the profound conflict between Catholics, Protestants and sectarians in the Reformation era. Protestants had vilified the Roman church since the 1520s: woodcuts portrayed demons sitting astride the gallows to defecate on the bodies of monks, while priests were depicted as cannibals or werewolves devouring the flesh of the faithful. Catholics responded in kind. A bishop claimed in 1563 that Luther was literally the spawn of the Devil, who assumed the shape of a man to seduce his mother, an innkeeper's daughter, "by means of coaxing words and other inducements to sensuality". Propagandists on both sides identified their opponents with criminality, greed, sodomy and witchcraft. These representations often conveyed a theological message, but they were also intended to shock and repel – to make people squirm at the foulness of their confessional enemies. Such negative images probably made a deeper impact on the European population than the more positive efforts at religious education promoted by Catholic and Protestant reformers, and the belief that religious dissenters were simply monstrous "outsiders" informed much of the intolerance of the age. In this respect, the bloodshed of the Reformation provides one further example of the dangers of dehumanising certain groups in the pursuit of a pure society.[2]

But this is only part of the story. It is tempting to view the religious intolerance that was taken for granted in medieval and Renaissance culture in purely negative terms, as no more than the hatred of "out groups" defined by creed. If we do so, however, we risk missing a more profound and challenging truth. There were also *positive* reasons for intolerance. The dehumanising propaganda of the reformers and their opponents emerged from a coherent and defensible worldview. Moreover, the desire to eradicate heresy could be highly principled and was sometimes inspired by compassion. This is a frightening idea. Some people may even find it offensive. It is necessary, therefore, to explain why we should take a sympathetic view of the persecuting mentality. First, there is a tendency among many Christians today to regard the heresy trials and religious conflicts of the past as an aberration from something called "true Christianity". In this view of history, the true spirit of religion was perverted by outside influences that led to its complicity in persecution and war. The liberal impulse behind this idea is admirable, and its practical consequence is a more tolerant society, but as an interpretation of the past it is deeply flawed. Far from being an aberration, intolerance was integral to medieval and Renaissance Christianity. It was a sincere expression of faith. When John Donne warned Henry Goodyear not to express his views on toleration so candidly, he was concerned that his friend might be accused of religious "indifferency". This was a common contemporary definition of "atheism".[3] The desire to defeat heresy was central to the Christian worldview for at least 600 years: if we ignore this fact, we risk dismissing as "false Christians" all the major figures in the church from the time of Charlemagne to the Enlightenment. We also avoid asking hard questions about why, exactly, intolerance should no longer be an essential part of Christianity. The men who ran the inquisition were sincere Christians. Those who wish to be sincere Christians today should have a clear idea why an inquisition is no longer needed.

The second reason for understanding the case for religious intolerance is political. The rise of religious fundamentalism, in both its Christian and Islamic forms, is a striking feature of our own time. In some cases fundamentalism has involved an aggressive rejection of western society, often aligned to political demands: groups like al-Qaeda and the US Christian militia movement are explosive examples. It is common for people outside these groups to describe their members as "fanatical", "bigoted" or "evil". Their behaviour is often explained in terms of "brainwashing". The psychologist Roy Baumeister has argued that these labels are emotionally satisfying because they provide an explanation for the behaviour of frightening outsiders that re-affirms our own goodness and rationality. But these labels are also unhelpful. By using them, we present intolerant people in wholly negative terms that that we would never apply to ourselves. As a result, we avoid any real understanding of their motives. The alternative approach is far riskier, but ultimately more rewarding: to try to understand why rational, well-intentioned people who have *not* been brainwashed might subscribe to the goals of these organisations. This is, of course, an undertaking far beyond the scope of this chapter. But we can at least take one positive step by appreciating that religious intolerance is sometimes based on sincere and defensible principles. A sympathetic knowledge of the history of western Christianity should make this abundantly clear.[4]

What, then, was the positive case for religious intolerance in pre-industrial Europe? The desire to eliminate heresy was based on three fundamental concerns: the need to preserve and defend true religion, the fate of the human soul after death, and the will of God. These concerns were, of course, developed and expressed in many different contexts over the centuries in which they dominated western thinking, and only the essential threads of the arguments can be considered here. We can begin by addressing the premise that underscored the whole ideal of intolerance: the existence of a "true church" whose teachings and practices were essential to salvation.[5]

THE SCIENCE OF EVERLASTING LIFE

It was the unquestioned assumption of most medieval and Renaissance thinkers that one true church existed in the world. This belief was implicit in the authoritative creeds of Christianity: it was spelt out succinctly in the affirmation of the Nicene creed that "we believe . . . in one holy Catholic and apostolic church". Much flowed from this idea. The teachings and sacraments of the church offered the faithful a way to salvation; this was, after all, the promise of scripture and the *raison d'être* of Christianity. But if there was only one church, it followed that salvation was possible only within the doctrinal and institutional framework of that church. Its enemies posed a threat to salvation and this threat had to be faced in some way. At first this reasoning may seem naive, but one needs only to accept its basic assumption for the argument to become compelling.

A modern analogy may be useful. Today it is widely assumed that there are "laws of nature" which govern physical phenomena. Only a relatively small number of people understand these laws at a sophisticated level, but very few would deny that they exist. It would seem ridiculous to most westerners to suggest that these laws are inconsistent: that the rules of geometry might change from day to day, or that water might occasionally flow uphill. Even professional scientists engaged in areas where the normal rules do not seem to apply – such as quantum mechanics – assume that there must be an underlying unity that is not yet fully understood. This is the fabled "theory of everything". The belief underpinning this view is that nature can work in only one way. Religion was understood in a similar fashion in medieval and Renaissance Europe. Through the diligent study of God's revelation, it was possible to map out the path to salvation. This could be done because the laws of God were constant and unified, just like the principles of nature. There was, of course, a correct way to understand these laws, and there were many ways to get them wrong. In modern societies, the correct knowledge of natural laws is believed to confer material benefits: effective medicine is one obvious example. Material advantages also flowed from the correct understanding of religion in the pre-industrial world, but the benefits of this knowledge also extended to the fate of the soul after death. Today we believe that poorly trained or misinformed doctors are a threat to physical health; in the sixteenth century, the threat posed by false doctors of religion was immeasurably worse. In the memorable phrase of the Elizabethan divine William Perkins, theology was "the science of living blessedly forever".[6]

Since there was only one correct version of this science, the religious disputes of the medieval and Renaissance period centred on the identity of the "true church". Very few people argued that true religion could be found in more than one set of practices and beliefs, just as few people today assume that every description of the natural world is accurate. The earliest heretics in western Europe presented themselves as the only authentic Christians. The twelfth-century Cathar movement in Italy and southern France established its own priesthood and bishops. In the eyes of its leaders, the Cathar community was emphatically separate from the counterfeit church of Rome, which belonged to the Devil. Later heretical groups like the French Waldensians, the English Lollards and the Hussites of Bohemia were equally convinced that they were the sole custodians of Christianity. The Protestant reformers of the sixteenth century took the same view. When Martin Luther reflected on the state of religion in Europe and the wider world, he concluded that true knowledge of God existed in only one tiny part of the earth: "If we make an account, we shall find that we have the Gospel now only in a corner. Asia and Africa have it not, the Gospel is not preached in Europe, in Greece, Italy, Hungary, Spain, France, England, or in Poland." Only the "little corner" of Saxony really understood God's word. This verdict was shocking, but it was not short-sighted or absurd. To return to the analogy with science, Copernicus and Galileo believed that their particular understanding of the movement of planets was the only interpretation that was possible; they also assumed that most of their contemporaries held false beliefs about the physical world. For Luther and the great majority of his educated peers, it was obvious that the laws of God were as unified and consistent as the laws that governed planetary motion. If only one person in the world understood these laws, their interpretation would still be the only accurate account that was possible.[7]

The experience of the sixteenth-century Anabaptists illustrates the prevalence of such thinking. The Anabaptist movement originated in Zurich during the 1520s, and established communities in central Europe, Germany and the Netherlands by the middle years of the century. Unlike the mainstream Protestant churches, the members of this group never enjoyed the protection of political elites; consequently, they suffered intensely at the hands of both Catholic and Protestant governments. Some 2,000 Anabaptists were executed for heresy across Europe between 1520 and 1565. More than any other religious faction in the period, the Anabaptists would have benefited from the idea that the path to salvation could be found in more than one set of beliefs. Nonetheless, the leaders of the movement accepted the plain fact that this notion was absurd. The firm conviction that Anabaptism was the one true church was set out in the statement of faith agreed by the "Swiss brethren" in 1527. If anything, this document went further than most Protestant and Catholic texts in asserting the danger posed by alternative creeds:

> Since all who do not walk in the obedience of faith, and have not united themselves with God so that they wish to do his will, are a great abomination before God, it is not possible for anything to grow or issue from them except abominable things. For truly all creatures are in but two classes, good and bad, believing and unbelieving, darkness and light, the world and those [who have] come out of the world, God's temple and idols, Christ and Belial; and none can have part with the other.

Anabaptists confirmed the validity of their church – and the falsehood of all others – by the act of adult baptism. This voluntary act implied that men and women were free to choose their own religion, but it did not mean that all such choices were correct. Rather, baptism marked the separation of the faithful from the fake creeds that dominated the world, and rescued them from the divine punishment that awaited those who chose to remain outside the church.[8]

The fact that Anabaptists held these views does not, of course, detract from the great courage they showed in the face of terrible persecution. It does, however, suggest that even the most oppressed religious groups in the pre-industrial age shared with their enemies the conviction that there was only one path to salvation. This truth raised a profound question for all Christians: how should those within the church treat those outside it? The Anabaptists' answer was to withdraw peacefully from the damned world that surrounded them; but other, less passive solutions were also possible. There was a moral case for the active suppression of heresy.

SPIRITUAL PESTILENCE AND THE WRATH OF GOD

On a December day in 1022, ten defrocked churchmen were led to the stake in the town of Orléans. One witness observed that they went steadfastly to their fate: they laughed as they were strapped to the pyre and boasted that the flames would leave their bodies unconsumed. According to the same source, "they were promptly reduced to ashes so completely that not a trace of their bones was found". This immolation was the climax of the first heresy trial in western Europe for which detailed records have survived. These records provide a fair account of the proceedings against the accused men, and occasionally allow their voices to be heard. When the bishop of Beauvais asked them to acknowledge the truth of the virgin birth, they offered instead an eloquent repudiation of the doctrinal claims of the church:

> You may spin stories in that way to those who have earthly wisdom
> and believe the fictions of carnal men, scribbled on animal skins. To
> us, however, who have the law written upon the heart by the Holy
> Spirit (and we recognize nothing but what we have learned from God,
> creator of all), in vain you spin out superfluities and things
> inconsistent with the divinity. Therefore, make an end and do
> whatever you wish with us. For we shall see our king in heaven, who
> will raise us in heavenly joys to everlasting triumphs at his right hand.

This early trial contained elements that were repeated in countless subsequent proceedings. The accused were subjected to strenuous efforts to convert them to an orthodox position, and they in turn asserted the correctness of their own views. It was this defiance that ensured their deaths: according to one account of the case, two other members of the group "recovered their senses" and were spared. The episode also provided an early instance of the readiness of orthodox churchmen to identify heresy with Satan. One report depicted the condemned men as necromancers, who summoned and adored the Devil "first as an Ethiopian, then as an angel of light, who daily brought them much money". The link between heresy and the Devil would later contribute to the emergence of Renaissance theories of witchcraft. For most of the Middle Ages, however, the idea of demonic intervention simply provided a plausible explanation for the appearance of false beliefs.[9]

The incident at Orléans also illustrated one of the central concerns of the authorities that dealt with heresy. They believed it killed souls. This idea followed logically from the knowledge that there was only one church: since the church existed to redeem souls, those who abandoned it were probably destined for Hell. In his account of the trial in 1022, Paul of Chartres noted that "an abode in hell with the devil was already waiting" for the condemned men. St Bernard of Clairvaux made a similar point in 1145 during another outbreak of heresy at Le Mans:

> Souls everywhere are snatched away to the dread tribunal, alas,
> unreconciled by penance, unfortified by Holy Communion. So long
> as the grace of baptism is denied them, the life of Christ is barred to

the children of Christians, nor are they allowed to draw near to salvation, although the saviour tenderly calls them, saying, "Suffer little children to come to me".

In the middle years of the thirteenth century, Yves of Narbonne described the deadly effects of heresy in northern Italy: through their missions to public fairs and noble households, Cathar preachers were "collecting a treasure of souls for Antichrist". In the same period, St Thomas Aquinas spelt out the implications of this idea for the punishment of the crime:

> It is a much more serious matter to corrupt faith, through which comes the soul's life, than to forge money, through which temporal life is supported. Hence if forgers of money or other malefactors are justly put to death by secular princes, with much more justice can heretics, immediately upon conviction, be not only excommunicated but also put to death.

This sentence was reserved for those heretics who refused to recant, or were reconciled briefly to the church before relapsing into false beliefs. In such cases, Aquinas noted, the execution of offenders was essential for "the safety of others". The belief that heresy constituted soul murder survived into the sixteenth century. In 1584 the English pastor George Gifford captured the moral force of this argument in a single question: "Who is the worst murderer? He who murders the body or he who murders the soul?"[10]

The pious desire to retrieve souls from damnation could, of course, conceal more worldly motives for suppressing dissent, but it would be unduly cynical to assume that this was normally the case. It appears that the first aim of those dealing with heretics was to reclaim them for the church. Accounts of early trials record the lengthy attempts that were made to convert dissenters from their errors, and later manuals of the Dominican inquisition identify this as the tribunal's primary goal. Around 1133, Peter the Venerable, the abbot of Cluny, noted that "Christian charity should put the greater effort on converting heretics than on driving them out". To this end, he argued, "let authority [of the scriptures] be cited to them, let reason be added, so that they may be compelled to yield – to authority if they choose to remain Christians, to reason if they choose to remain men". This point was amplified by Aquinas, who stressed that heretics should be "received by the church to penance, by means of which salvation is opened up to them". If they were sincerely converted, even formerly heretical clergy could be readmitted to their posts.[11]

The threat posed by false beliefs was magnified by their ability to reproduce themselves. Once an error was established, it could spread with alarming speed through whole communities. In the mid-thirteenth century, Stephen of Bourbon described how the heresy of the Waldensians was transmitted from house to house and village to village; its followers were "most hostile, infectious, and dangerous heretics, who wander everywhere". Stephen's remark illustrates one common way of representing heresy in the Middle Ages: as a kind of contagious disease that destroyed souls. The unorthodox beliefs discovered at Orléans in 1022 were described as a "pest" lurking in the kingdom of France. An early twelfth-century chronicle presented the philosophy of a false preacher at Le Mans as a plague that "entered the ears" to consume the body and spirit. "Like a potent poison, it penetrated to the inner organs [and] vented an inexorable hatred on life". Even when the preacher was expelled from the town, he continued to "spread infection by his poisonous breath". A few years later, Peter the Venerable called heresy "a serious pestilence [that] has slain many people and infected more". The capacity of false beliefs to spread by word of mouth ensured that the idea of infection continued to colour discussions of heresy for centuries. During the Reformation, Catholic and Protestant writers depicted false religion as a kind of spiritual cancer. Writing in 1628, the Oxford theologian John Doughtie warned that false beliefs "creep from man to man, until they have corrupted the church throughout". In the wake of the English civil war, the Presbyterian divine Thomas Edwards likened the spread of religious sects to the progress of gangrene.[12]

We can best understand the moral case for religious persecution by reflecting on the belief that heresy was like a disease. In common with the most serious viruses recognised by modern science, it had the capacity to kill individuals, and could contaminate large communities through face-to-face contact. Unlike any virus, however, it killed the eternal soul rather than the physical body, making it a more terrible threat than anything faced by modern medicine. From the earliest documented outbreak in 1022, the institutions that confronted this menace sought to cure individuals who carried the contagion. They did so by trying to convert them to "true religion", a process that would heal their souls and prevent them from infecting others. But at this point they faced a dilemma: many of the people who carried the disease did not want to be cured. Rather, in the words of Peter the Venerable, they wished to offer "the cup of death" to others in order to make them "their peers in misery". What was the right thing to do in such cases? The nearest modern equivalent is a person who refuses treatment for a lethal and contagious disease and expresses a desire to spread their infection as widely as possible. There are few readers, I suspect, who would object to the incarceration of such a person. From the perspective of orthodox churchmen in medieval and Renaissance Europe, the situation was considerably worse: it was *normal* for heretics to resist treatment for their condition, and some even pretended to be cured in order to spread the disease. Since the death penalty was the only sentence available for serious crimes in this period, the moral argument for executing unrepentant heretics was compelling.[13]

The implications of treating heresy as an infectious disease were crystallised in the work of Ephraim Pagitt, a London pastor during the English civil war. Pagitt's *Heresiography* (1645) was a pointed attack on the de-facto toleration of religious sects in the capital during the conflict. Addressing his argument to the city's magistrates, he developed a telling analogy with their response to earlier outbreaks of bubonic plague:

> [I have] seen your great care and provision to keep the city from infection, in the shutting up [of] the sick, and in carrying them to your pest-houses, [and] in making of fires and perfuming the streets . . . The plague of heresy is greater, and you are now in more danger than when you buried five thousand a week. [Yet] you have power to keep these heretics and sectarians from . . . schooling together to infect one another.

Pagitt increased the moral force of his argument by reminding his audience of the peculiar qualities of the "plague of heresy". Unlike other kinds of pestilence, its carriers deliberately set out to disseminate the infection, and its effects, of course, were deadlier than any physical disease. It was imperative, therefore, to deal more vigorously with "the sectarian cancer" than with other types of contagion. These considerations led Pagitt to demand the severest penalties for the leaders of the city's sectarian congregations: "If such [persons] as poison waters and fountains at which men and beasts drink deserve capital punishment, how much more they that . . . go about to poison men's souls?" The same argument was advanced two years later in an anonymous pamphlet on the verse in the Song of Solomon describing the "little foxes" that destroy God's vine (Song 2:15). The author warned that heresy was "like the plague of pestilence", and would infest "the whole city and kingdom" if its progress was not quickly arrested.[14]

These arguments were frightening – and in practice they were impossible to implement – but their logic and moral force were hard to deny. The analogy with infectious disease allowed Pagitt and others to stress the humanitarian and altruistic reasons for the suppression of heresy: many souls could be saved by restricting the spread of false beliefs, and thousands would be lost if magistrates stood selfishly by. This appeal belonged to a tradition of arguments for intolerance based on the spiritual welfare of humankind. But there was another, parallel tradition that held equal weight: the belief that persecution expressed the will of God.

Despite the ecumenical statements occasionally ascribed to Jesus in the New Testament, the Bible contains much material that enjoins religious intolerance. The second Psalm, for example, instructs rulers to suppress false religion in the most violent and unequivocal terms:

> Ask of me, and I shall give thee the heathen for thine inheritance,
> and the uttermost parts of the earth for thy possession. Thou shalt
> break them with a rod of iron; thou shalt dash them in pieces like a
> potter's vessel. Be wise now, therefore, O ye kings; be instructed, ye
> judges of the earth.
>
> (Ps. 2:8–10)

This message is reiterated in Psalm 105, which affirms that God gave his
people "the lands of the heathen . . . that they might observe his statutes, and
keep his laws". (Ps. 105:44–5). The Old Testament also provides examples
of godly rulers such as Darius and Nebuchadnezzar who imposed the
worship of God on their populations, and dealt harshly with those who
deviated from the faith. These examples had particular resonance in the
Christian culture of medieval and Renaissance Europe, since they offered the
clearest model in scripture for the principles of earthly government. The
dangers of heresy and schism were amplified in the New Testament, where
Jesus warned against "false prophets" and asserted that "he who is not with
me is against me" (Matt. 20:30). In response to the threat of schismatic
doctrines, St Paul instructed Titus to reproach and abandon those who erred
from the true faith (Titus 3:10–11). The New Testament also warned that
"false teachers" would assail the church as the Last Judgment approached.
They would speak "perverse things to draw away disciples after them", as
Jesus revealed to his disciples (Acts 20:29–30). Likewise, Paul's epistle to
Timothy predicts that "in the latter times some shall depart from the faith,
giving heed to seducing spirits and doctrines of devils" (1 Tim. 4:1).
Christian magistrates were obliged to defend the church from these wicked
teachers who, as Jesus warned, "would come to you in sheep's clothing, but
inwardly they are ravening wolves" (Matt. 7:15).

Thus medieval and Renaissance churchmen found compelling evidence in
scripture that God abhorred heresy and desired its suppression. They could
read the same lesson in the history of the early church and the work of its
greatest theologians. Medieval scholars cited the prophecy of Isaiah that
kings would be "nursing fathers" of the church (Isa. 49:23), and assumed that
this prophecy had been fulfilled with the conversion of the Roman Empire
in the fourth century. Subsequently, they pointed out that Christian emperors
had gloriously extended God's kingdom through the enforcement of true
religion. They also found in St Augustine a powerful advocate for the coercive
role of the state. The Church Father had argued in the early fifth century that
it was the duty of God-fearing rulers to compel their subjects to receive true
doctrines. Pope Innocent III enjoined this duty forcefully in 1209, when he
declared a crusade against the Cathar movement in southern France. Later
in the thirteenth century, St Thomas Aquinas argued that Christians were
obliged to strive towards the extirpation of false beliefs. It is likely that most

orthodox churchmen in the late Middle Ages regarded intolerance as a sign of their obedience to God, whose will was expressed clearly in scripture, church history and patristic texts. This attitude persisted in the sixteenth and seventeenth centuries, when the idea of toleration was often equated with religious indifference. Thus Thomas Edwards lamented in 1646 that "our father, our saviour and blessed spirit are wounded by damnable heresies", while the English parliament lacked sufficient zeal to suppress them. He observed darkly that this lax attitude was "the most provoking sin against God that ever parliament was guilty of in this kingdom".[15]

Edwards' talk of "provoking sins" affirmed an important consequence of the view that heresy was offensive to God: the fear that He would punish nations for the sins committed by "false brethren", and for the failure of their rulers to prevent them. In his second epistle to Peter, St Paul warned that "false teachers" would rise up to "bring in damnable heresies, even denying the Lord that bought them [salvation], and bring upon themselves swift destruction". He then listed examples of God's just retribution against the ungodly, such as the smashing of Sodom and Gomorrah (2 Pet. 2:1–6). This warning was not lost on orthodox divines in the Middle Ages. In 1214, for example, Yves of Narbonne explained the atrocities committed by Mongol invaders of Europe as divine punishment for the flourishing of heresy, for which "God has become a hostile destroyer and a terrible avenger". Such thinking was still common in the sixteenth and seventeenth centuries. When floods engulfed the English Midlands in 1647, the Coventry pastor John Bryan observed that "extraordinary public judgements do . . . point out some common sin in a nation that is notorious and unpunished". He suggested that lack of church discipline, and a consequent plague of blasphemy and falsehood, was the cause "of God's raining thus his wrath upon us". In this view, the repression of heresy by God-fearing magistrates was essential to please God and placate his just wrath against the community as a whole.[16]

This argument for the legal restraint of heresy was particularly important to Protestants after the Reformation, since it emphasised the majesty and judgment of God. In the late sixteenth century, the work of the English theologian William Perkins illustrated the consistent application of a theory of intolerance based on these principles. Perkins also showed how a desire for compassion could exist alongside a rigid understanding of the need to restrict religious freedom, and to fight those who appeared to be the enemies of God.

THE COMPASSIONATE PERSECUTOR

William Perkins was perhaps the most influential English theologian of the Elizabethan age, and one of the few to achieve an international reputation. The extensive translation of his published works led Thomas Fuller to note in 1642 that they "spoke more languages than their maker ever understood". One current that flowed through his writings was the nature of the law and its application in practical contexts. Perkins distinguished between divine law, which was revealed in scripture, and the "laws of man", which were needed to keep order in human communities. The latter, he insisted, should be tempered with "Christian moderation". Take the case of a young thief:

> Now suppose a young boy – pinched with hunger, cold and
> poverty – steals meat, apparel and other things for relief, being
> pressed to it by want and not having knowledge or grace to use better
> means. To put this person to death for this fact is the extremity of
> the law . . . The equity or moderation, I say, in this case is not to
> inflict death . . . but to determine a punishment less than death, yet
> such a one as shall be sufficient to reform the party for his sin.

Such moderation was essential for justice, as it mitigated the "general corruption of man's nature, which is always ready to deal too hardly with other men, as also too mildly with themselves". It was permissible to soften the penalty for theft in this way because it was a human creation, and the demands of Christian charity meant that it should be applied with compassion. Perkins suggested that Christians should not insist on the enforcement of their own rights over others in the higher interest of the "maintenance of peace and love amongst them". There was, however, a crucial exception to this rule:

> In the practice of this duty, one caution only must be remembered:
> namely, that we must distinguish between another's right and our
> own . . . This caution holds especially when the cause is not ours but
> God's, or his church's; for when it is such a truth which directly
> concerneth the honour of God or the good of his church, then must
> a man take heed that he yield not without warrant from God's word.
> For as it is equity often to yield thy right, so to yield in God's causes
> is to betray the truth.

In Perkins' view, people should normally surrender their own rights over others in the name of "Christian moderation", but they should never give way in matters that touched on the rights of the Lord.[17]

This principle precluded any relaxation in the international struggle against the Roman church, and justified the strict application of England's anti-Catholic laws. In *A Reformed Catholicke* (1597), Perkins asserted that alternative policies would betray the Gospel, which obliged Christians to join "ourselves always to the true church of God". Acts of reconciliation – even marriages between Protestants and Catholics – would surely invite divine chastisement: Christians should "eschew all the sins of the church of Rome, that they withal may escape her deserved plagues and punishments". The same reasoning applied to Anabaptists and other separatist groups. The nation was bound by the Lord to enforce laws against heresy, just as Israel had once been bound to protect the true faith from its enemies. This perspective led Perkins to extend the death penalty beyond Catholic priests and unrepentant sectarians to anyone who promoted idolatry. As he reminded his readers, this was expressly commanded in the book of Deuteronomy, which demanded the execution of those who "hath sought to thrust thee away from the Lord thy God" (Deut. 13:6–10).[18]

Perkins' standpoint produced some intriguing results. By stressing the priority of divine law over human interests, he contributed to the emergence of a Protestant theory of passive resistance. There were circumstances, his work implied, in which God's children might have to disobey princes who asked them to break God's laws. His view of Catholicism also appeared to set limits on the power of the crown. While Elizabethan England was at war with Spain, it was fairly unproblematic to state that a "league of amity . . . may not be made with those that be enemies of God"; but such claims would later rebound against the pro-Spanish foreign policy of the Stuart monarchs. Perhaps most strikingly, Perkins' insistence that crimes against God were more serious than crimes against human goods allowed him to combine severity with compassion. The theology that demanded the death penalty for idolaters also commended the lenient treatment of adolescent thieves.[19]

PRINCIPLES AND PERSECUTION

As Perkins developed his theory of intolerance in the 1590s, Europe was convulsed by religious conflicts of unprecedented violence. In France, a series of regencies and weak monarchs, combined with ruthless dynastic rivalries, had set the scene for civil wars between Catholics and Protestants for the best part of fifty years. Catholic Spain was at war with England and the rebellious subjects of the Netherlands, who were themselves divided into feuding religious camps. Paradoxically, these confessional wars encouraged the gradual emergence of arguments for toleration. In 1579, the Catholic Philip du Plessis-Mornay set out the pragmatic case for co-existence between the two parties in the Netherlands:

> I would like to ask those who oppose the existence of two religions in this country how they intend to get rid of one of them. Obviously by this, I mean the one which they think is the weakest. Clearly, you cannot eliminate religious practice without force and civil war . . . If

we set about destroying the Protestants we will destroy ourselves just
like the French did. It should be obvious that it is better to live
peacefully with them rather than to destroy ourselves by a civil strife
and a dangerous, disastrous, long and difficult, or rather a never-
ending, hopeless war.

These sentiments were echoed by Catholic *politiques* in France, who sought
a provisional accommodation with the Protestant minority in order to
preserve the kingdom. An uneasy settlement was finally achieved in 1598,
when the crown guaranteed the protection of autonomous Protestant regions.
While the arguments of du Plessis–Mornay and the *politiques* were essentially
practical, more principled theories of toleration began to circulate in the later
years of the Reformation. The Polish rationalist John Crell broke decisively
with the tradition that religious pluralism challenged the will of God, and
lauded the pacific ministry of Christ over the vengeful Lord of the Old
Testament. First published in Amsterdam in the 1630s, Crell's work was
translated into several European languages, appearing in English in 1646 as
A Learned and Exceeding Well Compiled Vindication of Liberty in Religion. A
year later, the anonymous author of a tolerationist pamphlet argued that
coercion actually set back the cause of faith: "Human violence may make men
counterfeit but cannot make them believe, and is good for nothing but to
breed form without and atheism within". For the proponents of this new
approach, the intolerance of the Renaissance churches proved they had
departed from the principles of early Christianity, and provided compelling
evidence that the world had entered the reign of Antichrist.[20]

The arguments of John Crell and many other advocates of religious
pluralism were idealistic. They were motivated by a sincere desire to advance
the cause of religion and the welfare of human communities. It is easy to
acknowledge this truth, since the ideal of religious toleration is now widely
accepted in our own culture. For the same reason, however, it is hard to see
that many of their opponents were equally idealistic. It is tempting instead to
assume that the case against pluralism was inspired by grubby politics or self-
interest. But from a Renaissance perspective, the same could be said of some
arguments for toleration. The views of du Plessis–Mornay and the French
politiques appeared shockingly cynical to many contemporaries: for purists like
William Perkins, they demonstrated an unprincipled elevation of political
concerns over Christian duty, and betrayed a casual willingness to condemn
souls to Hell. The theology of persecution is no longer tenable for most
western Christians, but this does not mean that its proponents were insincere.
Nor does it mean that their reasoning was flawed. They assumed that religion
required the maintenance of certain beliefs or practices – either to please God
or to obtain salvation. Religious toleration implied that it was possible to
please God or be saved through a wider range of beliefs; correspondingly, the

specific claims of any particular creed became less important. In so far as religion involved pleasing God or saving souls, more toleration meant less religion; complete toleration meant no religion at all. This view was summed up tartly by the English pastor Matthew Newcomen, who observed that "he that admits contrary religions believes neither of them". For any Christian who holds that beliefs are important to the fate of the soul, the problems raised by this argument are still relevant today.[21]

Like the participants in any human endeavour, those who implemented the laws against heresy and fought the religious wars of the sixteenth century were probably inspired by a wide range of motivations, from personal greed to the most sincere faith. But the more idealistic among them believed they were serving God's will and freeing souls from Hell. Their cause was more important than life and death: it touched on *eternal* life and death. Today it is generally accepted that some causes are sufficiently important to promote or defend with military force, even when this involves the loss of human life. These causes include abstract principles like "democracy", "human rights" and "self-determination". For those who participated in the religious conflicts of the pre-modern age, the issues at stake were inestimably greater. We should not be surprised that they were prepared to kill for them.

10

Conclusion

"The Edge of Wonder"

St Augustine believed that every day was an astonishing work of God. The ascent of the sun was a breathtaking act of creation, and the existence of life was a wonder that should rightly inspire feelings of awe. Surrounded by these marvels, men and women could be expected to gaze in grateful amazement at the world around them. But this was not the case. Instead, people tended to take the daily manifestations of God's glory for granted. The sun rose every day, so they forgot how astounding it was that the earth was illuminated at all. Only the sight of new marvels could rouse them from this comfortable inattentiveness. "If they happen to become acquainted with the diamond", the saint wrote, "they are indeed for a time filled with amazement at something unfamiliar; but daily familiarity gradually blunts the edge of wonder". In a land filled with precious stones, even diamonds would go unnoticed. The world, of course, was replete with marvellous things, but people saw them so often they did not marvel at all.[1]

Augustine was making a point about perspective. Routine exposure to things tends to make them unremarkable, even when they are truly astounding. Modern researchers into human consciousness could say much the same thing: there is nothing more stupefying than the fact of self-awareness, yet this fact is so close to our daily experience that we hardly give it a thought. Augustine proposed his own solution to this problem. He suggested that we open our minds to the "daily miracles" of creation by trying to contemplate the world from a fresh perspective. This was one of the aims of monasticism. To help us along, he added, God occasionally performed miracles to shake off our cosy familiarity and remind us of His power. By interrupting the "ordinary course of nature" from time to time, He forced us to look at more commonplace marvels with renewed awe. The study of alien belief systems can have a similar effect. By challenging our familiar way of seeing things, the ideas of other cultures can jolt us into a fresh perspective on the things we take for granted.

The study of "strange histories" can provide this fresh perspective. If rational people in the past could believe in demonically possessed apples, and execute pigs, witches and heretics, then rational people today should consider the potential "strangeness" of their own ideas. To put it another way, will people in the future find our beliefs as ridiculous as the ideas of witch-finders now seem to us? This shift in perspective has some fascinating implications. First, it draws attention to the process by which all people – including us – make sense of things around them. Clifford Geertz has made this point in the context of anthropology, where the study of "exotic" belief systems has produced the same effect. "If we look at the views of people who draw conclusions very different from our own by the mere living of their lives", he suggests, "we will rather quickly become aware that common sense is both a more problematic and a more profound affair than it seems from the perspective of a Parisian café or an Oxford Common Room".[2] The everyday use of "common sense", it turns out, is a complicated business involving a great deal of prior assumptions. These assumptions derive largely from beliefs that existed before we were born, and are communicated to us by other people.

This leads to another implication of apparently strange beliefs. If culture plays a major role in our understanding of the world, perhaps we should be cautious about things that seem self-evidently true. After all, the existence of witches was obvious to educated people in the sixteenth century. It appears that obviousness is not the same as truth. St Thomas Aquinas made this point in 1259. "Custom", he wrote, "especially that which dates from childhood, takes on the force of nature, and as a result the things with which the mind has been imbued from childhood take such firm root that it is as if they were naturally known of themselves". Ironically, Thomas wrote this to justify his attempt to prove the existence of God. One objection to this project was that it was pointless: it was simply self-evident to Thomas's contemporaries that God existed, so there was no need for a careful argument to prove it. For Aquinas however, it was not enough to accept things because they were taken for granted. The fact that the existence of God is no longer self-evident to many people in the twenty-first century bears out his insight. The things that were taken for granted in thirteenth-century Italy are no longer obvious to us.[3]

If this thought is unsettling, one further implication of the strange past is rather more reassuring. It reminds us that we are part of history. Just as the study of unfamiliar cultures has shown anthropologists that "we are all natives", so the exploration of vanished belief systems indicates that all of us live against the backcloth of the past. Our beliefs, like everything else in our society, have developed over time. While they may appear to be fixed and certain now, they reach us at a particular point in their development, and often result from arguments that were settled long before we were born. As the historian Quentin Skinner has observed, "the past is a repository of values we no longer endorse, of questions we no longer ask". By revisiting these forgotten questions, we can gain a better understanding of our present ideas. We may even revise them in the light of long-hidden alternatives. As Skinner goes on, the historian can act "as a kind of archaeologist, bringing buried intellectual treasure back to the surface, dusting it down, and enabling us to reconsider what we think of it". It would take another book to explore fully the value of these fresh perspectives. But this chapter can at least touch on some of the more interesting consequences of seeing the "strangeness" of our world.[4]

SEEING AND BELIEVING

"It is astonishing", wrote Henri Boguet in 1602, "that there should still be found today people who do not believe that there are witches". If we accept that Boguet was a well-intentioned man with a rational mind, we are forced to examine the intellectual process by which he arrived at this statement. How exactly did he come to believe such a thing? We would not ask the same question about other things he might have said. If you substitute the word "murderers" for "witches", the problem seems to disappear. Katharine Hodgkin has noted that to "study witchcraft is to study something we do not believe in"; and since we do not believe in witches, we need to explain how anyone else could. On the other hand, there is nothing mysterious about believing in murder. Boguet, however, probably believed in witches for the same reasons that most of us believe in murder: the crime was theoretically possible, its existence was testified by respected sources, and it was occasionally reported in his community. In fact, as a provincial judge in Franche-Comté, he had more first-hand experience of witchcraft than most of us will ever have of homicide. This example does not, of course, mean we should doubt the reality of murder – or witches for that matter. Rather, it indicates that similar processes may be at work in the formulation of belief in different cultures, though they only become obvious when they lead to ideas that surprise us.[5]

The philosopher C. A. J. Coady has recently affirmed the importance of shared information to our understanding of the world. Just like Boguet, we normally make judgments on the basis of what we already know. This knowledge, in turn, depends largely on the testimony of others. Coady makes the point with a simple illustration:

> I am visiting a foreign city that is new to me – Amsterdam will do.
> When I arrive at my hotel I am asked to fill in a form giving my name,
> age, date of birth, passport number, and so on, all of which is accepted
> by the hotel clerk as true because I say it is and will be accepted by
> others because he says it is . . . More interestingly still, a good deal of
> the information that I give so confidently and authoritatively is
> accepted as true *by me* on the word of others. That I am so many years
> old; that I was born on such and such a date; that number H11200
> does indeed correspond to the number the Australian passport

authorities have in their files – none of these are facts of my individual observation or memory or inference from them.

This episode could be multiplied a hundred times. It is simply impossible, Coady suggests, for us to verify much of what we believe by direct observation, so we rely to a large extent on opinions and information provided by other people. This leads him to conclude that "a great deal of the actual thinking, classifying, and recognizing that we do is heavily conditioned by our social existence, and by the observations, constructions, memories and theories of others".[6]

Not only do we rely on other people for much of what we know, but also our response to things around us is shaped by beliefs we have acquired in this way. We are more likely to accept new information if it fits with our existing beliefs. In some cases, fresh knowledge will be dismissed on this basis, even when it is based on direct observation. An avowed atheist could spend the night in a supposedly haunted house, and witness strange phenomena that she could not place comfortably within the framework of her established beliefs. Nonetheless, she might account for this experience in terms that preserve these beliefs: she could accept that whatever she saw or heard may appear to be "supernatural" for the time being, but assume that a natural explanation will emerge at some later time. By the same token, people are predisposed to accept new facts when they correspond with their existing beliefs. The discovery of "Piltdown Man" in 1912 provides a spectacular example. Hailed as the earliest specimen of a fossilised ape-man, this creature was accepted in academic texts until its exposure as a crude forgery in 1953: a human cranium had been joined to an orang-utan's jaw, and the teeth filed down to make them match. With hindsight, the fake seemed too obvious to have fooled any one. But Piltdown Man confirmed prevailing ideas about human evolution in the early twentieth century – namely that the growth of the brain was the driving force behind the transition from lesser primates to humans. Arthur Smith Woodward, who confirmed the authenticity of the find in 1912, was also the most eminent British supporter of this position.[7]

As well as influencing the acceptance or rejection of information, prior beliefs can shape our perception of the physical facts of life. The evidence of biology can be read in different ways in the context of different assumptions. To us, few things seem more obvious than the division of humankind into two physical types: women and men. But a significant minority of children are born with indeterminate genitals. Most commonly, these "inter-sex" individuals possess both a rudimentary penis and a vagina. The biological state of these infants is determined by nature, but the meaning of their condition depends entirely on the cultures in which they chance to be born. In Renaissance Europe, inter-sexuality was explained in various ways: as a supernatural judgment or a portent for the sins of others, or as an "imbalance" of male and female humours. In modern East Africa, the tribespeople of the Pokot regard inter-sex children as divine mistakes. The Native American Navaho, in contrast, perceive them as blessed. They are viewed as oracles and talismans of good fortune. Perhaps the most extraordinary response to inter-sexuality is found in our own society. Here inter-sex babies are routinely subjected to "gender-assignment" surgery. Based on the physical characteristics of the infant in question, a decision is made about its future gender. The child is then modified by surgical interventions so that its appearance approaches the "correct" state of either a boy or a girl. As a result, very few inter-sex adults exist in the western world.[8]

The phenomena surrounding death provide further illustrations of how preconceived ideas can frame our perceptions. In our own time, pathological research has found that bodies behave in various ways *post mortem*: they may be preserved in a relatively uncorrupted state, but can also assume a ruddy and bloated appearance for weeks after death. Blood sometimes fails to congeal, and can even reliquify, and the pooling of blood can cause it to spill from the mouth. When skin and fingernails drop away, apparently fresh skin and nails sometimes appear underneath. We explain these observations today in physical terms. For pre-modern people, supernatural explanations could be just as effective. In the right circumstances, an exceptionally preserved body might imply the sanctity of the dead person. Alternatively, the examination of an abnormally preserved cadaver could confirm the existence of a revenant. In 1723, a team of doctors examined corpses disinterred from a Serbian graveyard, and decided that several of them were vampires. A number of the bodies were swollen and red-faced. The corpse of one woman was "quite complete and undecayed": her lungs, liver and spleen were as "fresh as they would be in a healthy person", and new fingernails had formed on one of her hands. For modern pathologists and eighteenth-century physicians alike, it appears that the facts do not speak for themselves. The physical evidence of death may not change, but what it means depends largely on the intellectual context in which it is placed.[9]

Much the same can be said of the experience of bereavement. Psychological research indicates that recently bereaved men and women often experience visions of the dead: in one recent study, almost half the subjects recorded experiences of this kind, and many insisted the visitation was objectively real. Despite these claims, such reports are normally explained as hallucinations. In pre-modern societies, the same experiences were understood in several different ways: as true visions of the deceased, as angels appearing to comfort the bereaved, or as demons masquerading as the dead. Henry Howard favoured the latter possibility when he reported a visitation in 1583:

It chanced after the decease of a certain honest gentleman, whom I forbear to name . . . [that] the devil appeared first to one of his daughters in his wonted shape, and with a voice and countenance agreeable, and soon after to another, [and] brought the plain and well disposed maids into so strange a plight as would have grieved any man alive.

Were they reported today, the same experiences would be explained by the psychology of bereavement. The same is true of other visions of the dead that were understood in terms of witchcraft. After Margaret Moore was visited by spectres of her dead children one night, she came to believe they were familiar spirits asking for her soul. This vision formed part of her confession to witchcraft, for which she was hanged in 1647. During the trials at Salem, one of the victims of *maleficia* described a vision of "six children in winding sheets". These were her sister's dead infants, whom she believed had perished through the sorcery of her neighbour Rebecca Nurse.[10]

Such experiences were linked to another phenomenon that can be understood differently through the lens of modern and pre-modern beliefs. This is a condition known variously as sleep paralysis, "the mare", and "the hag". The syndrome involves a form of semi-conscious sleep, in which the sufferer awakes in a state of paralysis. Frequently, the experience also involves feelings of panic and the sensation of a suffocating weight bearing down on the chest. Victims also report visual hallucinations. These commonly take the form of a menacing figure standing beside them. Modern researchers have estimated that around a third of the population experience this syndrome at one time or another. Medical models have been advanced to explain it, based on the assumption that it involves a dysfunction in normal patterns of sleep. Very similar symptoms were described in pre-modern societies. In much of western Europe, demons or familiar spirits were held responsible for "the hag". In parts of central Europe in the seventeenth and eighteenth centuries, the same symptoms were understood as attacks by vampires. Henry More provided the following account of a Silesian vampire in 1652:

> Those that were asleep it terrified with horrible visions; those that were waking, it would strike, pull or press, lying heavy upon them . . . This terrible apparition would sometimes stand by their bedsides, sometimes cast itself upon the midst of their beds, would lie close to them, [and] would miserably suffocate them.

More described another victim who was "so squeezed and pressed when he was asleep, that wakening he found himself utterly spent". As the man gazed fearfully around him, he was suddenly gripped by a figure that held "him all over so fast that he could not wag a finger". In this and many other cases, the spectre appeared first to the immediate family of the deceased. This suggests that vampire beliefs explained two phenomena that are recognised today in medical terms: the "hallucinations" associated with bereavement, and the syndrome of sleep paralysis. The point of this observation is not to "explain away" vampires in terms of modern science. Rather, these examples show how the same phenomena can be understood differently – and effectively – within alternative systems of belief. In a world that believes in demons and spirits, "the hag" presents clear evidence of their activity; in a society that does not, it needs to be explained in terms of other acceptable ideas, such as hallucinations and sleep disorders.[11]

These illustrations help to illuminate the process by which we normally understand things. Much of our knowledge is received through other people, who inherit it – like us – from the culture in which they are born. Our established beliefs then frame our interpretation of what we see. This allows us to find "common sense" evidence that these beliefs are true. The mechanisms by which we receive and confirm our beliefs are much easier to see when we step outside our own culture, and appreciate how other people make different sense of the same evidence. At the same time, an awareness of this process should force us to reflect on the status of our own beliefs. At the very least, it should encourage us to look carefully at what we perceive to be the "facts of life".

MATTERS OF FACT

When the doctors opened the Serbian graveyard in 1723, the physical evidence they described resembled the findings of modern pathology. Similarly, Renaissance accounts of "hermaphrodites" would be recognised by doctors treating "inter-sex" children today. In these cases, the physical facts encountered by people in different cultures were not in doubt, though the belief systems through which they were filtered meant these facts did not speak for themselves. In other cases, things accepted as real by pre-modern people would now be dismissed as entirely false. In 1602, Henri Boguet confirmed the existence of witchcraft by reporting accounts of "the hag" that sleep psychologists would still recognise, but he also described witches' *sabbats* that never took place. Boguet's belief in an international conspiracy of Satanists was based on his reading of other authors and confirmed by the confessions of alleged witches to his own leading questions. The construction of historical beliefs in this way – and the fact that dangerous "false beliefs" can become widely accepted – should alert us to the possibility that the same thing could happen today. If this is the case, we should remember that these beliefs might appear just as self-evident as the witches' sabbat did to Boguet.

A fairly trivial example can illustrate the role of published opinion in creating and sustaining false beliefs. In 1993, a resident of Birmingham, England spotted a videocassette for sale at a comic-book fair. The film, *Cannibal Holocaust*, was at that time illegal in the United Kingdom because of its graphic depictions of violence. A year earlier, the same film had been described in the local press as a "snuff" movie in which a real murder was committed on screen. No evidence was provided to support this claim, and it happened to be untrue. Following the tip-off, trading standards officials seized the copy of the film. The Birmingham *Evening Mail* reported the event as the seizure of a snuff video. It claimed that the "foreign made movie – said to be one of the worst snuff films ever made – included scenes of gruesome mutilation and a genuine murder". Subsequently, the national press took up the report. In April 1993 the respected British newspaper the *Independent* presented the following account:

> Trading standards officers seized copies of a "snuff" video – said to include footage of an actual murder – at a children's fair in Birmingham . . . A spokesman for Birmingham's environmental services department said that it was the first known seizure in the city of a snuff video. He said he had no doubt that the death scene was genuine.

Apart from the seizure of the video, none of the claims reported here were correct. Even the statement that the film was found at a children's fair was inaccurate: the event was organised for adult collectors of comics. On a small scale, this episode illustrates the dependence of news-gatherers on the reports of other people. The *Independent* based its story on the *Evening Mail*, which accepted uncritically the claim that the video included a real-life murder, and the whole incident was sparked by a member of the public who presumably accepted earlier claims about the film as true. Without these prior assumptions, there would have been no story at all.[12]

The creation of this "news from nowhere" illustrates another general point. Fears for the safety of society can encourage the circulation of false information. The video was seized to protect a community from something believed to be harmful. More specifically, reports of the seizure presented the video as a danger to children: the headline in the *Evening Mail* was "Death Film on Sale to Kids". Threats to children have played a prominent role in many similar episodes. Sociologists have identified numerous "moral panics" involving children: the suppression of horror comics during the 1950s, "video nasties" in the early 1980s, and later allegations of "satanic child abuse". In each of these scares, concerns about child welfare appear to have overridden attempts to verify the information on which they were based. A similar desire to protect children was evident in pre-modern witch beliefs, as ritual infanticide was a common feature of the sabbat. In the case of snuff films, another parallel with witchcraft should be noted. The alleged crimes were believed to be theoretically possible, so even the exposure of mistaken allegations did not undermine the general acceptance of the threat. Even if no one is killed for real in *Cannibal Holocaust*, this does not prove that no murders have ever been committed for the camera. Reports of snuff movies still circulate in the western media – despite minimal evidence to support them – partly because the possibility of the crime makes it too frightening to ignore.[13]

False claims about the content of films may have practical results. A small number of movies have been censored, or even banned outright, on the basis of inaccurate information in the recent past. In other areas of public life, the uncritical acceptance of questionable claims may have much graver consequences. The current "war on drugs" is a striking example. Until 1914, the sale of opiates such as morphine and heroin was legal in America, and it was common for doctors to prescribe heroin on a long-term basis to men and women addicted to the drug. This allowed them to work despite their addiction. Dr Willis Butler ran a clinic for addicts in Shreveport, Louisiana, until he was forced to close it down in the 1920s. His patients included churchmen and doctors, a retired judge and the mother of the local police commissioner. Despite the American lead, the prohibition of opiates was resisted elsewhere in the western world: doctors in the United Kingdom continued to prescribe heroin to those who needed it until 1968. Enid Bagnold, the author of the classic children's novel *National Velvet*, was one recipient: she pursued a highly successful career despite being addicted to morphine for sixty years. As several researchers have noted, this historical evidence suggests that a clean supply of opium-based drugs is not lethal. Tragically however, contaminated supplies can be deadly and the risk of overdose is increased hugely by the unpredictable quality of heroin sold on the black market. In Britain alone, 790 heroin-related deaths were recorded in 2002. Virtually all deaths from heroin result from overdose or disease spread by dirty needles, but these dangers were relatively uncommon before the age of prohibition.[14]

Despite these shocking figures, the present war on drugs is characterised by almost complete silence on one central issue. How dangerous is heroin in normal doses? The drug can be highly addictive: many soldiers became addicts in the early 1900s, when opium-based painkillers were used during battlefield surgery. But the effects of this condition were not particularly malign. In one of the largest studies of opiate use, 861 patients were examined in Philadelphia General Hospital during the 1920s: they were found to suffer no ill effects from the drug, though many of the subjects had been addicted for five years or more. More recently, a programme backed by the Swiss government provided a clean supply of heroin to over a thousand addicts between 1994 and 1997. Researchers found that their physical health improved dramatically, and this improvement was sustained throughout the period of the programme. In the light of these findings, it is at least an open question whether heroin addiction in itself is a death sentence. Given the bleak life prospects of addicts forced to rely on the black market, this question has some moral urgency. Here again, the analogy with witchcraft is illuminating. At the height of witch persecutions in the sixteenth century, all the experts agreed that satanic forces threatened the world. Most advocated a regime of suppression: those who trafficked with demons were criminals and deserved punishment under the law. A few thinkers took a more liberal approach, while still insisting on the grave dangers posed by Satan. Johann Weyer, for instance, argued that witches should be treated as victims of the Devil rather than his accomplices. Viewed from a distance of 300 years, it seems strange that hardly any one asked the most obvious question: was the Devil a threat at all? In much the same way, the most basic question is seldom asked in the British and American war against heroin. How harmful is the drug itself? It was certainly not regarded as deadly in the 1800s, and our present belief that it is may appear strange – and tragic – when another century has passed.[15]

In this case and many others, the lesson from history is caution. We cannot be sure that things we take for granted are correct because they seem obvious to us. Indeed, the fact that we *do* take them for granted may be a good reason to think more carefully about them. It is extremely hard, as Quentin Skinner has observed, "to avoid falling under the spell of our own intellectual heritage". Sometimes we need to step back from the beliefs we have inherited and reflect on alternative possibilities. In the case of drugs policy, knowledge of the period before prohibition reveals that our present way of seeing things is not the only one, and our current attitudes have evolved – like everything else – through a historical process that is still going on. For Skinner, the historian's job is to open up these new perspectives:

> [The] historian can help us to appreciate how far the values
> embodied in our present way of life, and our present ways of
> thinking about those values, reflect a series of choices made at
> different times between different possible worlds. This awareness can
> help to liberate us from the grip of any one . . . account of those
> values and how they should be interpreted and understood.
> Equipped with a broader sense of possibilities, we can stand back
> from the intellectual commitments we have inherited and ask
> ourselves in a new spirit of enquiry what we should think of them.

The possible worlds described in this book seem strange because they are far removed from our accustomed ways of thinking. But they can also help us to look at our own world from a fresh point of view. If we can accept that people once took things seriously that now seem self-evidently absurd, and resist the temptation to dismiss them as crazy, we can better appreciate the historical context of our own assumptions. This may inspire a more critical approach to the things we think we know. It may even, from time to time, lead us to reflect on how strange we really are.[16]

NOTES

1 INTRODUCTION: STRANGE WORLDS

1 Krämer and Sprenger describe this episode in the *Malleus Maleficarum*, trans. Montague Summers (Dover, New York 1971), 235. Robert Bartlett identified the original case in *Trial by Fire and Water: The Medieval Judicial Ordeal* (Clarendon, Oxford 1986), 145–6.

2 Thomas Carlyle, *Selected Writings*, ed. A. Shelston (Penguin, Harmondsworth 1971), 267.

3 Peter Rushton, "Texts of Authority: Witchcraft Accusations and the Demonstration of Truth in Early Modern England", in Stuart Clark, ed., *Languages of Witchcraft* (Macmillan, London 2001), 26–7; Hans Peter Broedel, *The Malleus Maleficarum and the Construction of Witchcraft* (Manchester University Press, Manchester 2003), 100–1.

4 For a classic statement of the prevalence of oral communication in human societies, see Walter Ong, *Orality and Literacy* (Methuen, London 1982).

5 Clifford Geertz, *The Interpretation of Cultures* (London, Fontana, 1993), 145; Clifford Geertz, *Local Knowledge* (London, Fontana, 1993), 76.

6 David E. Stannard, *The Puritan Way of Death* (Oxford University Press, Oxford 1977), 69.

7 For the *ars moriendi* and rituals associated with death, see Eamon Duffy, *The Stripping of the Altars* (Yale University Press, New Haven, Conn. 1992), 313–27, and Stephen Wilson, *The Magical Universe: Everyday Ritual and Magic in Pre-Modern Europe* (Hambledon, London 2000), Chapter 11. For an excellent survey of the precarious lives of Renaissance villagers, see Keith Wrightson, *Earthly Necessities: Economic Lives in Early Modern Britain* (Yale University Press, New Haven, Conn. 2000).

8 R. W. Southern, *Western Society and the Church in the Middle Ages* (Penguin, Harmondsworth 1970), 15.

9 Andrew Joynes, ed., *Medieval Ghost Stories* (Boydell, Woodbridge 2001), 56; Caesarius of Heisterbach, *Dialogue on Miracles*, trans. H. Von E. Scott and C. C. Swinton-Bland (George Routledge, London 1929), 327. For the recording of wonders in medieval chronicles, see Carl Watkins, "Memories of the Marvellous in the Anglo-Norman Realm", in Elizabeth van Houts, ed., *Medieval Memories: Men, Women and the Past, 700–1300* (Longman, London 2001).

10 An English translation of Lavater's text was published in 1572. Ludwig Lavater, *Of Ghostes and Spirites Walking by Nyght* (London 1572), 19, 49, 53, 78, 97.

11 ibid.,161, 163; Henri Boguet, *An Examen of Witches*, trans. E. A. Ashwin (Frederick Muller, London 1971), 11–12.

12 ibid., 74. Boyle's research into subterranean demons is cited in Stannard, *Puritan Way of Death*, 67.

13 Henry Howard, *A Defensative Against the Poison of Supposed Prophecies* (London 1583), D *verso*, Y i *recto*, Bb i *v*, Ll iii, *r–v*.

14 Christopher Hill, *England's Turning Point: Essays on Seventeenth-Century English History* (Bookmarks, London 1998), 197–8; Richard Gross, *Psychology: The Science of Mind and Behaviour* (3rd edn, Hodder & Stoughton, London 1996), 183.

15 Jean-Claude Schmitt, *Ghosts in the Middle Ages: The Living and the Dead in Medieval Society*, trans. T. Lavender Fagan (University of Chicago Press, Chicago, Ill. 1998), 39–40.

16 *Newes From Scotland* (1591), 21–3.

17 For a sensitive and accessible introduction to theories of magic, see Graham Cunningham, *Religion and Magic: Approaches and Theories* (Edinburgh University Press, Edinburgh 1999). Stephen Wilson provides an excellent survey of the subject in the introduction to *The Magical Universe*.

18 For the prevalence of magical thinking in pre-modern culture and the interplay between magic and religion, see Wilson, *Magical Universe*, and Duffy, *Stripping of the Altars*.

19 Michael Camille, "Visual Art in Two Manuscripts of the *Ars Notoria*", in Claire Fanger, ed., *Conjuring Spirits: Texts and Traditions of Medieval Ritual Magic* (Sutton, Stroud 1998); Willem de Blécourt, "Witch-Doctors, Soothsayers and Priests", *Social History*, 19, 3 (1994), 300–1; Michael Hunter, *John Aubrey and the Realm of Learning* (Duckworth, London 1975), 106; *A New Fortune Book* (1720), title page.

20 St Augustine, *On Christian Teaching*, trans. R. P. H. Green (Oxford University Press, Oxford 1997), 51. For Johannes Nider, see Michael Bailey, *Battling Demons: Witchcraft, Heresy and Reform in the Late Middle Ages* (Pennsylvania State University Press, Philadelphia, Pa. 2003). Robert Mathiesen, "A Thirteenth-Century Ritual to Attain the Beatific Vision", in Fanger, *Conjuring Spirits*, 148. Selections from Agrippa can be found in Englander, Norman, O'Day and Owens, eds, *Culture and Belief in Europe, 1450–1600* (Blackwell, Oxford 1990), 208–12.

21 Martin Luther, *Commentary on the Epistle to the Galatians*, trans. T. Graebner (Zondervan, Grand Rapids, Mich. 1949), Gal. 5:20.

22 Cajetan's method appears to have worked. His companion Roberto Bellarmino later claimed that the "story of the ambush was true in every detail". Wilson, *Magical Universe*, 389.

23 For the tricky business of distinguishing between "superstition" and true religion, see Helen Parish and William G. Naphy, eds, *Religion and Superstition in Reformation Europe* (Manchester University Press, Manchester 2002). R. W. Scribner describes the magical uses of images of Luther in *Popular Culture and Popular Movements in Reformation Germany* (Hambledon, London 1987), Chapter 15.

24 James VI, *Daemonologie* (Edinburgh 1597), 81; Matthew Hopkins, *The Discovery of Witches* (London 1647), 6.

25 James VI, *Daemonologie*, 80–1; Bartlett, *Trial By Fire and Water*, 26, 33. Hugh of Poitiers's account is reproduced in W. L. Wakefield and A. P. Evans, eds, *Heresies of the High Middle Ages* (Columbia University Press, New York 1969), 249.

26 Thomas Aquinas, *Summa Theologica*, Part 2.2, Question 8, Article 98.

27 The torture of alleged witches not only increased the chances of individual convictions, but also encouraged the naming of other suspects in cases where judges assumed that witchcraft was a collective activity. The quote from Aquinas is from *Summa*, 2.2, Question 8, Article 98.

28 Bartlett, *Trial By Fire and Water*, 165–6.

2 ANGELS ON A PINHEAD

1   For Bede's life of Cuthbert, see D. H. Farmer, ed., *The Age of Bede* (Penguin, Harmondsworth 1998), 53–4.
2   John Calvin, *Commentary on Genesis* (Banner of Truth Trust, Edinburgh 1965), 504–5. The punishment of Gabriel Harding is described in *Strange and True News From Westmoreland*, in *The Euing Collection of English Broadside Ballads* (University of Glasgow Publications, Glasgow 1971), 565–6.
3   St Augustine, *City of God*, trans. H. Bettenson (Penguin, Harmondsworth 1984), X, 12; XXI, 6.
4   Joseph Glanville, *Saducismus Triumphatus* (London 1689), 427–8.
5   For attitudes towards the corporeality of angels, see Dyan Elliott, *Fallen Bodies: Pollution, Sexuality and Demonology in the Middle Ages* University of Pennsylvania Press, Philadelphia, Pa., especially Chapter 6. Aquinas's discussion of angels is in Part 1 of the *Summa Theologica*, Questions 50–64.
6   Aquinas, *Summa*, Part 1, Question 51: Articles 2–3.
7   Sex between angels and humans offered proof that celestial beings could interact physically with mortals. This idea was important to the development of witchcraft theory in the 1400s. Walter Stephens considers the religious implications of demonic sex in *Demon Lovers: Witchcraft, Sex and the Crisis of Belief* (University of Chicago Press, Chicago, Ill. 2002). Augustine, *City*, XV, 23; Aquinas, *Summa*, I, Q. 63: Art. 2.
8   Aquinas, *Summa*, I, Q. 57: Art. 3–4.
9   Ludwig Lavater, *Of Ghostes and Spirites Walking by Nyght* (London 1572), 196.
10 For the *Sworn Book* of Honorius of Thebes, see Robert Mathiesen, "A Thirteenth-Century Ritual to Attain the Beautific Vision", in Claire Fanger, ed., *Conjuring Spirits: Texts and Traditions of Medieval Ritual Magic* (Sutton, Stroud 1998); Richard Kieckhefer, *Forbidden Rites: A Necromancer's Manual of the Fifteenth Century* (Sutton, Stroud 1997).
11 For Jerome's life of Hilarion, see Caroline White, ed., *Early Christian Lives* (Penguin, Harmondsworth 1998), 92; for Catherine of Sweden, see Richard Kieckhefer, *Unquiet Souls: Fourteenth-Century Saints and Their Religious Milieu* (University of Chicago Press, Chicago, Ill. 1984), 132; Julian of Norwich, *Revelations of Divine Love*, ed. Clifton Walters (Penguin, Harmondsworth 1966),182; Caesarius of Heisterbach, *Dialogue on Miracles*, trans. H. Von E. Scott and C. Swinton-Bland (Routledge, London 1929), I, 327.
12 Augustine, *City*, VIII, 22; White, *Early Christian Lives*, 92; Kieckhefer, *Unquiet Souls*, 176; Fernando Cervantes, *The Devil in the New World* (Yale University Press, New Haven, Conn. 1994), 35–6.
13 Stuart Clark describes the limits of demonic power in his magisterial *Thinking with Demons: The Idea of Witchcraft in Early Modern Europe* (Oxford University Press, Oxford 1997), 153–6. William Gouge, *The Whole Armour of God* (2nd edn London 1619), 33–5.
14 Augustine, *City*, XVIII, 18; Heinrich Krämer and James Sprenger, *Malleus Maleficarum*, trans. Montague Summers (Dover, New York 1971), 119–20; Nicolas Rémy, *Demonolatry*, trans. E. A. Ashwin (John Rodker, London 1930), 172.
15 Caesarius, *Dialogue*, I, 335, 364. The story of the Prussian carter is in R. W. Scribner, *Popular Culture and Popular Movements in Reformation Germany* (Hambledon, London 1987), 88.
16 Stephen of Bourbon described this incident. Caesarius of Heisterbach recorded similar tales of repentant demons in Germany. See Elliott, *Fallen Bodies*, 138–40.

Aquinas describes the suffering of demons in *Summa*, I, Q. 64, Art. 3.

17 The best overview of Christian ideas about the afterlife is probably Colleen McDannell and Bernhard Lang, *Heaven: A History* (2nd edn, Yale University Press, New Haven, Conn. 2001). On the general resurrection, see Caroline Walker Bynum, *The Resurrection of the Body in Western Christianity, 200–1336* (Columbia University Press, New York 1995). Gerardesca's vision is quoted in McDannell and Lang, *Heaven*, 76.

18 Augustine, *City*, XXII, 20; Bynum, *Resurrection*, 118–19; Aquinas, *Summa*, Supplement, Q. 80: Art. 2.

19 Augustine, *City*, XIII, 23; XXII, 14; Aquinas, *Summa*, Supplement, Q. 81: Art. 1.

20 Augustine, *City*, XXII, 19; Aquinas, *Summa*, Supplement, Question 84: Article 1–2; Thomas Watson, *A Body of Divinity* (Banner of Truth Trust, Edinburgh 1970), 309–10.

21 Aquinas, *Summa*, Supplement, Q. 86: Art. 1; Bynum, *Resurrection*, 131.

22 Aquinas, *Summa*, Supplement, Q. 97: Art 6; Thomas Head, "Saints, Heretics and Fire", in Sharon Farmer and Barbara Rosenwein, eds, *Monks and Nuns, Saints and Outcasts* (Cornell University Press, Ithaca, NY 2000).

23 Aquinas, *Summa*, Supplement, Q. 97, Art. 7. For the debate about the dimensions of hell in seventeenth-century Italy, see Piero Camporesi, *The Fear of Hell: Images of Damnation and Salvation in Early Modern Europe*, trans. L. Byatt (Polity, Cambridge 1990), 30–2. Samuel Lee is quoted in David E. Stannard, *The Puritan Way of Death* (Oxford University Press, Oxford 1977), 67–8.

24 Aquinas, *Summa*, Supplement, Q.69, Art. 2; Bynum, *Resurrection*, 132; Dante, *Divine Comedy*, Purgatorio, Canto 14.

25 White, *Early Christian Lives*, 82; Farmer, *Age of Bede*, 49–50; Caesarius, *Dialogue*, II, 247; Philip Stubbes, *A Christall Glasse for Christian Women* (London 1591), C4 r.

26 Caesarius, *Dialogue*, II, 272, 306; William of Malmesbury's story is reproduced in Andrew Joynes, ed., *Medieval Ghost Stories* (Boyndell Press, Woodbridge 2001), 60–1.

27 For the concept of the empyrean, see McDannell and Lang, *Heaven*, 80–8.

28 Aquinas, *Summa*, Supplement, Q.70, Art. 3. For Protestant ideas about the appearance of spirits of the dead, see Bruce Gordon, "Malevolent Ghosts and Ministering Angels: Apparitions and Pastoral Care in the Swiss Reformation", in Bruce Gordon and Peter Marshall, eds, *The Place of the Dead* (Cambridge University Press, Cambridge 2000).

29 The argument that some theological questions are "divine mysteries" best left alone was often invoked to prevent heresy or close off potentially divisive arguments within the church. For examples from seventeenth-century England, see my *Religion and Society in Early Stuart England* (Ashgate, Aldershot 1998), Chapter 2.

3 THEY HANG HORSES, DON'T THEY?

1 E. P. Evans, *The Criminal Prosecution and Capital Punishment of Animals* (1906; reprinted by Faber & Faber, London 1987), 153–4, 298–303; Esther Cohen, "Law, Folklore and Animal Lore", *Past and Present* 110 (1986), 10–11.

2 Evans, *Criminal Prosecution*, 295, 307. I am grateful to Carroll Phillips for translating these texts. Ervin Bonkalo, "Criminal Proceedings Against Animals in the Middle Ages", *Journal of Unconventional History* 3:2 (1992), 27.

3 Evans, *Criminal Prosecution*, 37–50.

4 Cohen, "Law", 15; Evans, *Criminal Prosecution*, 41; Bonkalo, "Criminal Proceedings", 25.

5 Joyce E. Salisbury, *The Beast Within: Animals in the Middle Ages* (Routledge,

London 1994), 40–1; William Bradford, *Of Plymouth Plantation*, ed. F. Murphy (Random House, New York 1981), 356; Joad Raymond, ed., *Making the News: An Anthology of the Newsbooks of Revolutionary England* (Windrush Press, Moreton-in-Marsh 1993), 151. For a highly readable account of pre-modern views on bestiality, see William Naphy, *Sex Crimes: From Renaissance to Enlightenment* (Tempus, Charleston, SC 2002), Chapter 9.

6   Thomas Aquinas, *Summa Theologica*, Part 2 (Second part), Question 76: Article 2; Donald Davidson, *Inquiries into Truth and Interpretation* (Oxford University Press, Oxford 1984), 199.

7   Jean Bodin, *On the Demon-Mania of Witches*, trans. R. A. Scott (Centre for Reformation and Renaissance Studies, Victoria University, Toronto 1995), 203.

8   Esther Cohen, "Animals in Medieval Perceptions", in Aubrey Manning and James Serpell, eds, *Animals and Human Society* (Routledge, London 1994), 72.

9   Evans, *Criminal Prosecution*, 45.

10 The egg of an aged cockerel, it was believed, could hatch a into a monstrous creature called a basilisk. This was half-serpent and half-fowl, and was thought to be deadly poisonous. Fear of this beast probably spurred the magistrates of Basle into action. Cohen, "Law", 34–5; H. Krämer and J. Sprenger, *Malleus Maleficarum*, trans. M. Summers (Dover, New York 1971), 65; Salisbury, *Beast Within*, 141; Norman Cohn, *Europe's Inner Demons* (2nd edn, Pimlico, London 1993), 203–4.

11 Cohen, "Law", 28–30; Bonkalo, "Criminal Proceedings", 27–8.

12 Evans, *Criminal Prosecution*, 65; Cohen, "Law", 31–2.

13 Evans, *Criminal Prosecution*, 20.

14 For the theatre of judicial violence, see Susan Dwyer Amussen, "Punishment, Discipline and Power", *Journal of British Studies* 34 (1995), 1–33. For speeches from the gallows, see J. A. Sharpe, "Last Dying Speeches: Religion, Ideology and Public Execution in Seventeenth-Century England", *Past and Present* 107 (1985), 144–67.

15 Walter Wakefield and Austin Evans, eds, *Heresies of the High Middle Ages* (Columbia University Press, New York 1969), 75; Martín Del Rio, *Investigations Into Magic*, trans. P. G. Maxwell-Stuart (Manchester University Press, Manchester 2000), 238; Henri Boguet, *An Examen of Witches*, trans. E. A. Ashwin (Frederick Muller, London 1971), 164. For details of the sentence passed on the Marquis de Sade, see Sade, *Justine, Philosophy in the Bedroom and Other Writings*, translated by R. Seaver and A. Wainhouse (Grove, New York 1965), 83.

16 Evans, *Criminal Prosecution*, trans. Phillips, 296–7.

17 Nicholas Humphrey, Preface to Evans, *Criminal Prosecution*, xxii–iii; 309.

18 *The Newgate Calendar*, ed. Norman Birkett (J. M. Dent, London 1974), 179; Salisbury, *Beast Within*, 153; Cohen, "Animals in Medieval Perceptions", 69–70.

19 Salisbury, *Beast Within*, 39; Cohen, "Law", 21–4, 36–7.

20 Evans, *Criminal Prosecution*, xxvi, 308–9.

21 Erica Fudge, *Perceiving Animals: Humans and Beasts in Early Modern English Culture* Macmillan, London 2000), 121; Blake Morrison, *As If* (Granta, London 1997), 37–8, 241.

22 Simon Hattenstone, "They Were Punished Enough By What They Did", *Guardian*, October 30, 2000.

23 Wolfgang Behringer, "Weather, Hunger and Fear: Origins of the European Witch-Hunts in Climate, Society and Mentality", in D. Oldridge, ed., *The Witchcraft Reader* (Routledge, London 2002).

24 *Little Flowers of St Francis*, Book XX; Evans, *Criminal Prosecution*, 28–9.

25 D. H. Farmer, ed., *The Age of Bede* (Penguin, Harmondsworth 1998), 70; Evans, *Criminal Prosecution*, 92.

26 ibid., 96.
27 Racine's play, *The Litigants*, features a dog sentenced to the gallows for theft. In one scene, a lawyer pleads for this sentence to be lifted for the sake of its abandoned litter.

4 THE ROAMING DEAD

1 This extract from William of Newburgh's *History of the Events of England* is reproduced in Andrew Joynes, ed., *Medieval Ghost Stories* (Boydell, Woodbridge 2001), 99–100.
2 In parts of central Europe, belief in revenants survived at all social levels well into the nineteenth century. See John V. Fine, "In Defence of Vampires", *East European Quarterly*, 21:1 (1987). For the role of the dead in late medieval culture, see Jean-Claude Schmitt, *Ghosts in the Middle Ages: The Living and the Dead in Medieval Society*, trans. T. Lavender Fagan (University of Chicago Press, Chicago, Ill. 1998). The activity of revenants in medieval Europe is explored in Nancy Caciola, "Wraiths, Revenants and Ritual in Medieval Culture", *Past and Present* 152 (1996). For the early modern period, see Bruce Gordon and Peter Marshall, eds, *The Place of the Dead: Death and Remembrance in Late Medieval and Early Modern Europe* (Cambridge University Press, Cambridge 2000). For a classic study of twentieth-century revenant beliefs, see Agnes Murgoci, "The Vampire in Roumania", *Folklore* 37 (1926). Joynes, *Medieval Ghost Stories*, 56–8, 100.
3 Christina Larner, "The Crime of Witchcraft in Early Modern Europe", in Darren Oldridge, ed., *The Witchcraft Reader* (Routledge, London 2001), 207.
4 Roger Bacon, for instance, argued that Christians should remain physically intact in preparation for the general resurrection. See Paul Binski, *Medieval Death: Ritual and Representation* (British Museum Press, London 1996), 63–9, 199–203. *The Acren Riwle: A Treatise on the Rules and Duties of Monastic Life*, trans. J. Morton (Camden Society, London 1853), 361.
5 On the "holy dead" and the culture of pilgrimage, see Ronald C. Finucane, *Miracles and Pilgrims: Popular Beliefs in Medieval England* (2nd edn, Macmillan, London 1995). For the protections and judgments of St James, see Benedicta Ward, *Miracles and the Medieval Mind* (2nd edn, Wildwood House, Aldershot 1987), 110–17.
6 Caesarius of Heisterbach, *Dialogue on Miracles*, trans. H. Von E. Scott and C. C. Swinton-Bland (George Routledge, London 1929), II, 323–5; Bartolomea Riccoboni, *Life and Death in a Venetian Convent: The Chronicle and Necrology of Corpus Domini*, ed. D. Bornstein (University of Chicago Press, Chicago, Ill. 2000), 72, 77.
7 Caesarius, *Dialogue*, II, 287–8; Schmitt, *Ghosts*, 138; Walter Map, *De Nugis Curialium: Courtier's Trifles*, ed. and trans. M. R. James, revised by C. N. L. Brooke and R. A. B. Mynors (Clarendon, Oxford 1983), 203–5.
8 Since the wandering of the dead was viewed as a penalty for sin, Caesarius of Heisterbach placed most of his stories about revenants in Book V of his *Dialogue* on the "punishment" of the dead. The stories from Wales and Scotland are cited in Caciola, "Wraiths", 19, 23; Joynes, *Medieval Ghost Stories*, 98.
9 Augustine Calmet, *Treatise on Vampires and Revenants*, trans H. Christmas (Desert Island, Brighton 1993), 90–1, 177; James VI *Daemonologie* (Edinburgh 1597), 80; Joynes, *Medieval Ghost Stories*, 102. For the physical signs of vampirism in eighteenth-century Europe, see Paul Barber, *Vampires, Burial and Death* (Yale University Press, New Haven, Conn. 1988).

10 For the life of Wilfrid, see D. H. Farmer, ed., *The Age of Bede* (Penguin, Harmondsworth 1998), 126–7. Silvano Cavazza, "Double Death: Resurrection and Baptism in a Sevententh-Century Rite", in Edward Muir and Guido Ruggiero, *History From Crime* (Johns Hopkins University Press, Baltimore, Md. 1994), 12.

11 Ward, *Miracles*, 114–15; Calmet, *Treatise*, 35–7.

12 For representations of the raising of Lazarus, see Binski, *Medieval Death*, 8–9, 137. Calmet, *Treatise*, 37.

13 Caesarius, *Dialogue*, II, 269, 300.

14 An alternative reading was also possible. The episode could have been a true resurrection of the kind that awaits the damned at the Last Judgment. If so, it was presumably intended by God as a warning to the rest of us! William of Malmesbury, *Deeds of the English Kings*, in Joynes, *Medieval Ghost Stories*, 56–8.

15 Joynes, *Medieval Ghost Stories*, 99, 100, 123.

16 The intensely physical nature of demonic possession is considered in Chapter 7. Map, *De Nugis*, 203; Caciola, "Wraiths", 11–13; Caesarius, *Dialogue*, II, 292.

17 For the purgative properties of fire in the late Middle Ages, see Margaret Aston, *Faith and Fire: Popular and Unpopular Religion, 1350–1600* (Hambledon Press, London 1993), 300–2. Joynes, *Medieval Ghost Stories*, 98; Map, *De Nugis*, 203–5.

18 For attacks on purgatory in Protestant propaganda, see R. W. Scribner, *For the Sake of Simple Folk: Popular Propaganda for the German Reformation* (Cambridge University Press, Cambridge 1981), 89–93. Ludwig Lavater, *Of Ghostes and Spirites Walking by Nyght* (London 1572), 72.

19 See Bruce Gordon, "Malevolent Ghosts and Ministering Angels", in Gordon and Marshall, *The Place of the Dead*, 87–109; Jürgen Beyer, "A Lübeck Prophet in Local and Lutheran Context", in Bob Scribner and Trevor Johnson, eds, *Popular Religion in Germany and Central Europe, 1400–1800* (Macmillan, London 1996), 171; Lavater, *Of Ghostes*, 170–1; James VI, *Daemonologie* (Edinburgh 1597), 59–60.

20 Carleton Cunningham, "The Devil and the Religious Controversies of Sixteenth-Century France", *Essays in History*, 35 (1993), 36–7; Martín Del Rio, *Investigations Into Magic*, trans. P. G. Maxwell-Stuart (Manchester University Press. Manchester 2000), 109; Francesco Maria Guazzo, *Compendium Maleficarum*, trans. E. A. Ashwin (Dover, New York 1988), 60, 68–70; Nicolas Rémy, *Demonolatry*, trans. E. A. Ashwin (John Rodker, London 1930), 88.

21 In 1563 the Protestant Johann Weyer presented the whole incident as a popish fraud. George Mora and Benjamin Kohl, eds, *Witches, Devils and Doctors in the Renaissance: Johann Weyer, De Praestigiis Daemonum* (Binghampton, New York 1991), 439–41. For the reform of Protestant funeral rites, see Andrew Spicer, "Rest of their Bones: Fear of Death and Reformed Burial Practices", in William Naphy and Penny Roberts, eds, *Fear in Early Modern Society* (Manchester University Press, Manchester 1997), 167–83.

22 Henry More, *An Antidote to Atheism* (2nd edn, London 1655), 209–27. Another version of the story from Breslau is reproduced in Barber, *Vampires*, 10–13.

23 *The Declaration of John Robins*, ed. Andrew Hopton (Aphoria, London 1992), 27; *George Fox's "Book of Miracles"*, ed. H. Cadbury (New York 1973), 14–15. The examination of Dorcas Erbury is included in Ralph Farmer, *Satan Inthron'd in his Chair of Pestilence* (London 1657), 18–19. A slightly different version was recorded in William Grigg, *The Quakers Jesus* (1658).

24 Cavazza, "Double Death", 1–31.

25 H. Krämer and J. Sprenger, *Malleus Maleficarum*, trans. M. Summers (Dover, New York 1971), 109–11; Rémy, *Demonolatry*, 88; Henri Boguet, *An Examen of Witches*, trans. E. A. Ashwin (Frederick Muller, London 1971), 21; Ludovico

Maria Sinistrari, *Demoniality*, trans. M. Summers (Benjamin Blom, New York 1972), 11.

26 Del Rio, *Investigations*, 111–12; Boguet, *Examen*, 21.

27 Rémy, *Demonolatry*, 89–90, 92; Calmet, *Treatise*, 104–5.

28 Nider is quoted in Michael Bailey, *Battling Demons: Witchcraft, Heresy and Reform in the Late Middle Ages* (Pennsylvania State University Press, Philadelphia, Pa. 2003), 40; Jean Bodin, *On the Demon-Mania of Witches*, trans. R. A. Scott (Centre for Reformation and Renaissance Studies, Victoria University, Toronto 1995), 105; Rémy, *Demonolatry*, 87.

29 More, *Antidote*, 227.

5 "A SHIPWRECK OF SOULS": UNDERSTANDING WITCHCRAFT

1 Hawthorne's description of Gallows Hill sets the scene for his story "Alice Doane's Appeal". Thomas Maule, *Truth Held Forth and Maintained* (1695), 185.

2 Increase Mather's sermon against the trials was preached to a congregation of fellow clergy in Cambridge, Massachusetts. It was subsequently published as *Cases of Conscience Concerning Evil Spirits* (Boston 1693). The quote is from the preface.

3 Paul Boyer and Stephen Nissenbaum, *Salem Possessed: The Social Origins of Witchcraft* (Harvard University Press, Cambridge, Mass. 1974), 19.

4 The idea of collective witchcraft had some roots in popular culture. There is strong evidence from Germany that ordinary people feared the collective activity of witches, associated mainly with *maleficium* affecting the weather. But these beliefs did not normally involve the idea of devil worship or ritual attacks on Christianity. See Wolfgang Behringer, "Weather, Hunger and Fear: Origins of the European Witch-Hunts in Climate, Society and Mentality", in D. Oldridge, ed., *The Witchcraft Reader* (Routledge, London 2002).

5 St Augustine, *The City of God*, VIII, 18, 22. For the biblical and classical sources for witchcraft belief, see Sydney Anglo, "Evident Authority and Authoritative Evidence", in S. Anglo, ed., *The Damned Art* (Routledge & Kegan Paul, London 1976).

6 Martín Del Rio, *Investigations Into Magic*, trans. P. G. Maxwell-Stuart (Manchester University Press, Manchester 2000), 126; *The Examination of John Walsh*, reproduced in Barbara Rosen, ed., *Witchcraft in England, 1558–1618* (University of Massachusetts Press, Amherst, Mass. 1969), 70; P. G. Maxwell-Stuart, ed., *The Occult in Early Modern Europe* (Macmillan, London 1999), 124–5.

7 Jean Bodin, *On the Demon-Mania of Witches*, trans. R. A. Scott (Centre for Reformation and Renaissance Studies, Victoria University, Toronto 1995), 138; Del Rio, *Investigations*, 119.

8 David P. Phillips et al., "The Hound of the Baskervilles Effect: Natural Experiment on the Influence of Psychological Stress on Timing of Death", *British Medical Journal*, 323, 22–9 Dec. 2001; Robin Briggs, *Witches and Neighbours* (HarperCollins, London 1996), 64.

9 Cotton Mather described this episode in *Memorable Providences Relating to Witchcrafts and Possessions*, reproduced in George L. Burr, ed., *Narratives of the New England Witchcraft Cases* (Dover, New York 2002), 100–2.

10 Caesarius of Heisterbach, *Dialogue on Miracles*, trans. H. Von E. Scott and C. C. Swinton-Bland (George Routledge, London 1929), 315–18. For necromancers in the clerical underworld, see Richard Kieckhefer, *Magic in the Middle Ages* (Cambridge University Press, Cambridge 1989), Chapter 7.

11 John Rogers, *Ohel or Beth-Semesh* (London 1653), 433; Nicolas Rémy, *Demonolatry*,

trans. E. A. Ashwin (John Rodker, London 1930), 4–5; Francesco Maria Guazzo, *Compendium Maleficarum*, trans. E. A. Ashwin (Dover, New York 1988), 22; Rosen, *Witchcraft*, 115. For the case of Margaret Moore, see Malcolm Gaskill, "Witchcraft and Power in Early Modern England", in Jenny Kermode and Garthine Walker, eds, *Women, Crime and the Courts* (University College London Press, London 1994).

12 Henry Howard, *A Defensative Against the Poyson of Supposed Prophecies* (London 1583), Y i *recto* – Y ii *recto*.

13 ibid., Y i *v*; Del Rio, *Investigations*, 117.

14 Michael Bailey, *Battling Demons: Witchcraft, Heresy and Reform in the Late Middle Ages* (Pennsylvania State University Press, Philadelphia, Pa. 2003), 41–4.

15 Henri Boguet, *An Examen of Witches*, trans. E. A. Ashwin (Frederick Muller, London 1971), 55–60.

16 For the Italian *benandante*, see Carlo Ginzburg, *The Night Battles: Witchcraft and Agrarian Cults in the Sixteenth and Seventeenth Centuries*, trans. John and Anne Tedeschi (Routledge, London 1983); on fears of collective witchcraft in Salem, see Elaine G. Breslaw, *Tituba: Reluctant Witch of Salem* (New York University Press, New York 1996).

17 Boguet, *Examen*, 44–6.

18 The literature on Satanic abuse is huge. For an excellent account of the British experience, see J. S. La Fontaine, *Speak of the Devil: Tales of Satanic Abuse in Contemporary England* (Cambridge University Press, Cambridge 1998). Work by supporters and sceptics of ritual abuse allegations is included in Oldridge, *Witchcraft Reader*, Part 10. Michelle Smith and Lawrence Pazder, *Michelle Remembers* (Michael Joseph, London 1981), 159.

19 Patrick Casement, "The Wish Not to Know", in Oldridge, *Witchcraft Reader*, 435.

20 Hans Peter Broedel, *The Malleus Maleficarum and the Construction of Witchcraft* (Manchester University Press, Manchester 2003), 92–101; Alan Macfarlane, *Witchcraft in Tudor and Stuart England* (2nd edn, Routledge, London 1999), 135–8.

21 Bodin, *Demon-Mania*, 43; Gustav Henningsen, *The Witches' Advocate: Basque Witchcraft and the Spanish Inquisition* (University of Nevada Press, Reno, Nev. 1980), 30–4; E. William Monter, "The Sociology of Jura Witchcraft", in Oldridge, *Witchcraft Reader*, 93–5.

22 Reginald Scot, *The Discoverie of Witchcraft* (Dover, New York 1972), 21; Boguet, *Examen*, 211–12, 217, 220; Alasdair Palmer, "The US is Ready to Use Torture Against Terrorism", *Sunday Telegraph*, 15 Dec. 2002; Tim Reid, "Defiant Prisoner Starts Months of Questioning", *The Times*, 16 Dec. 2003.

23 Bodin, *Demon-Mania*, 43; Rémy, *Demonolatry*, 12–13, 78, 79.

24 Alan Kors and Edward Peters, eds, *Witchcraft in Europe: A Documentary History* (University of Pennsylvania Press, Philadelphia, Pa. 1972), 341.

25 ibid., 251–2. For the persecutions at Würzburg, see Robert Walinski-Kiehl, "The Devil's Children: Child Witch Trials in Early Modern Germany", *Continuity and Change* 11:2 (1996).

26 Kors and Peters, *Witchcraft*, 336, 351–7.

27 George Mora and Bejamin Kohl, eds, *Witches, Devils and Doctors in the Renaissance: Johann Weyer, De Praestigiis Daemonum* (Medieval and Renaissance Texts and Studies, Binghampton, NY 1991), 34, 310–12, 315, 522.

28 For Weyer's pessimism about using human laws to defeat the Devil, see Elisa Slattery, "To Prevent a 'Shipwreck of Souls': Johann Weyer and *De Praestigiis Daemonum*", *Essays in History*, 36 (1994). Scot, *Discoverie*, 9, 81; James VI, *Daemonologie* (Edinburgh 1597), preface, ix.

29 Mather published his account of the two cases in *An Essay for the Recording of*

Illustrious Providences (1684). This is reproduced in Burr, *Narratives*, 18–23. For the more radical denial of demonic interventions in the mid-1600s, see Andrew Fix, "Angels, Devils, and Evil Spirits in Seventeenth-Century Thought", *Journal of the History of Ideas*, 50:4 (1989).

30 ibid., 148; Boyer and Nissenbaum, *Salem Possessed*, 9, 11–12.
31 Mather, *Cases of Conscience*, 6, 15, 20, 29, 34, postscript.

6 WEREWOLVES AND FLYING WITCHES

1 *Bite Me*, issues 5, 10, 21. The interview with a psychic vampire is in issue 4.
2 For French werewolves, see E. W. Monter, *Witchcraft in France and Switzerland* (Cornell University Press, Ithaca, NY 1976), 145–51, and Caroline Oates, "The Trial of a Teenage Werewolf, Bordeaux, 1603", *Criminal Justice History*, 9 (1988), 1–24. For lycanthropy in the British Isles, see Joyce E. Salisbury, *The Beast Within: Animals in the Middle Ages* (Routledge, London 1994), 163–4. Francesco Maria Guazzo, *Compendium Maleficarum*, trans. E. A. Ashwin (Dover, New York 1988), 52; *A True Discourse Declaring the Damnable Life and Death of One Stubbe Peeter* (London 1590), 2; Jean Bodin, *On the Demon-Mania of Witches*, trans. R. A. Scott (Centre for Reformation and Renaissance Studies, Victoria University, Toronto 1995), 122; James VI, *Daemonologie* (Edinburgh 1597), 61–2; Edward Fairfax, *Daemonologia: A Discourse on Witchcraft*, ed. W. Grainge (Harrogate 1882), 97.
3 Sabine Baring-Gould, *The Book of Werewolves* (Senate, London 1995), 130–1.
4 St Augustine, *City of God*, trans. H. Bettenson (Penguin, Harmondsworth 1984), XVIII, 18; James VI, *Daemonologie*, 61; Bodin, *Demon-Mania*, 124.
5 Monter, *Witchcraft*, 149; Guazzo, *Compendium Maleficarum*, 51; Nicolas Rémy, *Demonolatry*, trans. E. A. Ashwin (John Rodker, London 1930), 108; Bodin, *Demon-Mania*, 124; Martín Del Rio, *Investigations Into Magic*, trans. P. G. Maxwell-Stuart (Manchester University Press, Manchester 2000), 101–2; Éva Pócs, *Between the Living and the Dead*, trans. S. Rédy and M. Webb (Central European Press, Budapest 1999), 44–6; *Dr Lambs Darling: or Strange and Terrible News From Salisbury* (London 1653), 7; John Clare, "The Shepherd's Calendar", 'January', II.
6 Bodin, *Demon-Mania*, 126; Henry More, *An Antidote to Atheism* (2nd edn, London 1655), 234–5.
7 Henri Boguet, *An Examen of Witches*, trans. E. A. Ashwin (Frederick Muller, London 1971), 143–5.
8 George Mora and Benjamin Kohl, eds, *Witches, Devils and Doctors in the Renaissance: Johann Weyer, De Praestigiis Daemonum* (Medieval and Renaissance Texts and Studies, Binghampton, NY 1991), 516; Reginald Scot, *The Discoverie of Witchcraft* (Dover, New York 1972), 28–9, 51–8; Bodin, *Demon-Mania*, 123–4, 127.
9 H. Krämer and J. Sprenger, *Malleus Maleficarum*, trans. M. Summers (Dover, New York 1971), 122–4; Rémy, *Demonolatry*, 111.
10 ibid., 112–13.
11 Boguet, *Examen*, 140–1; Del Rio, *Investigations*, 101–2; Guazzo, *Compendium*, 52–3.
12 ibid., 51; Del Rio, *Investigations*, 100.
13 This account is based on the excellent reconstruction of Grenier's case by Caroline Oates in "The Trial of a Teenage Werewolf", especially 15–19.
14 James VI, *Daemonologie*, 39–40; Robert Walinski-Kiehl, "The Devil's Children: Child Witch Trials in Early Modern Germany", *Continuity and Change* 11 (1996), 177.
15 Carlo Ginzburg, *The Night Battles: Witchcraft and Agrarian Cults in the Sixteenth*

and Seventeenth Centuries, trans. John and Anne Tedeschi (Routledge, London 1983); Darren Oldridge, ed., *The Witchcraft Reader* (Routledge, London 2002).

16 Boguet, *Examen*, 48–9; James VI, *Daemonologie*, 41.

17 Krämer and Sprenger, *Malleus*, 106; Rémy, *Demonolatry*, 182; Bodin, *Demon-Mania*, 121; James VI, *Daemonologie*, 38.

18 Mora and Kohl, *Witches*, 197–9; Scot, *Discoverie*, 58–9.

19 For the possible role of drugs in witchcraft confessions, see Richard Rudgley, *The Alchemy of Culture: Intoxicants in Society* (British Museum Press, London 1993). Bodin, *Demon-Mania*, 115; Rémy, *Demonolatry*, 6; Del Rio, *Investigations*, 94.

20 Ginzburg, *Night Battles*, 1–3; Walinski-Kiehl, "Devil's Children", 178.

21 Boguet, *Examen*, 51; James VI, *Daemonologie*, 41–2; Boguet, *Examen*, 50–1; Del Rio, *Investigations*, 120.

22 Rémy, *Demonolatry*, 43–4; Boguet, *Examen*, 50; Guazzo, *Compendium*, 33–4.

23 More, *Antidote*, 236–7; James, *Daemonologie*, 38, 40.

7 RAPTURES AND FORBIDDEN WORDS

1 Samuel Clarke, *A Mirrour or Looking Glasse both for Saints and Sinners* (2nd edn, London 1654), 231–8.

2 Richard Baxter claimed that Quakers were possessed in *The Certainty of the Worlds of Spirits* (London 1691), 175–6. Critics of witch trials also noted Satan's fondness for deception. Cotton Mather cited Clarke and Baxter in his *Cases of Conscience Concerning Evil Spirits* (Boston 1693), 11, 23.

3 For the culture of prophecy in early sixteenth-century Italy, see Ottavia Niccoli, *Prophecy and People in Renaissance Italy*, trans. L. G. Cochrane (Princeton University Press, Princeton, NJ 1990). The acceptance of demonic affliction and possession among charismatic Christians is described in Michael W. Cuneo, *American Exorcism* (Bantam, New York 2001).

4 For the case of Marthe Brossier, see D. P. Walker, *Unclean Spirits: Posssession and Exorcism in France and England in the Late Sixteenth and Early Seventeenth Centuries* (Scolar, London 1981), 15, 33–42. Clarke Garrett, *Spirit Possession and Popular Religion* (Johns Hopkins University Press, Baltimore, Md. 1987), 4–5; Alison Weber, "Between Ecstasy and Exorcism: Religious Negotiation in Sixteenth-Century Spain", *Journal of Medieval and Renaissance Studies* 23 (1993), 231.

5 Bartolomea Riccoboni, *Life and Death in a Venetian Convent: The Chronicle and Necrology of Corpus Domini*, ed. D. Bornstein (University of Chicago Press, Chicago, Ill. 2000), 26–7, 31, 90.

6 Anthropologists have also found that possessed individuals in spirit-believing societies are usually invaded by spirits of the opposite gender. God and the Devil were normally assumed to be male in pre-modern culture. I. M. Lewis, *Religion in Context: Cults and Charisma* (2nd edn, Cambridge University Press, Cambridge 1996), Chapter 3; Mary Douglas, *Natural Symbols* (Penguin, Harmondsworth, 1973), 112; Riccoboni, *Life and Death*, 26.

7 Julian of Norwich, *Revelations of Divine Love*, ed. Clifton Walters (Penguin, Harmondsworth 1966), 112.

8 Richard Kieckhefer, *Unquiet Souls: Fourteenth-Century Saints and Their Religious Milieu* (University of Chicago Press, Chicago, Ill. 1984), 27–8, 152–3; Patricia Crawford, *Women and Religion in England, 1500–1720* (Routledge, London 1993), 108; Jane Turner, *Choice Experiences of the Kind Dealings of God* (London 1653), 2; Richard Francis, *Ann the Word* (Fourth Estate, London 2000), 40–5.

9 For hallucinations related to sleep loss, see Stanley Coren, *Sleep Thieves: An Eye-Opening Exploration into the Science and Mysteries of Sleep,* (Free Press, New York 1996). Richard Gross, *Themes, Issues and Debates in Psychology* (Hodder & Stoughton, London 1995), 143; Thomas Szasz, *The Myth of Mental Illness* (Paladin, London 1972).

10 George Fox, *Journal* (J. M. Dent, London 1962), 44, 57, 87.

11 ibid., 169; Garrett, *Spirit Possession*, 162, Chapter 10.

12 David Genticore describes this episode, which he explains as an instance of repressed guilt, in *From Bishop to Witch: The System of the Sacred in Early Modern Terra d'Otranto* (Manchester University Press, Manchester 1992), 114–16.

13 For the implantation of demonic thoughts, see Darren Oldridge, *The Devil in Early Modern England* (Sutton, Stroud 2000), 45–7.

14 Jean Bodin made the lurid and memorable observation in 1580 that possessing spirits could speak "through the shameful parts" of women's bodies. Bodin, *On the Demon-Mania of Witches*, trans. R. A. Scott (Centre for Reformation and Renaissance Studies, Victoria University, Toronto 1995), 109; George L. Burr, ed., *Narratives of the New England Witchcraft Cases* (Dover, New York 2002), 162.

15 William Weston, *The Autobiography of an Elizabethan*, trans. P. Caraman (Longmans, Green & Co, London 1955), 24; Henri Boguet, *An Examen of Witches*, trans. E. A. Ashwin (Frederick Muller, London 1971), 173; Burr, *Narratives*, 28.

16 James VI, *Daemonologie* (Edinburgh 1597), 70–1; Boguet, *Examen*, 173; Francesco Maria Guazzo, *Compendium Maleficarum*, trans. E. A. Ashwin (Dover, New York 1988), 167; Weston, *Autobiography*, 25; John Darrel, *The Triall of Maist. Dorrell* (London 1599), 34; Walker, *Unclean Spirits*, 32–3.

17 For a later account of the testing of Marthe Brossier, see Augustin Calmet, *The Phantom World*, trans. H. Christmas (Wordsworth, London 2001), 87; Ludovico Maria Sinistrari, *Demoniality*, trans. M. Summers (Benjamin Blom, New York 1972), 14; Walker, *Unclean Spirits*, 31.

18 For the caution of some Protestants regarding bodily possession, see Lyndal Roper, *Oedipus and the Devil* (Routledge, London 1994), Chapter 8. James VI, *Daemonologie*, 70; Thomas Wright, *Narratives of Sorcery and Magic*, II (London 1851), 143; Burr, *Narratives*, 110.

19 Bodin, *Demon-Mania*, 109.

20 ibid., 171; Calmet, *Phantom World*, 89; Roper, *Oedipus*, 175–6; Jacqueline Eales, "Thomas Pierson and the Transmission of the Moderate Puritan Tradition", *Midland History* 20 (1995), 81–2.

21 A contemporary account of the possession of William Sommers is reproduced in Oldridge, *Devil*, 180–6. Wright, *Narratives*, 139, 140–1; Boguet, *Examen*, 3, 11–12; Barbara Rosen, ed., *Witchcraft in England, 1558–1618* (University of Massachusetts Press, Amherst, Mass. 1969), 297; Burr, *Narratives*, 21.

22 E. William Monter, "The Sociology of Jura Witchcraft", in Oldridge, *Witchcraft Reader*, 90; Walker, *Unclean Spirits*, 53; Burr, *Narratives*, 27, 30–1.

23 Ottavia Niccoli, "The End of Prophecy", *Journal of Modern History* 61 (1989), 667–82; Weber, "Between Ecstasy and Exorcism", 221–5.

24 Gary K. Waite, *Heresy, Magic and Witchcraft in Early Modern Europe* (Palgrave Macmillan, Basingstoke 2003), 110–12; Martin Luther, *Commentary on the Epistle to the Galatians*, trans. T. Graebner (Zondervan, Grand Rapids, Mich. 1949), Gal. 3:1.

25 Moshe Sluhovsky, "A Divine Apparition or Demonic Possession", in Oldridge, *Witchcraft Reader*, Chapter 19; Walker, *Unclean Spirits*, 19–28.

26 Edward Fairfax, *Demonologia: A Discourse on Witchcraft*, ed. W. Grainge (Harrogate 1882), 61–4.

27 Burr, *Narratives*, 161.

28 Rosen, *Witchcraft*, 269; Guazzo, *Compendium*, 111; *A Booke Declaring the Fearfull Vexasion of one Alexander Nynde* (London 1573), 5–6.

29 Lauderdale described his trip to Loudon in a letter to Richard Baxter, who published it in *The Certainty of the Worlds of Spirits* (London 1692), 92; Boguet, *Examen*, 181; Roper, *Oedipus*, 172–3, 175–6.

30 Baxter, *Certainty*, 89–92; James VI, *Daemonologie*, 71–2; Darrel, *Triall*, 34.

31 Fox, *Journal*, 26; Roy Porter, *The Social History of Madness* (Weidenfeld & Nicolson, London 1987), 89.

8 SUFFERING SAINTS

1 Marquis de Sade, "Dialogue Between a Priest and a Dying Man", in *Justine, Philosophy in the Bedroom and Other Writings*, translated by R. Seaver and A. Wainhouse (Grove, New York 1965), 165–75.

2 St Athanasius, "Life of Anthony", in Caroline White, ed., *Early Christian Lives* (Penguin, London 1998), 12, 15; Vern Bullough, Dwight Dixon and Joan Dixon, "Sadism, Masochism and History", in Roy Porter and Mikuláš Teich, eds, *Sexual Knowledge, Sexual Science* (Cambridge University Press 1994), 54.

3 Bartolomea Riccoboni, *Life and Death in a Venetian Convent: The Chronicle and Necrology of Corpus Domini*, ed. D. Bornstein (University of Chicago Press, Chicago, Ill. 2000), 72, 93; Antonia Pulci, *Florentine Drama for Convent and Festival* (University of Chicago Press, Chicago, Ill. 1996), 193–4.

4 Simons' hymn is reproduced in Michael Driedger, "Crossing Max Weber's Great Divide: Comparing Early Modern Jewish and Anabaptist Histories", in Werner Packull and Geoffrey Dipple, eds, *Radical Reformation Studies* (Ashgate, Aldershot 1999), 166.

5 For a more sympathetic account of Puritan sensibilities, see Patrick Collinson, "Elizabethan and Jacobean Puritanism as Forms of Popular Culture", in Christopher Durston and Jacqueline Eales, eds, *The Culture of English Puritanism* (Macmillan, London 1996).

6 Samuel Clarke, *A Generall Martyrologie* (London 1651), 391; John Gough, *A Godly Book Wherein is Contained Certain Fruitful, Godly and Necessary Rules* (London 1561), title page.

7 Robert Harris, *Works* (London 1654), 279; William Perkins, *Works*, ed. Ian Breward (Sutton Courtenay, Appleford 1970), 151, 158; Goodwin is quoted in David E. Stannard, *The Puritan Way of Death* (Oxford University Press, Oxford 1977), 41–2; Richard Sibbes, *The Saints Safetie in Evill Times* (1634), 17; Samuel Clarke, *The Saints Nose-Gay* (London 1642), 45.

8 John Calvin, *Institutes of the Christian Religion: 1536 Edition*, trans. Ford Lewis Battles (William Eerdman, Grand Rapids, Mich. 1975), 34; Warwick County Record Office, Journals of Richard Newdigate, M1/351/5/21, 391, 453, 619; CR136/A14, 221.

9 Philip Stubbes, *The Anatomie of Abuses* (1583), Q ii; WCRO, M1/351/5/21, 43, 391, 423, 482–5.

10 WCRO, CR136/A7, 54; M1/351/5/21, 620; Samuel Clarke, *A Mirrour or Looking Glasse, Both for Saints and Sinners* (London 1646), 20; Joad Raymond, ed., *Making the News: An Anthology of the Newsbooks of Revolutionary England* (Windrush, Gloucester 1993), 192; Joanna Moody, ed., *The Private Life of an Elizabethan Lady: The Diary of Lady Margaret Hoby, 1599–1605* (Sutton, Stroud 1998), 173–4.

11 William Lamont, *Puritanism and Historical Controversy* (University College London Press, London 1996), 19.

12 Perkins, *Works*, 392, 402, 405, 406; Arthur Hildersam, *Lectures upon the Fourth of John* (London 1629), 311–12.

13 Vavasor Powell, *The Life and Death of Mr Vavasor Powell* (London 1671), 12; John Rogers, *Ohel or Beth-Shemesh* (1653), 429–30; Richard Baxter's account of Nalton's despair and recovery is recorded in *The Life and Times of Richard Baxter*, ed. William Orme (1880), I, 243–4; Perkins, *Works*, 406–7.

14 William Bradford, *Of Plymouth Plantation*, ed F. Murphy (Random House, New York 1981), 13–14, 66; Virginia DeJohn Anderson, *New England's Generation* (Cambridge University Press, Cambridge 1991), 83; Increase Mather, *Cases of Conscience Concerning Evil Spirits* (Boston 1693), 10.

15 Thomas Shepard, *God's Plot*, ed. M. McGiffert (University of Massachusetts Press, Amherst, Mass. 1972), 57.

16 *The Book of the General Lawes and Libertyes Concerning the Inhabitants of Massachusetts* (facsimile edition, Harvard University Press, Cambridge, Mass. 1929), iii, 5, 6, 24, 30–1.

17 Ephraim Huitt, *The Anatomy of Conscience* (London 1626), dedication, 5–6; Thomas Hooker, *The Poor Doubting Christian Drawn to Christ* (East Windsor 1845), 36; David D. Hall, *Worlds of Wonder, Days of Judgment: Popular Religious Belief in Early New England* (Harvard University Press, Cambridge, Mass. 1989), 39–41.

18 Cotton is quoted in Edmund S. Morgan's classic study of attitudes towards church membership in New England, *Visible Saints: The History of a Puritan Idea* (Cornell University Press, Ithaca, NY 1963), 90; *Watertown Covenant* (Boston 1630).

19 Ephraim Huitt, *The Whole Prophecy of Daniel Explained* (London 1643), 226; *The New England Primer* (Wallbuilder Press, Aledo, Tex. 1991), "Verses for Children".

20 This painful aspect of Puritan spirituality is addressed with great sensitivity in Stannard, *Puritan Way of Death*, 55–6, 61–9; *New England Primer*, "Dialogue Between Christ, Youth and the Devil".

9 THE CASE FOR KILLING HERETICS

1 Goodyear's poetry is deservedly unpublished. The full text of his "Eulogie and Admiration of his Jorney into Spaine" can be found among the state papers in the Public Record Office, Kew: SP14/145/12A. John Donne, *Letters to Severall Persons of Honour* (London 1651), 100–1; Thomas Cogswell, "England and the Spanish Match", in Richard Cust and Ann Hughes, eds, *Conflict in Early Stuart England* (Longman, London 1989), 107–33; George Gifford, *A Briefe Discourse of Certaine Points of Religion* (London 1584), 34; Samuel Clarke, *A Mirrour or Looking Glasse both for Saints and Sinners* (London 1646), 65.

2 Johann Weyer reported the story about Luther in 1583. George Mora and Benjamin Kohl, eds, *Witches, Devils and Doctors in the Renaissance: Johann Weyer, De Praestigiis Daemonum* (Binghampton, New York 1991), 243–4; William Monter, "Heresy Executions in Reformation Europe, 1520–1565", in Ole Peter Grell and Bob Scribner, eds, *Tolerance and Intolerance in the European Reformation* (Cambridge University Press, Cambridge 1996), 48–64; R. W. Scribner, *Popular Culture and Popular Movements in Reformation Germany* (Hambledon, London 1987), 277–99. For the persecution of heretics as dangerous "others" akin to witches, see Gary K. Waite, *Heresy, Magic and Witchcraft in Early Modern Europe* (Macmillan, London 2002).

3 Donne, *Letters*, 101.

4 Roy Baumeister, *Evil: Inside Human Violence and Cruelty* (Freeman, New York 1996).

5 For more detailed studies of the idea of persecution, see John Christian Laursen, ed., *Histories of Heresy in the Seventeenth and Eighteenth Centuries* (Macmillan, London 2002), and Grell and Scribner, eds, *Tolerance and Intolerance*. For Reformation England, see John Coffee, *Persecution and Toleration in Protestant England, 1558–1689* (Longman, London 2000).

6 William Perkins, *Works*, ed. Ian Breward (Sutton Courtenay, Appleford 1970), 177.

7 For excellent overviews of the Cathar movement, see Malcolm Barber, *The Cathars* (Longman, London 2000) and Malcolm Lambert, *The Cathars* (Blackwell, Oxford 1998); Martin Luther, *Table Talk*, trans. W. Hazlitt (Fount, London 1995), 364.

8 Mark A. Knoll, ed., *Confessions and Catechisms of the Reformation* (Apollos, Leicester 1991), 52–3.

9 Almost all the major documents relating to heresy in western Europe before 1200 can be found in Walter Wakefield and Austin Evans, eds, *Heresies of the High Middle Ages* (Columbia University Press, New York 1969). For the episode at Orleans, see pp. 74–81.

10 Wakefield and Evans, *Heresies*, 80, 123, 186–7; Henry Bettenson, ed., *Documents of the Christian Church* (2nd edn, Oxford University Press, Oxford 1963), 134; Gifford, *Briefe Discourse*, 8.

11 Wakefield and Evans, *Heresies*, 119; Bettenson, *Documents*, 134–5.

12 Wakefield and Evans, *Heresies*, 76, 110, 114, 119, 209–10; John Doughtie, *Touching Church Schisms, but the Unanimity of Orthodox Professours* (Oxford 1628), 5.

13 Wakefield and Evans, *Heresies*, 121.

14 Ephraim Pagitt, *Heresiography* (London 1645), Epistle Dedicatory; anon., *The Hunting of the Fox, or The Sectaries Dissected* (London 1648), 28.

15 For Augustine's defence of religious persecution, see Serge Lancel, *St Augustine* (SCM Press, London 2002), 302–4. Thomas Edwards, *Gangraena* (London 1646), Epistle Dedicatory, 120.

16 Wakefield and Evans, *Heresies*, 187; John Bryan, *A Discovery of the Probable Sin Causing This Great Judgement of Rain and Waters* (London 1647), 9–10, 17.

17 This argument is taken from Perkins' *Epieikeia, or A Treatise of Christian Equity and Moderation*, first published in 1604. Perkins, *Works*, 487–8, 496–7; Thomas Fuller, *The Holy State* (Thomas Tegg, London 1841), 83.

18 Perkins presented the most extreme formulation of this view in *A Discourse on the Damned Art of Witchcraft* (London 1608), which defined all magicians as idolaters and traitors against God. Since this was the highest possible form of treason, he argued that it should always be punished by death. Perkins, *Works*, 570, 577.

19 Perkins, *Works*, 577–8.

20 For an excellent survey of the theological arguments for toleration, see Coffey, *Persecution and Toleration*, 51–68. William G. Naphy, *Documents on the Continental Reformation* (Macmillan, London 1996), 116–7; *Heretickes, Sectaries and Schismaticks* (London 1647), 19.

21 Coffey, *Persecution and Toleration*, 34.

10 CONCLUSION: "THE EDGE OF WONDER"

1 For Augustine's theory of miracles, see Benedicta Ward, *Miracles and the Medieval Mind* (2nd edn, Wildwood House, Aldershot 1987), Chapter 1. The

quote is from Augustine, *City of God*, trans. H. Bettenson (Penguin, Harmondsworth 1984), XXI, 4.

2 Clifford Geertz, *Local Knowledge* (Fontana, London 1993), 77.

3 The quote from St Thomas is from the *Summa Contra Gentiles* of 1259. The most accessible modern edition is Thomas Aquinas, *Selected Writings*, ed. R. McInerny (Penguin, Harmondsworth 1998), 246.

4 Geertz, *Local Knowledge*, 151; Quentin Skinner, *Liberty Before Liberalism* (Cambridge University Press, Cambridge 1998), 112.

5 Henri Boguet, *An Examen of Witches*, trans. E. A. Ashwin (Frederick Muller, London 1971), xxxix; Katharine Hodgkin, "Reasoning with Unreason: Visions, Witchcraft, and Madness in Early Modern England", in Stuart Clark, ed., *Languages of Witchcraft* (Macmillan, London 2001), 217.

6 C. A. J. Coady, *Testimony: A Philosophical Investigation* (Oxford University Press , Oxford 1992), 6–7, 170.

7 Other leading supporters of Piltdown Man were inspired by the belief that human evolution was predestined by the increasing complexity of the brain. The French theologian Pierre Teilhard de Chardin, who participated in the original find, later achieved fame by arguing that God directed the process of evolution. See Ronald Millar, *The Piltdown Men* (Gollancz, London 1972) and John Evangelist Walsh, *Unravelling Piltdown* (Random House, New York 1996).

8 For ideas about inter-sexuality in the seventeenth and eighteenth centuries, see Ian McCormick, ed., *Secret Sexualities* (Routledge, London 1997); Geertz, *Local Knowledge*, 80–4.

9 Paul Barber, *Vampires, Burial and Death* (Yale University Press, New Haven, Conn. 1988), 16–17, 109–10, 115–16.

10 For an excellent discussion of the context and meaning of visionary experiences, see Hodgkin, "Reasoning with Unreason". Malcolm Gaskill, "Witchcraft and Power in Early Modern England", in Jenny Kermode and Garthine Walker, eds, *Women, Crime and the Courts* (University College London Press, London 1994), 132–3, 135; Henry Howard, *A Defensative Against the Poison of Supposed Prophecies* (London, 1583), Bb ii recto; Paul Boyer and Stephen Nissenbaum, *Salem Possessed: The Social Origins of Witchcraft* (Harvard University Press, Cambridge, Mass. 1974), 14.

11 J. A. Cheyne, et al., "Hypnagogic and Hypnopompic Hallucinations during Sleep Paralysis: Neurological and Cultural Construction of the Night-Mare", *Consciousness and Cognition* 8 (1999); Henry More, *An Antidote to Atheism* (London, 1655), 211–12, 220.

12 "Death Film on Sale to Kids", Birmingham *Evening Mail*, April 5, 1993; "Officers Seize 'Snuff' Video", the *Independent*, 6 April 1993.

13 Satanic abuse is discussed in Chapter 5 of this book. Martin Barker, *A Haunt of Fears* (Pluto, London 1984); Martin Barker, ed., *The Video Nasties: Freedom and Censorship in the Media* (Pluto, London 1984); David Kerekis and David Slater, *Killing for Culture* (Creation, London 1994).

14 Victoria Berridge and Gareth Edwards, *Opium and the People: Opiate Use and Policy in Nineteenth and Early Twentieth Century Britain* (Allen Lane, London 1981); Caroline Jean Acker, "From All Purpose Anodyne to Marker of Deviance: Physicians' Attitudes Towards Opiates in the US from 1890 to 1940", in Roy Porter and Miculás Teich, eds, *Drugs and Narcotics in History* (Cambridge University Press, Cambridge 1995); Nick Davies, "Make Heroin Legal", the *Guardian*, June 14, 2001.

15 Given the high profile of heroin in the war on drugs, surprisingly little medical research has been published on the effects the drug in normal dosage. An article in the *British Medical Journal* in 1983 claimed that the prescribed use of heroin was

harmful to addicts, but several experts in the field challenged these findings. The much larger Swiss study found that addicts were healthier when they received a regular supply of the drug under medical supervision. Ann Dally, "Anomalies and Mysteries in the War on Drugs", in Porter and Teich, *Drugs*; A. Uchtenhagen, et al., *Programme for a Medical Prescription of Narcotics* (Institute for Social and Preventative Medicine, University of Zurich, Zurich 1997).

16 Skinner, *Liberty*, 116–17.

INDEX